Dr Ian Maxwell is a graduate of the Queen's University of Belfast where he completed his PhD on Sir Wilfrid Spender in 1991. He was a Records Officer at the Public Record Office of Northern Ireland, 1991-96, and during this time as head of the Public Search Room he pioneered a series of leaflets on genealogy which are now available on the Internet. His book, *Tracing Your Ancestors in Northern Ireland*, was published in 1997. Ian works in Lands and Legislation Branch, Roads Service and takes an evening course on genealogy at the Upper Bann Institute.

For Scott

RESEARCHING
ARMAGH
ANCESTORS

A practical guide for the family
and local historian

IAN MAXWELL

SERIES EDITORS
W·H. CRAWFORD
BRIAN TRAINOR

ULSTER HISTORICAL FOUNDATION

First published 2000
by the Ulster Historical Foundation
12 College Square East, Belfast, BT1 6DD
Email: enquiry@uhf.org.uk
Website: www.ancestryireland.com

ISBN 0-901905-89-5

Cover and Design by Dunbar Design
Typeset by UHF
Printed by ColourBooks Ltd

Front cover illustration:
St. Patrick's Catholic Cathedral photographed from the new
graveyard on Sandy Hill after the Sacristy and Synod Hall were
built in 1896. From the Allison Collection, PRONI,
courtesy of the Deputy Keeper of the Records, PRONI.

CONTENTS

ACKNOWLEDGEMENTS

I have had the support and encouragement of a great many people during the production of this book. I would like to thank Dr Brian Trainor for his enthusiastic support and invaluable advice. My thanks are also due to Shane McAteer, Executive Director of the Ulster Historical Foundation, for his continued interest in the project, and to Trevor Parkhill, Aideen Ireland, Colette O'Flaherty, W. H. Crawford, Roger Weatherup, Grace Greer, Mary McVeigh, Joseph Downey, Kieran McConville, Joan Petticrew, Ken Abraham, Michele Neill, Mrs C. Carey, Valerie Adams and Gerard MacAtasney for their helpful contributions. I would like to express my gratitude to Anne Trimble, editor of PRONI's, *Guide to County Sources for County Armagh* for her advice. I would also take this opportunity to pay tribute to Philip Wilson whose enthusiasm and generosity of spirit inspired a whole generation of local and family historians. I am also most grateful to Armagh City and District Council for their generous financial contribution to help defray the costs of publication. Finally I would like to thank my wife Valerie for spending her holidays with me in County Armagh rather than France or Spain, and my sister Fiona who wanted me to mention her at some point in the book.

Ian Maxwell

ABBREVIATIONS

OF REPOSITORIES

AA   Armagh Ancestry (Armagh)
GO   Genealogical Office (Dublin)
GRO   General Register Office (Belfast)
LDS   Latter Day Saints (Belfast)
NAI   National Archives of Ireland (Dublin)
NLI   National Library of Ireland (Dublin)
PRONI   Public Record Office of Northern Ireland (Belfast)
RCB   Representative Church Body (Dublin)
UHF   Ulster Historical Foundation (Belfast)

The vast majority of records for County Armagh are held by the Public Record Office of Northern Ireland (PRONI). All references, unless otherwise stated, are for documents held by PRONI.

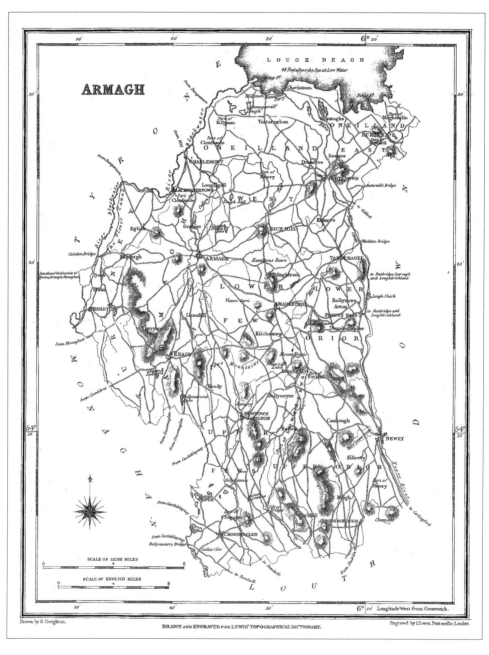

Map of County Armagh, 1837, from Samuel Lewis'
Atlas of the Counties of Ireland (1837)

INTRODUCTION

Armagh is the smallest county in Northern Ireland. It is a famous fruit-growing area and its rich rolling hills have something of the appearance of the English shires. The north of the county is dominated by the market towns of Lurgan and Portadown and the new city of Craigavon. Close to the town of Lurgan is the flat marshy land that forms part of the Lough Neagh basin. The county is more hilly to the south with small enclosed fields and standing on several small hills is the ecclesiastical city of Armagh. The apple-growing region to the north-east of the county is known as the orchard of Ireland. Many of the seventeenth-century settlers here came from Worcestershire and they laid out the orchards on the same pattern as those in the Vale of Evesham.

Much of Ulster's colourful early history has taken place in and around the ancient ecclesiastical settlement of Armagh. The name is the English version of the Irish Ard Macha – the Hill of Macha

– the legendary queen who built her fortress about 600 BC on the hill around which the city would develop. More than six hundred years later another queen of that name built the palace of Emain Macha a few miles from the city at the site now known as Navan Fort. It became the ancient seat of the Kings of Ulster. Archaeologists have discovered at Navan the traces of a giant temple, the largest prehistoric building in Britain, which was erected for the purpose of ritual destruction and burial beneath the mound that can be seen today. There was a royal settlement with an enclosure and archaeologists have unearthed ancient weapons, jewellery and the bones of people and animals including the skull of a barbary ape. Here too the legendary exploits of Cuchulainn and the Red Branch Knights were preserved in the oral tradition.

They were supposed to have lived around the time of the birth of Christ and are the heroes of a series of stories known as the Ulster Cycle. These stories, among the oldest in Europe, tell of the heroic battles fought between the Kingdom of Ulaidh, who gave their name to Ulster, and the armies of Queen Meadhbh of Connacht. The greatest warrior amongst the knights was Cuchulainn, whose birth was the result of the union of the Dé Danaan god, Lugh, and a Red Branch girl called Dechtire. Cuchulainn's heroic deeds kept Ulster independent and in his final battle he refused to give way asking instead to be tied in an upright position so that he could face the enemy sword in hand. Otters came from the river and drank his blood and ravens came to eat his flesh, but only when the men of Connacht were defeated, did Cuchulainn drop his sword and die.

According to tradition, Emain Macha was the capital of the Ulaidh for more than eight hundred years, but was finally overthrown by the armies of Connacht around the middle of the fifth century A.D. Ulaidh was confined to Counties Down, Antrim and Louth and they would establish a colony in Argyll whose rulers would one day become kings of Scotland. Armagh became part of the kingdom of Airgialla (Oriel) and it flourished under the patronage of the Ui Neill. They were a powerful tribal group claiming descent from the fifth century monarch Niall of the Nine Hostages. Out of the Ui Neill came other surnames such as O'Doherty, O'Hagan and O'Donnell.

After the destruction of Navan, the centre of power moved to the present site of Armagh, probably in the 5th century A.D. The abandonment of Emain Macha seems to be connected with the establishment of a very early church at Armagh by Patrick and his followers.

Around 445 Saint Patrick persuaded Daire, the local chieftain, to grant him the hilltop site where Macha had established her fortress nearly a thousand years before. Patrick established his most important church at this site and around it colleges and schools were founded so that it became a centre of learning from which missionaries were sent to England and the Continent. Patrick was credited by later generations with bringing Christianity to Ireland. In fact Christianity had already spread to the south of Ireland as a result of the regular trading contacts with the empire. So it was in the north of the country that he probably did most of his work. Very little is known about him, neither the dates of his birth or death, nor where exactly he came from or where he preached. It seems likely that Patrick was a native of late Roman Britain. Two Latin texts written by Patrick are the oldest documents in Irish history. Unfortunately neither is autobiographical. *The Book of Armagh* contains a complete New Testament, bound up with accounts of Patrick's life and his 'Confession'; all aimed at asserting Armagh's association with the saint and its pre-eminence as a church in Ireland. The book was written by Ferdomnach (described as 'a wise and excellent scribe of Armagh' in the Annals of Ulster). The Confession is a defence of Patrick's mission in answer to his detractors. His mission was to bring the Christian faith to the Irish who lived 'at the ends of the earth'. Patrick identifies himself as the son of a deacon and the grandson of a priest. He mentions his capture at the age of sixteen during a raid on his father's estate, his enslavement for six years in Ireland, his escape from the country and his eventual decision to return. The second text is a letter of excommunication to the soldiers of Coroticus, a British chief (presumably resident in Britain, but possibly in Ireland) who had murdered some of his converts and enslaved others.

Around Patrick's church in Armagh monastic settlements, colleges and schools were founded so that it became a centre of learning from which missionaries were sent to England and the Continent.

Aldfrith, King of the Northumbrian Saxons between 685 and 704, celebrated his time as a student at the ancient school of Armagh in verse:

> I found in Armagh the splendid,
> Neatness, wisdom and prudence blended,
> Fasting as Christ hath recommended,
> And noble councillors untranscended.

From the eighth century the abbot-bishops of Armagh pressed their claims as the inheritors of Patrick's mission for the primacy of Armagh and this primacy was formally recognised by Brian Boru as High King in 1004. The wealth of the monastic foundations, however, was to attract the Norsemen or Vikings during the ninth and tenth centuries and the city suffered further destruction during the wars between the natives and the Anglo-Normans during the late twelfth and thirteenth century. The Reformation and the suppression of the abbeys ensured that Armagh had by Plantation times declined beyond all recognition from its former ecclesiastical importance.

Until the end of the sixteenth century Ulster remained unaffected by the piecemeal conquest of the rest of Ireland. Armagh was, however, on the edge of the most successfully anglicised colony in the island from the twelfth century. To the north Gaelic culture and society remained intact. The O'Neills were the dominant family in County Armagh having by the thirteenth century driven out among others the MacMurphys from the barony of Fews, where they established their supremacy over the territory chiefly inhabited by the Garveys, O'Callaghans and the Hanrattys. Meanwhile the Magennis, O'Hanlon, MacMahon and O'Reilly lordships separated the O'Neills from the Anglo-Norman settlements in County Down and the Irish midlands.

During the fifteenth century Henry VIII extended his policy of surrender and re-grant into Ulster where the frontier of mountain and lake had allowed the Gaelic system to remain intact. In 1542 Conn O'Neill accepted a royal grant of his lands with the title of the earl of Tyrone. When Conn died in 1559 he was succeeded by his younger son, Shane, who assumed the traditional title of 'The O'Neill' and asserted his independence from the English Crown. He also managed to alienate his neighbours, the O'Donnells of

Tyrconnell and the MacDonnells of north Antrim, and was defeated and killed in 1567.

For the next twenty years Armagh was relatively peaceful as Hugh O'Neill, Conn's grandson, established himself in the earldom. He had been brought up in England and, when war had broken out between the crown and Shane O'Neill in 1566, had fought with the English forces. In 1585 he was formally recognised by the Crown as the earl of Tyrone but he was proclaimed a traitor when he declared himself 'The O'Neill' ten years later. During the closing years of the reign of Queen Elizabeth I, a protracted and bloody war took place with the native Irish forces scoring a succession of victories over the English armies. A great battle was fought in 1598 between O'Neill's forces, assisted by those of O'Donnell and other chiefs, and the English forces commanded by Sir Henry Bagenal. The battle of the Yellow Ford took place two miles to the north of the city of Armagh where Bagenal and 800 of his men were killed forcing English garrisons to withdraw from Armagh and Blackwater.

With the arrival of Lord Mountjoy as governor in 1600, the war began to turn in favour of the English Crown. By using a scorched earth policy which included devastating the Fews in South Armagh, Mountjoy undermined the Irish forces. Hugh O'Neill, earl of Tyrone and the chief general of the Irish forces, surrendered shortly after the accession of James I in 1603. During the war with O'Neill a network of fortified posts had already been established in Armagh. By this time the province of Ulster was also divided into counties with O'Neill's land shired separately into County Armagh. By the beginning of the seventeenth century, Armagh was divided into the five baronies of Oneilland, Armagh, Tiranny, Orior and Fews.

Hugh O'Neill signed the Treaty of Mellifont in 1603 and was allowed to retain his lands in Ulster. However, his position was undermined by the presence of English officials and by garrisons stationed at Armagh and throughout his territories. Therefore in 1607, along with his family, retainers and fellow lords, he fled to the continent. Since they had reneged on their allegiance to the King, their lands were seized by the Crown and in January 1608 a plan which called for the plantation of much of Ulster was published. In the plantation scheme for County Armagh, Oneilland barony was assigned to English undertakers, Lower Fews to Scottish undertakers and Orior to servitors (former soldiers) and natives. Trinity College was granted half of Armagh barony and the other half went to the Church of Ireland and other servitors. The barony of Tiranny was given over to the church and to natives. Some Irish were exempt from the plantation. One of the most prominent was Sir Turlough MacHenry O'Neill – who was granted the barony of Upper Fewes.

As a result of the plantation the Irish were to be heavily concentrated in the south Armagh area and they retained the Irish language and their Catholic religion. The north of the county was dominated by a Protestant, English-speaking community. It is therefore hardly surprising that so much of the violence that accompanied the 1641 rising took place in that area. In 1641 a number of Irish chieftains, who had earlier been dispossessed of their land or feared that such a fate was about to befall them, attempted to drive the settlers from Armagh as Ulster was plunged into more than ten years of bloody fighting. In the course of the campaign the town of Lurgan and the castles at Markethill and Tandragee were destroyed.

In the summer of 1649 Oliver Cromwell arrived in Ireland with an army with the object of regaining control of Ireland and avenging the colonists who had been massacred in 1641. This he did with characteristic ruthlessness. During the Cromwellian confiscations that followed, 34 per cent of the land in County Armagh was seized and granted to soldiers and 'adventurers' who had subscribed towards the cost of the reconquest of Ireland. Most soldiers sold their land cheaply to their officers and returned to their homes. At the same time many Catholic tenantry drifted back to the confiscated territories. Nevertheless, Catholic landowners had been replaced by army officers and those Protestant landowners already established since the plantation. They were reinforced by a new wave of immigrants towards the end of the century. The new settlers were divided into those, usually of English descent, who were Church of Ireland, and those lowland Scots who brought with them their Presbyterianism. Generally speaking the northern portion of the county was dominated by the established church while the Presbyterians dominated the middle third.

The distribution of names in County Armagh illustrates the limited success of the plantation in the region. The most popular surnames are almost equally divided between Irish and settler surnames. Murphy, the most common surname throughout Ireland, is also the most popular found in County Armagh. This is followed by Hughes, Wilson and Campbell, representing settler families, then by the Irish name O'Hare, and Smith, the commonest name in England and Wales. The Irish names McCann and Donnelly are followed alternately by settler and Irish names. These are Watson, Quinn, Johnston, Kelly and Thompson.

One should not take it for granted that an English or Scottish surname invariably means that an ancestor was of settler stock. For example the name Hughes, the second commonest in County Armagh and widespread in Wales and England, is not exclusive to those whose ancestors migrated to Ulster in the seventeenth century. A significant number are in fact from Irish stock, descendants of the several O hAodha (O' Hugh) septs or of the Mac Aodha (Mc Hugh) septs, whose forebears adopted Hughes as their surname. The same may be said of the surname Campbell, one of the commonest in Scotland. Some who bear this surname may be descended from the native Irish sept based in County Tyrone, Mac Cathmhaoil.

Despite the prolonged wars of the seventeenth century that had devastated much of its countryside, County Armagh was to become one of the most prosperous and densely populated counties in Ulster during the following century. Landlords such as Arthur Brownlow, the major landowner in the Lurgan area, encouraged their tenants to weave their linen yarn into cloth. He established a market at Lurgan and promised to purchase all the linen offered for sale.

North Armagh therefore became the heart of the 'linen triangle', which extended to Dungannon to the west and Lisburn to the east. Between 1776 and 1778 the prominent agriculturist Arthur Young toured Ireland. He found that the farms in County Armagh were very small and given over to the linen manufacture. At Maghan he had a chance to take a close look at the everyday life of the weaver. 'Their food is stir-about, potatoes, bread of maslin [i.e. mixed grain] or wheat, and some meat once a fortnight. They are well clothed and have plenty of fuel. The weavers universally earn

much more than the few labourers there are...As to health, from
the sedentary life, they rarely change their profession for that. They
take exercise of a different sort, keeping packs of hounds, every
man one, and joining; they hunt hares: a pack of hounds is never
heard, but all the weavers leave their looms, and away they go
after them by hundreds.'

The linen industry also encouraged continuous migrations of
settlers into County Armagh during the eighteenth century. Arthur
Young found that 'About Armagh, the farms are very small; the
only object the linen manufacture. This is the case all the way to
Newry, also to Monaghan, but in that county the farms are
somewhat larger ... Scarce any of them have potatoes and oats to
feed their families; great importations from Louth, Meath,
Monaghan, Cavan and Tyrone, besides what comes occasionally
from England and Scotland.'

This very prosperity contributed to the intense rivalry in the county
between the Catholic and Protestant populations which were almost
equal in numbers. Faction fighting between rival groups developed
into sectarian conflict. In north Armagh strong Catholic parishes
clashed with neighbouring Protestant parishes. This had taken on a
more organised form by the late eighteenth century in the Protestant
Peep-of-Day boys and Catholic Defenders, and culminated in the
'Battle of the Diamond' in September 1795 which led to the
formation of the Orange Order. Chevalier De Latocnaye, a former
Royalist officer of cavalry, who was forced to flee his native France
because of the revolution, visited Ireland in the mid-1790s. He
found the Armagh countryside much disturbed and blamed the
trouble on the high quality of the agricultural land and the
quarrelsome nature of the locals: 'This country, which is, certainly,
the most beautiful in Ireland, is also that in which the inhabitants
are the least tractable, and approach nearest to the character which
the English call "Wild Irish". The animosity between the different
sects certainly contributes to this savagery, but if this pretext for it
were not available, another would soon be found. The real reason
is that the fertility of the country attracted a great many
strangers, who, having multiplied exceedingly, have become too
numerous to allow of equitable division of the land with the
descendants of the ancient stock, and therefore wish to expatriate

these, and to remain alone the occupiers. The others, naturally, wish to see the expulsion of the colonists or settlers, and the land remaining in their sole possession. Hence the continual quarrels between neighbours, such as are not found elsewhere. Sides are taken, disputes multiply, the sticks rattle, and the side which the Government for the moment favours profits by the sense of protection, and does its best to inflict the greatest possible injury on the other.'

Despite the intense sectarian rivalry, the population of the county continued to grow as the Napoleonic Wars during the late eighteenth and early nineteenth centuries led to an increase in the price of agricultural produce. Sir Charles Coote in his survey of 1804 wrote that: 'Armagh is indisputably, in proportion to its size, the most populous county in Ireland. Although much of the surface is covered with mountains, yet the greater part of the wildest country is very thickly inhabited, and it is on this account that its superior population is allowed.' He was most impressed by the quality of life enjoyed by the people of the county, commenting, 'I must confess, that the extraordinary comforts, so eminently enjoyed by the people of this county, both of the middle and the lower class, was a matter of astonishment to me, who had been well acquainted with the relative situation of those classes in other counties in this province, where their pursuits, both in and out of doors, so exactly corresponded'. He put this down to the fact that 'more money can be earned by the manufacture of fine, than of coarse linen; Armagh being more engaged in fine webs, than the other counties of Ulster which lie west of it'. More improbably he found that the people were 'more industrious and sober, and their earnings are seldom spent in the dram-shop'.

A feature of the County Armagh countryside that has remained to this day is the patchwork of small farms which dominates the landscape. The success of the linen industry in the county had enabled many weavers to take on small farms to supplement their income. Coote commented on this: 'The soil being excellent, the pursuit of manufacture, and the population very numerous, are the causes of the small size of farms, which are of so little extent as to leave the average of the county at less than five acres'. It is worth taking a drive to the top of Carrigatuke Mountain on the road from Markethill to Keady, where this landscape of small farms and abundant hedgerows can still be seen.

Mr and Mrs Hall, who toured Ireland in 1840, were favourably impressed by what they saw of the county: ... 'while it may be surpassed by many in picturesque beauty, it is surpassed by none in the sturdy, independent character of its peasantry. Along the high roads and also among the by-ways very little poverty is encountered; the cottages are for the most part neat, clean and comfortable, and few of them are without orchards added to the ordinary garden, and the continual click-clack of the shuttle betokens the industry that is securing humble luxuries within, and the whole of its inmates, from the very aged to the very young, are made useful in some degree.'

Within a few years of Mr and Mrs Hall's visit the county was devastated by the impact of the Great Famine. Much of County Armagh was severely affected by the devastation caused by the potato blight and the fever that followed in its wake. The distress brought about by the famine was all the more marked for it happened during a slump in the linen and cotton trade, putting further pressure on an industry already suffering from the impact of rapid industrialisation. In 1845 the potato crop had been badly affected by the blight. Henry John Porter, agent on the Duke of Manchester estates at Tandragee and Portadown, described the devastation caused by the blight in a letter to Sir T. Freemantle, Dublin Castle, dated 27 October 1845:

> Having returned from Dublin on Saturday night I was anxious to ascertain the state of potato crops on the farm of [the] Duke of Manchester's within his demesne and find the greater part of the crops had been dug, and put into pits or bins in the field and a portion housed. The steward had got some put up in this way about 10 days ago and on opening the pits they were found to be in a state of decomposition, and a smell that of decayed refuse from the garden.

However, when in July and August 1846 blight struck again the impact was devastating throughout the county. The workhouses, set up to deal with the destitute poor that were a feature of Ireland at the time, were soon overwhelmed.

The impact of the Great Famine can be seen in the dramatic fall in the population. In 1821, the year of the first properly organised census, the population of County Armagh stood at 197,427. Within twenty years it had reached 232, 393. By 1851, the first census to be held after the most catastrophic years of famine and fever, the population had fallen by more than 15 per cent to 196, 084. It continued to fall until the Second World War. The 1951 census returns showed an increase in the pre-war figures by 5.0 per cent. The population figure stood at 114, 254, less than half that of 1841.

During the late 1840s and in the years immediately after the Great Famine some families were evicted from their smallholdings by landlords in need of rents which could not be paid or anxious to consolidate the farms on their estates. Many sought employment in Lurgan and Portadown, which had become manufacturing centres. Lurgan's population, numbering 2207 in 1820, had more than doubled by the end of the Great Famine and by 1888 was somewhere in the region of 15,000. Portadown also grew rapidly during the nineteenth century. In 1816 its population was estimated to be 600, while the *Belfast and Ulster Street Directory* for 1897 calculated that it had reached 10,000. The ancient city of Armagh, better known for its architecture than its industries, also continued to grow but at a much less dramatic rate than its northern rivals.

The industrial heart of County Armagh is centred around the market towns of Lurgan and Portadown. The prosperity of these towns was based around the linen industry. Lurgan, a plantation town established on the Brownlow estate, was destroyed during the 1641 rising. Despite this setback, by the eighteenth and nineteenth centuries it became one of the chief centres of the linen industry in Ireland. One visitor to the town in the late eighteenth century declared:

> This is one of the prettiest little market towns in the Kingdom. The inhabitants are genteel, sensible and friendly. They seem, indeed, to exert themselves to support the reputation of their town which, from the similarity of its inhabitants to those of the English, had for many years acquired the name of Little England, and an Englishman at Lurgan indeed will think himself in his own country.

Portadown, or as it was originally called, Port-ne-doon ('the port of the fortified eminence') derived its name from the ancient castle of the McCanns or McCanes, who occupied this very important station commanding the pass of the river Bann. It was the Rebellion of 1641 that first brought Portadown to national prominence. This was due to the massacre of settlers at the bridge of Portadown during that year. A group of settlers from Armagh, Kilmore and Loughgall parishes were forced into the river Bann at Portadown and shot, stabbed or struck as they tried to escape. The number of deaths has been variously estimated but it was probably in the region of two hundred.

In spite of its troubled beginnings Portadown was to become one of the most prosperous market towns in Ulster. With the arrival of the railway in 1842, Portadown became an important railway junction with lines from Belfast to Dublin, Londonderry, Armagh, Cavan and the midlands of Ireland running through the town. Today the town clusters round its main street which crosses the river Bann at one end. Portadown's prosperity was the result of the growth in the linen industry and the establishment of weaving and spinning in the homes of labourers and farmers all over the province.

William Makepeace Thackeray, author of *Vanity Fair,* visited the area in 1842 and recalled that the ten miles from Armagh to Portadown was 'not the prettiest, but one of the pleasantest, drives I have had in Ireland, for the county is well cultivated along the whole of the road, the trees in plenty, and villages and neat houses always in sight. The little farms, with their orchards and comfortable buildings, were as clean and trim as could be wished; they are mostly of one storey, with long thatched roofs and shining windows, such as those that may be seen in Normandy and Picardy.'

Thackeray also noticed a change in the character of the people from those he had encountered further south. However, his impressions of the people of County Armagh were largely gathered on his coach trip one Sunday evening as he made his way from Armagh to Belfast and from an encounter with a northern and southern waiter he had come across at an inn at Armagh:

> the girls have their hair neatly braided up, not loose over their faces as in the south; and not only are bare feet very rare, and stockings extremely neat and white, but I am sure I saw at least a dozen good silk gowns upon the women along the road, and scarcely one which

was not clean and in good order. The men for the most part figured in jackets, caps, and trousers, eschewing the old well of a hat which covers the popular head at the other end of the island, the breeches and the long ill-made tail coat.'

He also found the accent very different. 'The people speak with a Scotch twang, and, as I fancied, much more simply and to the point.'

Many of the towns and villages in County Armagh were established during the plantation. These were usually established by the new landowners on their estates. Loughgall, Richhill, Markethill and Newtownhamilton were all established in this way. Others such as Tandragee had an older pedigree. This town owes its origins to the O'Hanlons who built a castle where the present Tandragee Castle stands and dominated the region until deprived of their lands during the reign of James I. The lands passed into the hands of Sir Oliver St John, who rebuilt the town.

Each landlord encouraged colonists from the motherland to settle on these new estates, which explains the preponderance of English surnames in the county. The religious outlook of the landowner could also have an effect on the character of a settlement. This can be seen in the case of the village of Bessbrook. Situated in a valley between Keggal Mountain and Slieve Gullion, three miles from Newry, the 'Model Village' of Bessbrook was founded in 1759 by John Pollock, a linen merchant. However it was the Richardson family who imposed their Quaker outlook on the village, providing free medicine and non-sectarian education to its inhabitants. Planned on the lines of a William Penn settlement, the village represents an experiment in social reform begun in 1845 by John Grubb Richardson. High quality houses were built but it was the absence of a police station, public house or pawn shop which aroused the curiosity of visitors. George Bernard Shaw visited Bessbrook in 1879, commenting that 'Bessbrook is a model village where the inhabitants never swear nor get drunk and look as if they would very much like to do both'.

By the end of the nineteenth century County Armagh was to become one of the major centres for opposition to the Home Rule Bills, which sought to give a measure of self-government to Ireland by establishing a parliament based in Dublin. During the late eighteenth century right through to the late twentieth century, North Armagh has been a hotbed of sectarian conflict. The journalist, F. Frankfort Moore, published a book in 1914 in which he tried to explain the resistance to Home Rule in Ulster. He studied all aspects of the situation in the North and took a particular interest in the phenomenon of the sectarian riot. He noted that street fighting in Ulster was not carried out in a haphazard way. Moore described how he learned 'the proper way to conduct a street riot' in Portadown in 1869. 'Every boy and girl in the crowd understood the art thoroughly. When the police charged in military fashion, they hurried to one side or the other, refraining from obstructing them in the least, but returned immediately afterwards to the place they had occupied before the "charge".'

With the partition of Ireland in 1921 Armagh was one of the six northern counties to opt for a separate parliament in Belfast which would retain its close links with the rest of the United Kingdom. The sectarian conflict which has been a feature of Northern Ireland for much of the twentieth century has left its mark on many of the Province's towns and villages. South Armagh is perhaps better known as one of the world's trouble spots. Nevertheless, the city of Armagh remains the ecclesiastical capital of Ireland and many of its finer buildings have been preserved and its history highlighted in a number of museums and visitors' centres. And if you are driving along a country road in the south of the country you may well come across another legacy of the past. The game of bullets, played in Armagh and Cork, emerged as a sport amongst the weavers and consists of throwing an iron ball along about two and a half miles of county road. The winner is that person who takes the least number of throws to complete the circuit!

HOW TO BEGIN

Although many records relating to County Armagh were destroyed as a result of the destruction of the Public Record Office, Dublin, in 1922, much has survived to aid the dedicated family historian. The purpose of this book is to highlight the most important records relating to Armagh, some of which are unique to the county. No single volume can hope to include all the relevant records; however, *Researching Armagh Ancestors* should help to take some of the mystery out of genealogical research.

Searching through old records, although often rewarding, can be time-consuming. Often even the best researcher will take a wrong turn and end up spending valuable time ploughing through records which make no mention of the relevant name. In order to ensure that you are on the right track it is essential to gather as much information as possible from old family bibles, legal documents such as wills or leases, and inscriptions from family gravestones.

This can help to pinpoint the right location and the correct dates to add to names which family historians are often disappointed to find were all too common in Ireland at the time. It is also usual to talk to relatives, especially those from an older generation whose memories, however inaccurate, may point you in the right direction. Only after gathering, and documenting such information should the family historian begin his or her search through old records.

GRAVESTONE INSCRIPTIONS

In Ireland the practice of erecting a headstone to mark the last resting place of a relative dates in most areas from the seventeenth century. If you know where your ancestor lived it is worth paying a visit to the local graveyard, as a headstone may provide important information such as names and dates of births and deaths, which will make easier the search through old records. A walk round a graveyard can often save wading through endless pages of a church register for the birth or death dates of a particular ancestor. The style of the headstone also can give a clue to the economic circumstances of the family at a particular period in history. Other valuable information can include place of birth, occupation and even cause of death.

Because so many headstones can be illegible it is worth checking at your local library to find out if the gravestones in a particular cemetery have been transcribed and published. A number of gravestone inscriptions for County Armagh are available at the Public Record Office of Northern Ireland, reference number T/808/14917–14924. The Ulster Historical Foundation has transcribed and computerised inscriptions for all cemeteries in County Armagh and Armagh Ancestry in Armagh City and Heritage World, based in Donaghmore, also hold transcripts for a number of cemeteries. Transcripts for Mullaghabrack and St. Patrick's are held by the Armagh County Museum and those inscriptions for Creggan (Vol 6, No. 2, 1972) and Sandy Hill (Vol 11, No. 2, 1985) have been published in *Seanchas Ardmhacha*.

BIRTHS, DEATHS AND MARRIAGES

Having obtained as much information as possible (particularly dates and location) from old bibles, gravestones etc it is now possible to begin to trace back through the generations using the public records. The best place to start is the records of births, deaths and marriage. It was not until 1 January 1864 that state registration of all births, deaths and marriages began in Ireland, although the registration of all marriages, except those celebrated by Roman Catholic clergy, began as early as 1 April 1845. Therefore it should be possible to obtain a copy of not only your own birth certificate, but also those of your parents, grandparents and great grandparents. These will provide such important details as the mother's maiden name, the father's name and occupation and their address at the time.

Marriage certificates provide details of the occupations of both parties, the names and occupations of their fathers and their addresses. Death certificates, although less interesting, do include details such as age at time of death, former occupation, address at time of death and the name, address and qualification of the informant.

Birth and death registers for County Armagh are available from 1 January 1864. They are located at the General Register Office, Oxford House, 49–55 Chichester Street, Belfast. Marriage registers are available there only for marriages from 1 January 1922. Marriage registers, dating from 1 April 1845 for non-Catholic marriages, and 1 January 1864 for all marriages, are located at the District Registrars' offices at one of the following locations:

- Armagh City and District Council, Registrar of Births, Deaths and Marriages, The Palace Demesne, Armagh
- Craigavon Borough Council, Registrar of Births, Deaths and Marriages, Civic Centre, Lakeview Rd, Craigavon.

Although based in County Down, the following councils are responsible for small specific areas of County Armagh:

- Banbridge District Council, Downshire Road, Banbridge
- Newry & Mourne District Council, Monaghan Road, Newry.

The registers themselves are not open to inspection. Once you have established the date of birth, death or marriage it is possible to visit the General Registrar Office in Belfast in order to obtain the relevant information in the form of certificates. If you require the assistance of a member of staff there is a waiting list for this service and bookings may need to be made six months in advance.

If you are unable to establish the exact date of an ancestor's birth, death or marriage the following indexes are available:

Birth Indexes	1864 – to date
Death Indexes	1922 – to date
Marriage Indexes	1922 – to date

It is also possible to apply for birth, death or marriage certificates by post to the General Register Office. Application forms are available from the General Register Office, Registrars' Offices and Citizens' Advice Bureaux. Staff at the General Register Office will undertake a search provided they are given sufficient information about the person concerned. Searches will be made in the year quoted plus the two years either side unless a wider search is requested. A further fee will be required for each extra five years searched.

The Church of Jesus Christ of Latter Day Saints (Mormons) have extensive microfilms both of indexes and certificates from the GRO. They can be searched at their Family History Centres in Dublin, Belfast and elsewhere in the world.

From 1948 the Mormon Church began microfilming documentary material in Ireland and their holdings include some baptismal and marriage registers for Roman Catholic parishes and some other denominations. The most important resource acquired at that time were the registers of births, deaths and marriages as well as the indexes to these records held in the Registrar General's Office, Custom House, Dublin. Unfortunately the Mormons were not able to complete the filming of all registers. As can be seen below copies of births 1882–1899 and 1911–1921 are wanting as well as marriages and deaths 1871–1921. Apart from these years microfilm copies of the actual official registers are available worldwide in Mormon family history centres. This is a vital resource to have accessible because in the Registrar's Offices in Dublin, Belfast and London the public have no right of access to the actual original records. The Mormon Church have indexed most of the two million reels of microfilms that they hold and these indexes are made available in an International Genealogical Index (IGI). This index is arranged both by county and surname and is available in many libraries and record offices and also on the Internet. Access to the IGI is free of charge as is the viewing of films held in Mormon Family History Centres. The LDS collection of GRO microfilms is as follows:

Births	Indexes	1864–1959
Births	Registers	1864–1881; 1900–1913
Marriages	Indexes	1845–1959
Marriages	Registers	1845–1870
Deaths	Indexes	1864–1959
Deaths	Registers	1864–1870

Armagh Ancestry has on its computerized database civil births, 1864–1922 and marriages, 1845–1922 for County Armagh.

ADMINISTRATIVE DIVISIONS

Government, both central and local, and the law courts arranged their records by county, parish, barony and townland and official maps recording each area are available from the 1830s onwards.

THE TOWNLAND

Ireland and its counties are sub-divided as follows: counties into baronies, baronies into parishes, and parishes into townlands. The townland is a unique feature of the Irish landscape and is one of the most ancient divisions in the country. They existed long before the parishes and counties were organised and laid down in their anglicised form. There is considerable variation in scale from the largest, which is more than 7,000 acres, to the smallest of 1 acre which is Mill Tenement in County Armagh.

From the seventeenth century onwards land was let by landlords on a townland basis and townland names were recorded in a variety of documentation concerning land. Estate rentals were organised by townlands, as were surveys such as the tithe applotment books. It was the smallest division and it was used as a basis of the census returns from 1821 and for the first official valuation of Ireland in the 1830s, known as the townland survey, and for Griffith's Valuation of 1848–64. For a complete list of townlands in County Armagh, see Appendix 3.

UNOFFICIAL PLACENAMES

Even the most experienced researcher can be confused by references to placenames in old documents which do not correspond with any local townland. These are usually old gaelic names for sub-divisions of land which ceased to be used in official documents after standardised names were given to each townland during the Ordnance Survey mapping of Ireland in the 1830s. The list of unofficial placenames reproduced in Appendix 4 should prove invaluable. The placenames are listed along with the townlands and civil parishes to which they belong and the Ordnance Survey map sheet number is given.

THE COUNTY

The county was and still is the principal unit of local government. During the second half in the sixteenth century Ireland's four provinces of Ulster, Connaght, Leinster, and Munster were divided into 32 counties which were based on older lordships. During the seventeenth century the county was a key unit of measurement when framing the plantation of Ulster. The importance of the county was confirmed by the subsequent mapping of Ireland which established the county system.

THE BARONY

During the late sixteenth century, Armagh was divided into the baronies of Armagh, O'Neilland East and West, Upper and Lower Fews, Upper and Lower Orior, and Tiranny. (See Appendix 3.)

The barony was an important county subdivision and is the Irish equivalent of the English hundred. A barony could occupy part of two counties in which case it is known as a half-barony in each. Within the boundary of the barony the local landowner was granted the right to administer justice. These rights were inherited along with the land. From the sixteenth to the nineteenth centuries the barony was used in surveys, official census returns etc. The various valuations of Ireland carried out in the nineteenth century were organised and published by barony and it was not until the reorganisation of local government in 1898 that the barony ceased to be included as an important territorial division.

THE PARISH

The parish in the past has been both an ecclesiastical and a civil unit. In England and Wales it was developed as a unit of local government by the Crown and grew in importance as the manor declined. Until the 1830s the parish was responsible for the relief of poverty, the collection of tithes and the provision of recruits for the army.

Since the Reformation the Church of Ireland and the Roman Catholic churches have had two separate parochial structures. The Church of Ireland retained the medieval parochial divisions and the civil parishes used in early census returns, tax records and maps are almost identical to the Church of Ireland parishes. (See map of civil parishes, Appendix 6.)

As a result of the confiscation of its buildings and land during the Reformation, Roman Catholic parishes were formed later and are larger and more cumbersome. This is illustrated by the fact that in County Armagh there are 23 Roman Catholic parishes and 29 Church of Ireland. The creation of new Catholic parishes in the nineteenth century may mean that the registers relevant to a particular area may be split between two parishes, as is the case with the Parish of Kilclooney, for example. (See map of Roman Catholic parishes, Appendix 7.)

THE POOR LAW UNION

In February 1837, the government introduced a 'Bill for the more effectual relief of the destitute poor in Ireland'. The Bill, which became law on 1 July 1838, provided for the division of the country into a series of poor law unions to be based on market towns. In England the units on which the poor law was administered were civil parishes. In Ireland the size of the unions varied considerably, the largest ones being in the west of Ireland and the small ones in the eastern part of Ulster where the population was most dense.

Each union was to have a workhouse that would be paid for

from rates levied on the property owners. The only previous general valuation of the country had been made under an Act of 1826 for the purpose of levying the Grand Jury cess charge levied on land and premises.

The Poor Law Relief Act also provided for a separate survey of Ireland in order to provide a basis for the calculation of rates, which were needed to pay for the upkeep of the new workhouses. This Primary Valuation, better known as the Griffith Valuation after its director Richard Griffith, was carried out between 1847 and 1864. The results were printed in bound volumes and include the names of occupants of land and houses, the persons from whom the land was leased, and their area and value. These, as we shall see later, are an invaluable source for genealogists.

DISTRICT ELECTORAL DIVISIONS

Poor Law Unions were in turn sub-divided into District Electoral Divisions for electoral purposes. Each poor law union was administered by local boards of guardians elected by rate-payers of the district, together with ex-officio members who were made up of Justices of the Peace, but who were not 'a stipendiary magistrate or assistant barrister, or a person in Holy Orders or a regular Minister of any religious denomination'. (See list of poor law unions and district electoral divisions, Appendix 3.)

THE RECORDS

Many researchers are impatient to work their way through records dating back to the sixteenth and seventeenth century. This is not the best place to start, however, because by jumping back several generations it is almost impossible to prove whether or not the James Calvert or Patrick Murphy listed in Griffith's Valuation or a seventeenth century Muster List is the direct ancestor they may appear to be. It is easier to start with records dating from the early part of this century when most people can be sure of their ancestor's location and surname.

CENSUS RECORDS

Occasionally these returns can provide details of two or three generations of a single family and on some occasions include details of overseas places of births of individuals including America, Australia and even Argentina.

THE TWENTIETH CENTURY

Although the 1901 and 1911 censuses may seem too recent to interest family historians, they do in fact include details of many individuals who were born early in the nineteenth century and before the devastation of the Great Famine.

1901 CENSUS

On 31 March 1901, a census was taken of the whole island of Ireland. Fortunately this census has survived. The original returns are deposited at the National Archives in Dublin while microfilm copies are available at the Public Record Office of Northern Ireland. The census records the name; relationship to the head of the household; religion; literacy; occupation; age; marital status; county of birth; ability to speak English or Irish. Every town, village and townland for County Armagh is represented and those inhabitants who were at home on 31 March 1901 are listed.

The original census returns are held at the National Archives in Dublin. The 1901 Census Catalogue is on the shelves of the Reading Room. Each county is listed in a separate volume and within each volume the district electoral divisions are arranged numerically. Before consulting the 1901 census returns you must establish in which district electoral division the relevant townland or street is situated. The district electoral division (DED) was based on the subdivision of the old poor law union for electoral purposes. The DED can be found in the 1901 Townland Index which is available on the shelves of the Search Rooms at both the National Archive and PRONI. Simply look up the relevant townland, village or town and you will find it listed along with the barony and poor law union. Appendix 3 provides a handy listing for County Armagh.

Within each DED the townlands are arranged numerically. In order to request the returns for a particular townland you must include the name of the county, the number of the DED and the number of the townland. The returns for 1901 are bound into large volumes. The DEDs for some of the more important towns in County Armagh include:

Armagh Town	2/DED
Armagh Town	3/DED
Keady Town	14/DED
Hamilton's Bawn	21/DED
Markethill	23/DED
Richhill	26/DED
Tandragee Urban	34/DED
Crossmaglen	37/DED
Newtownhamilton	43/DED
Lurgan Urban	47/DED
Portadown Urban	53/DED

The 1901 Census Returns for County Armagh are available on microfilm at the Public Record Office of Northern Ireland. It is not possible, with the limited space available, to include a complete listing of the 1901 census; the following references relate to the major towns and villages in county Armagh:

Armagh City	MIC/354/2/2–3
Keady	MIC/354/2/7
Loughgall	MIC/354/2/8
Hamilton's Bawn	MIC/354/2/10
Markethill	MIC/354/2/11
Richhill	MIC/354/2/13
Tandragee	MIC/354/2/17
Crossmaglen	MIC/354/2/18
Newtownhamilton	MIC/354/2/20
Lurgan	MIC/354/2/21
Portadown	MIC/354/3/26

Heritage World, based in Donaghmore, hold the 1901 census on their computerised database.

1911 CENSUS

The 1911 census was taken on 1 April on that year and contains additional information including the number of years a wife was married, with the number of children born and number still living. This census is not yet available at the Public Record Office of Northern Ireland because of the more restrictive 100-year UK rule on access, but the original census returns can be viewed at the National Archives in Dublin.

Many of the numbers allocated to District Electoral Divisions changed between 1901 and 1911. There is a slim official publication listing all the numbers given for each townland in the Townland Index published along with the volumes of the 1901 census report and also the new altered numbers used in the arrangement and cataloguing of the 1911 census. If in difficulty ask the staff in the National Archives search room to show you a copy of this publication.

Unlike the 1901 census returns which are available in large

volumes, those for 1911 are still unbound and stored in boxes. The returns for the major towns in County Armagh can be located under the following District Electoral Divisions:

Armagh East Urban	2/DED
Armagh North Urban	3/DED
Armagh South Urban	4/DED
Keady	13/DED
Hamilton's Bawn	22/DED
Markethill	24/DED
Richhill	28/DED
Tandragee	35/DED
Tandragee Urban	36/DED
Crossmaglen	39/DED
Lurgan Urban	49/DED
Portadown Urban	54/DED

Both censuses are arranged by poor law union, district electoral division, county, barony, parish, townland and street if in a town or city.

The 1901 and 1911 census returns for all Ireland have been filmed by the Church of Jesus Christ of Latter Day Saints (Mormons).

THE NINETEENTH CENTURY

The first properly organised census in Ireland commenced in 1821. The surviving census returns for 1821 and 1831 are unique for it was not until 1841 that a census was taken for the rest of the United Kingdom. Thereafter, with some exceptions, a census was taken every ten years. These census returns gave names, ages, occupations and relationships to the heads of household as well as the acreage of land and the number of storeys in the house.

Unfortunately, the census returns from 1861 to 1891 were pulped by government order and those from 1821 to 1851 were destroyed in the destruction of the Public Record Office of Ireland in 1922. However, returns for a small number of parishes have survived, particularly for the 1821 census. Of particular interest are the following which are deposited at the Public Record Office of Northern Ireland:

1821 Extracts from the Portadown census   PRONI T/281/7,
                                             SLC 258511, 258621
1821 Census returns for the Parish of Kilmore PRONI, T/450,
                                             SLC 258511, 258621
1821 Returns for Derryhale   *Ulster Folklife,* vol 7, 1961

The census returns for Kilmore, containing the townlands of Derryhale, Corcreevy, Balleney, Crewcat, Drumnahushin and Maynooth, are also available in bound typescript copies at the Irish History Library, Armagh and the Armagh County Museum. The original enumerator's notebook is held in the Armagh Public Library.

Extracts from the 1841 and 1851 census returns were prepared during the early twentieth century to assist applicants for old age pension claims (see below).

OLD AGE PENSION CLAIMS

Although it is a long shot, it is worth checking the old age pension search forms, for they contain extracts from the 1841 and 1851 census which were completely destroyed. The old age pension was introduced on 1 January 1909 for those over seventy years of age. For many born before 1864, when the state registration of births began in Ireland, it was necessary to pay for a search to be made of the 1841 and 1851 census in order to prove their entitlement to the pension. The forms submitted by the claimant include such information as the names of parents, location at the time of the 1841 or 1851 census, and age at the time of the claim and during the relevant census year. Individual application forms completed by or on behalf of the applicant are known as 'Green Forms'. They contain the applicant's name, contact address, age, parents' names and address at the time of the census. The result of the search was then added in the form of a brief statement as to whether or not the applicant's name had been located in the census. The Green Forms for County Armagh are held at the National Archives, Dublin. The reference for County Armagh is CENS/2/1–109.

CENSUS YEAR FOR WHICH SEARCH IS REQUESTED

1851

CLAIMANT	Mary Boyle
CLAIMANT'S FATHER	John O'Neill
CLAIMANT'S MOTHER	Elizabeth
TOWNLAND	Cavanakill
PARISH	Ballymyre
BARONY	Fews Upper County Armagh
AGE	as stated on claim 70
	As stated in census return eight

1851

JOHN O'NEILL	40 years, head, mar. 1831
ELIZA "	40 years, wife " "
OWEN "	16 years, son
CHARLES "	12 years, son
MARY "	8 years, daughter
JOHN "	6 years, son
JAMES "	4 years, son
PATT "	1 year, son
	none absent or dead

Another form of evidence related to the old age pension returns are 'Form 37s' which were submitted by local pensions offices. These contain information on a number of applicants including the name, stated age, parents' names and address at the time of the census. Details of the search were added to the form and each claim for County Armagh was bound according to baronies in a series of volumes now deposited in the Public Record Office of Northern Ireland. The following volumes should be consulted:

Armagh Barony	T/550/11
Fews Barony	T/550/12
Oneilland Barony	T/550/13
Orior Barony	T/550/14
Tiranny Barony	T/550/15
Mixed Baronies	T/550/16

A partial index is available on microfiche (reference MF/ 9/1/1–9); however, these entries relate to the Mormon microfilm copy and as a result do not always correspond to the originals. It is also worth taking a look at certified copies of census returns for County Armagh which are bound together with some entries for County Antrim, reference T/550/1A.

Certified copies of census returns for County Armagh, dating from the period 1916–22, are also available at PRONI reference T/550/1.

CENSUS SUBSTITUTES

NINETEENTH CENTURY

THE TITHE SYSTEM, 1824–1838

The tithe system, which nominally earmarked one-tenth of the produce of the land for the maintenance of the clergy, was introduced in England as early as the eighth century. Tithes were introduced in Ireland during the reign of Henry II although they were not paid outside the area around Dublin until the sixteenth century.

Originally the tithes were payable in kind such as the tenth cow or sheep etc. This created a great deal of ill-feeling and not only in Ireland. In England there was a great deal of opposition to payment in kind, and this became part of the movement for reform during the 1830s. In Ireland, because the tithe system was used for the upkeep of the Established Church, it caused a great deal of unrest among Roman Catholics and Presbyterians. Examples of early tithe records have survived for County Armagh. The most useful for family historians are:

Co. Armagh, tithe payers, 1737   PRONI T/808/15298
Tithe payers, Drumcree, 1737   NLI 920041 p1

The following extract illustrates the limited amount of information to be found in tithe records. Only the name of the head of the tithe payer is given:

DRUMCREE TITHE PAYERS

1737

	p	s	d
TULLYMAKANNY			
William Todd	–	13	11
Francis Morrow	0	7	11½
TROUGHAN			
Chris Thornbury	0	10	0
Neal O Donely	0	2	2
Dennis McFall	0	5	0
Edw O Neill		2	5
William McSaweny	4	6	
DRUMHERIF			
Widow Todd	0	4	7½
Eliz Donely	0	1	6
Richard Lapon	0	0	9
Jas McChohlin	0	3	2
Richard Wright	7	0½	
[ ] Mullen	8	6	
Joseph Mullen	6	2	
AUGHANENGALL			
Sol. Cullen	0	13	0
Dennis McKinny	0	6	8
Denis Lappen	0	2	11
Murtagh Conlon	0	4	11

The commutation of tithes into a money payment was introduced in Ireland more than a decade before it became law in England. The Tithe Applotment Act of 1823 was a recognition of the unpopularity of payment in kind and of the practical difficulties faced by those attempting to secure payments. As a result it was necessary to carry out a valuation of the entire country, parish by parish, in order to determine how much would be payable by each landowner. These assessments were carried out by local surveyors and there is considerable variation in the quality of the records from place to place. Sometimes only the names of large landowners are given and in the parish of Armagh the surviving survey only gives names for five townlands. However in general the tithe applotment books provide a country-wide survey giving names of occupiers or leaseholders and valuations for individual holdings prior to the devastation of the Great Famine.

The tithe survey books list the farmers occuping titheable land and therefore labourers, weavers and all purely urban dwellers were omitted. In 1838 the tithe payment was reduced by 25 per cent and transferred from the tenant to the landowner. It was finally abolished in Ireland in 1869.

The researcher can face problems in using the tithe books. In some areas, for example, the land was of such poor quality that no tithe could be levied. Other areas were tithe-free for other reasons, usually because the land was owned outright by the Church. Another more serious complication is that the subsequent dividing up and renaming of townlands and the transfer of townlands from one parish to another, and even from one county to another, is the cause of some confusion. Some parishes appear not to be represented at all in the series of applotment books when, in fact, they do exist but under another name or merely as part of a then larger parish. For example, Kildarton was a new parish, formed in 1840 out of the parishes of Armagh, Lisnadill, Loughgall and Mullaghbrack, and for Kilclooney the tithe entries will be found in the parish of Mullaghbrack which was surveyed in 1834. At the front of the tithe applotment catalogue in the search room of PRONI details of such parish and boundary changes are noted. The Householders' Index (a rough surname index compiled by the National Library of Ireland and available in typescript volumes for each county) on the shelves of the Public Search Room, can be used as a guide to the surnames listed in the Tithe Applotment Books (FIN/5A). A searchable database of the Householders' Index (for all nine counties of Ulster) can be found on the Ulster Historical Foundation website.

For a complete list of PRONI references for County Armagh Tithe Records see Appendix 5. An index to the Tithe Applotment Books for County Armagh (and the other five counties of present day Northern Ireland) is available on CD-ROM from Heritage World, Donaghmore.

VALUATION RECORDS

During the nineteenth century a series of valuations was carried out for the whole of Ireland. Every piece of land and every building was assessed and its financial value estimated. In theory the value was set at the amount the owner would expect should the property or land be hired out for one year. In fact, Richard Griffith, who supervised the Primary Valuation of Ireland, admitted that the land was valued 'from twenty-five to thirty per cent under its letting value...according to a scale of agricultural prices, not according to rents'.

THE TOWNLAND VALUATION, 1830

The 1830 valuation is an under-used source for family historians. Although it was primarily a valuation of land and the valuation of houses is often only a few pages at the end of the valuer's manuscript field book, many houses in towns were substantial enough to be subject to valuation. Houses for inclusion had to be valued at £3 or more and in 1838 this ceiling was raised to £5 but by then most of Ulster had been surveyed.

Unfortunately major towns and villages are not listed separately, but under the heading of the parish and barony they happen to be in. For example, Tandragee can be found in this valuation book of the parish of Ballymore in the barony of Orior Lower. The following references relate to the major towns and villages in County Armagh and can be found at the Public Record Office of Northern Ireland:

GOVERNMENT VALUATION.

ANNUAL VALUE, ONE-THIRD BEING DEDUCTED.

MARKET-STREET.

		£	s	d
1	Messrs. Heaton & Knox, house, offices and yard,	51	0	0
2	William Johnston, do. do. do.	39	0	0
3	George Scott, do. do. do.	48	0	0
4	Mrs. Greaves, house, offices, stores and yard,	56	0	0
5	G. M. Nelson and Henry Dickson, do. do. do. do.	80	0	0
6	Henry M'Kean, house,	17	0	0
7	John Simpson, house, offices and yard,	28	0	0
8	George Corry, house and yard,	27	0	0
9	James Riggs, house,	32	0	0
10	George Armstrong, house, offices, stores and yard,	46	0	0
11	William Christian, house, offices and yard,	27	0	0
12	Ezekiel Bruce, house and office,	12	0	0
13	John Robinson, house, offices and yard,	21	0	0
14	William Donnelly, house and yard,	8	0	0
15	Moses Eager, house, offices and yard,	9	0	0
16	John Long and G. Williamson, do. do. do.	12	0	0
17	N. Montgomery, do. do. do.	6	0	0
18	James M'Williams, do. do. do.	3	14	0
19	Hugh Treanor and others, house and yard,	7	0	0
20	Philip M'Gunty, house, offices and yard,	4	18	0
21	Three Houses (rear of No. 20) exempt.			
22	William Robb, stores,	4	6	0
23	William Kerr, house and yard,	6	6	0
24	Charles Baker, do. do.	6	10	0
25	John Conroy and Others, house, offices, store and yard,	30	0	0
26	Thomas Eager and William Lyons, house, office and yard,	14	0	0
27	William M'Caffry and another, do. do. do.	7	10	0
28	Owen Hughes, do. do. do.	4	4	0
29	Peter O'Donnell, do. do. do.	4	4	0
30	Miss O'Neill and John Jackson, do. do. do.	7	10	0
31	Pat. Morris and Thomas Hughes, house and yard,	5	4	0
32	John Jackson, house, offices and yard,	18	0	0
33	James M'Lerish, house and yard,	5	4	0
34	Daniel M'Allen, do. do.	8	12	0

* All Holdings, when of £5 or less Annual Value (before deducting the third) are said to be exempted.

Government Valution of Armagh City, 1839. Copies are available at the Irish Studies Library, Armagh and at the National Library, Dublin, NLI Pos.99.

Armagh	VAL/1B/ 21A
Crossmaglen	VAL/1B/240 A
Keady	VAL/1B/246 E
Loughgall	VAL/1B/234
Lurgan	VAL/1B/223B
Markethill	VAL/1B/210 A&B
Newtownhamilton	VAL/1B/242A
Portadown	VAL/1B/234
Tandragee	VAL/1B/214

A set of these field books is also available in the National Archives, Dublin. A copy of the valuation for Armagh city is available in typescript in the relevant calendar on the shelves of the PRONI Public Search room. A copy is also available at the Irish Studies Library, Armagh.

A complementary set of annotated Ordnance Survey maps on the scale of 6" to one mile is also available at the Public Record Office of Northern Ireland, reference VAL/1A. Town plans are located under VAL/1D.

GOVERNMENT VALUATION OF ARMAGH CITY, 1839

A valuation of the city of Armagh was published in 1839. It contains the name and annual value of every holding in the city. A copy is available at the Irish Studies Library, Armagh and at the National Library, Dublin, NLI Pos. 99.

BANBROOK HILL

1 Patrick Murphy, **house,** office **and** yard.
2 John Robinson, do. do. do.
3 John Mitchell, do. do. do.
4 John Jamieson, do. do. do.
5 James Wood, house and office.
6 Four houses at front and two at rear, exempt.
7 Eight houses exempt.
8 Francis M'Cormick, house, offices and yard.
9 Eight houses exempt.

MILL-STREET

1 John Drenan, house and office, –

2   Thomas Wright, house, offices and yard.

3   Felix Hughes,   do.   do.   do.

4   Gardens (valued with the land).

5   Two houses exempt.

6   James Bennett, offices and yard.

7   Five houses exempt.

8   Cholera Hospital, offices and yard.

9   John Adams, house, offices and yard.

DAWSON STREET

1   The Shambles and Market Yard.

2   William Elliott, house, office and yard.

3   Henry M'Laughlin, do. do.   do.

4   Henry M'Cune,   do. do.   do.

5   Henry Wilcox,   do. do.   do.

6   Bernard Donnelly, house, forge and yard.

7   Thomas Gilchrist, house, offices and yard.

8   Four houses exempt.

9   Henry Lamb, house, office and yard.

10   James Nugent, do. do.   do.

11   Three houses exempt.

12   Robert Fulton, offices and yard.

13   Cornelius Hackett, house and yard.

14   One Tenement in ruins, exempt.

15   John Carbry, house and yard.

16   James Murphy, do. do.

17   Three houses exempt.

THE FIRST GENERAL VALUATION (GRIFFITH) 1848–64

Also known as the Primary Valuation and popularly as Griffith's Valuation, this is a complete survey of all occupiers of land, tenements and houses. Unlike census records, where the names and ages of the entire family are included, Griffith's Valuation only lists the name of the head of the household. Arranged by counties and within counties by poor law union divisions and within unions by parishes, it is available in manuscript form at the Public Record Office of Northern Ireland, Reference Number VAL /2B.

Bound and printed summary versions are available on the shelves

No. and Letters of Reference to Map.	Townlands and Occupiers.	Immediate Lessors.	Description of Tenement.	Area. A. R. P.	Land. £ s. d.	Buildings. £ s. d.	Total Annual Valuation of Rateable Property. £ s. d.
	KNOOK—continued.						
14	James Joyce,	Duke of Manchester,	House, offices, and land,	9 3 31	11 10 0	5 0 0	16 10 0
15	. .	. .	Water, . .	1 1 0	—	—	—
			Total, .	105 1 6	120 10 0	37 0 0	157 10 0
	KNOCKNAMUCKLY. (Ord. S. 10.)						
1	John Weir, jun.,	Alexander Richmond,	Land, . .	9 3 0	10 5 0	—	10 5 0
— a	Rachel Gracey,	John Weir, jun.,	House, . .	—	—	1 0 0	1 0 0
— b	Robert Weir,	Alexander Richmond,	House and land,	0 0 10	0 15 0	0 15 0	1 10 0
2				0 2 10			
— a	James Weir,	Robert Weir,	House, . .	—	—	0 10 0	0 10 0
3 A				2 3 0	3 0 0	1 10 0	
— B	John Weir, sen.,	Alexander Richmond,	House, offices, & land,	2 0 20	2 10 0		6 15 0
— c				1 3 20	1 15 0		
B a	William Cherry,	John Weir, sen.,	House and sm. garden,	—	—	1 0 0	1 0 0
— b	Noble Weir,	Same,	House, . .	—	—	1 0 0	1 0 0
4	Jane Gracey,	Alexander Richmond,	House, offices, and land,	3 1 0	3 10 0	1 10 0	5 0 0
5	Thomas Gracey, jun.,	Same,	House and land,	3 2 25	4 0 0	1 0 0	5 0 0
6 a	John M'Cann,	Same,	House and land,	1 1 10	1 10 0	1 5 0	2 15 0
— b	Arthur O'Neill,	John M'Cann,	House and land,	0 2 0	0 15 0	0 10 0	1 5 0
7							
8	Anne Gracey,	Alexander Richmond,	House, offices, and land,	1 0 20	1 10 0	1 10 0	3 0 0
9 a	Robert M'Kerr,	Same,	House and land,	1 2 10	1 15 0	1 0 0	2 15 0
— b	Thomas England,	Same,	House and garden,	0 0 35	0 10 0	0 15 0	1 5 0
10	John Spence,	Same,	Land, . .	4 3 20	6 0 0	—	6 0 0
11	James Fletcher,	Same,	House, offices, and land,	4 0 0	4 15 0	2 0 0	6 15 0
12	Jno. Patten (Hacknahay)	Same,	Land, . .	1 2 30	2 0 0	—	2 0 0
13 A a	Thomas Patten,	Same,	House, offices, & land,	5 2 20	6 10 0	1 10 0	9 0 0
— B				0 3 10	1 0 0		
A b	James Winchester,	Thomas Patten,	House, . .	—	—	0 15 0	0 15 0
— c	Lucy Patten,	Same,	House, . .	—	—	0 15 0	0 15 0
14 A a	Greenway Patten, sen.,	Alexander Richmond,	House, offices, & land,	9 0 10	10 0 0	2 0 0	13 10 0
— D				1 1 20	1 10 0		
A b	James Moore,	Greenway Patten, sen.,	House and garden,	0 0 25	0 5 0	1 0 0	1 5 0
— c	James M'Cann,	Same,	House and sm. garden,	—	—	1 0 0	1 0 0
15	Thomas Spence,	Alexander Richmond,	Land, . .	14 2 10	17 0 0	—	17 0 0
— a	Henry Geddis,	Thomas Spence,	House and garden,	0 0 20	0 5 0	0 15 0	1 0 0
— b	Thomas M'Cormick,	Same,	House and garden,	0 2 0	0 5 0	0 15 0	1 10 0
16	Patrick Murphy,	Alexander Richmond,	House, offices, and land,	12 2 5	14 10 0	1 10 0	16 0 0
17 a	John Patten,	Same,	House, offices, and land,	4 0 15	4 15 0	2 0 0	6 15 0
— b	Edward Patten,	Same,	House and office,	—	—	1 0 0	1 0 0
18 A a	Jane Maze,	Same,	House, offices, & land,	7 1 30	7 15 0	3 0 0	17 0 0
— E				5 0 25	6 5 0		
— b	Rachel Lockhart,	Jane Maze,	House, . .	—	—	1 10 0	1 10 0
— c	Timothy Kennedy,	Same,	House, . .	—	—	1 10 0	1 10 0
19 A a	William Duffy,	Alexander Richmond,	House and land,	3 2 35	4 10 0	0 15 0	6 0 0
— B				0 3 0	0 15 0		
A b				0 0 20	0 5 0	0 10 0	
20 A	Margaret Duffy,	Same,	House and land,	1 2 0	1 10 0	—	4 5 0
— B				2 0 0	2 0 0	—	
21 A				0 2 20	0 15 0		
A a	John Maguire,	Same,	House and land,			0 15 0	1 5 0
B a	Thomas M'Conville,		House and land,			0 10 0	1 5 0
— B				0 1 35	0 10 0		
22 A	John Duffy,	Same,	House and land,	0 3 30	1 3 0	0 15 0	3 5 0
— B				1 1 0	1 7 0		
23	Margaret Corr,	Same,	House, office, and land,	4 2 0	4 10 0	1 0 0	5 10 0
24 A a	James Corr,	Same,	House and land,	0 1 10	0 7 0	1 0 0	3 10 0
— B				1 3 15	2 3 0		
A b	John Corr,	Same,	House, . .	—	—	0 10 0	0 10 0
25 a	Michael Corr, sen.,	Same,	House and land,	2 3 10	2 15 0	1 0 0	3 15 0
— b	Michael Corr, jun.,	Michael Corr, sen.,	House, . .	—	—	0 10 0	0 10 0
26	Bernard M'Evoy,	Elizabeth Carleton,	House, office, and land,	1 2 20	1 15 0	1 5 0	3 0 0
27 a	Thomas M'Evoy,	Same,	House, offices, and land,	8 2 5	9 0 0	1 5 0	10 5 0
— b	Lucas M'Evoy,	Thomas M'Evoy,	House, . .	—	—	0 15 0	0 15 0
28	James Rogers,	Elizabeth Carleton,	House, office, and land,	4 1 35	4 10 0	0 10 0	5 0 0
29	Greenway Patten, jun.,	Same,	House and land,	5 0 25	6 0 0	1 0 0	7 0 0
30 a	James Watson,	Same,	House, offices, and land,	10 1 30	11 10 0	2 10 0	14 0 0

Griffith's Valuation for the townland of Knocknamuckley
(Printed copies of Griffith's Valuation are available at the Linen Hall
Library, Central Library, PRONI, and the Irish Studies Library, Armagh).

of the Public Search Room for County Armagh and indeed for all
of Ulster. These volumes are arranged by poor law union, within
union by county, and then into parishes and townlands. The
boundaries of some unions overlap with county boundaries: the
union of Lurgan, for example, extends into counties Armagh,
Down and Antrim, and there are separate volumes of valuation
for each of these. There is an index at the front of each volume
which enables searchers to identify the page or pages in which a
specific townland may be found.

Again, the valuer's annotated set of ordnance survey maps
showing the location of every property is available at the Public
Record Office of Northern Ireland, reference VAL/ 2A.

Bound printed volumes of Griffith's Valuation for those unions
in County Armagh are available at the Linen Hall Library and Central
Library, Belfast, and the Irish Studies Library at Armagh and also
on the open shelves in PRONI. Copies may also be found in some
local libraries. An index to Griffith's Valuation for all of Ireland
(providing first name, surname, townland, parish and county
information) is available on CD-ROM from Heritage World in
Donaghmore. A CD-ROM set comprising page scans of the
printed Griffith's Valuation has been produced by Irish
Microforms Media Ltd in Dublin.

Griffith's Valuation for County Armagh was completed in 1864.
The valuer's manuscript books, held by PRONI, were updated
annually and these books up to c.1930 are available in PRONI
(VAL/12B). The so-called 'cancelled books' consist of notebooks
kept by the valuation office and include details of when a holding
was passed from one person to another; the name of the original
holder was crossed off, the new owner's name was written above
it and the date of the transfer was written in the margin. This helps
to establish significant dates in family history, such as dates of death,
sale or emigration. By the closing years of the nineteenth century
and the first two decades of the twentieth century most of the
occupiers of land had become landowners, thanks to a series of
land purchase acts. This explains the initials L.A.P. (Land Act
Purchase) which may be found stamped on an entry in the revision
lists. The corresponding maps are also available, reference VAL/
12D.

A complete list of references for County Armagh Valuation Records is available in Appendix 5.

1837

List of illiterate voters, known as 'Marksmen', of the Borough of Armagh, Parliamentary Papers, 1837, *Reports from Committees, Vol. II (1) Appendix A*. Parliamentary Papers, commonly called the 'blue books', of the late 18th and 19th centuries include reports from committees and royal commissions. Reprints by the Irish Universities Press are available at major public and university libraries. See Joseph Canning's article 'Nineteenth Century British Parliamentary Papers' as a source for local history published in *Ulster Local Studies*, Vol 11, No 1 (1989).

LIST OF RATEPAYERS 1840

A list of ratepayers for the Union of Armagh giving area, value and situation of property rated is available at the Public Record Office of Northern Ireland, reference D/1670/13/6.

THE EIGHTEENTH CENTURY

1740 PROTESTANT HOUSEHOLDERS

In 1740 the Irish House of Commons required the compilation of returns of Protestant Householders in the North of Ireland. The work was undertaken by Hearth Money Collectors in their various 'walks'. The original records of this survey were destroyed in PROI in 1922 but copies survive for part of the survey in transcripts prepared by Tenison Groves. These transcripts provide the names of 14,400 Protestant householders mainly in County Londonderry but covering 6 parishes in County Armagh.

The householders' list is simply a list of names. Returns have survived for the parishes of Shankill (Lurgan listed separately), Mullaghbrack, Derrynoose, Creggan, Loughgall and Tynan in County Armagh, and are located at the Public Record Office for Northern Ireland under the reference T/808/15258. A transcript is also available on the shelves of the Public Search Room.

```
Protestant Householders in 1740

County Armagh    Turany barony    TYNAN parish  1

Jn Morrow,  Tho Stewart,  Jn Fee,  Jam M'Crath,
Jn Keenan,  Neal Mulligan,  Jn Lenan,  Jn Mitchell,
Jn Mitchell,  Geo Mitchell,  Geo Mitchell,  Jn Mitchell,
Char Conan,  Wm Mitchell,  Jam Mitchell,  Jam Mitchell,
Jn Farier,  Allex Kane,  Sam Browne,
Jos Wmson,  Nath Kennedy,  Jn Orr,  Nath Kane,
Geo Mitchell,  Tho Mitchell,  Unfry M'Connell,  Tho Smith,
Jn Hamilton,  Her Wright,  Tho M'Cay,  Jn Parkes,
Thos Rushill,  Jam Morrison,  Jn Morrison,  Jn Bucock,
Robt Bucock,  Rob Irwin,  Jn Stringer,  Rob Grasen,
Jam M'Clare,  Wm Farbis,  Wm Clerke,  Dav Lawson,
Sam Lawson,  Jam Parkbry,  Allex Parkley,  Robt Gordon,
Jn Barkley,  Wm Reily,  Allex M'Cleery,
Rob Harrison,  Jn Harris,  Jn Grasen,  Tho Grasen,
Mr Huston,  Geo Hardman,  Jn Leawis,  Fran Mullan,
Mr Nivan,  Jam Martan,  Jn Roger,  Pa Camill,
Rob Grasen,  Jn Kelly,  Jam Caraboo,  Jos Frikelton,
Rob Parke,  Allex Chambers,  Rob Graham,  Jam M'Cleland,
Jn Mecklin,  Val Gregory,  Captain Gregory,  Jn Reily,
Jn M'Clure,  Rob Leman,  Walt Young,  Rob Mullan,
And Bryans,  Rich Stuart,  Jn Wilson,  Jn Crookshanks,
Jn Ferguson,
Wm Graham,  Tho Finlay,  Jam Betty,  Rich Johnston,
Wm Crookshanks,  Jam Hamilton,  Tho Clinton,  Caster Clinton,
Wm Hamilton,  Jn Burinston,  Jam Bucock,  Mr Leburn,
Jam Brown,  Jn Gormly,  Pa Goftony,  Pett Carr,
Hary Camill,  Wm Conry,  Wm Martin,  Jam Moore,
Jn Mecklain,  Walt Stewart,  Jn Brownlee,  Edw Bond,
Jam Moore,  Jam Grear,  Ham Howey,  Tim Marshall,
Tho Brownlee,  Tho Mathews,  Allex M'Bwy,  Hery Groes,
Hen Hamilton,  Rich Huston,  Moris Fox,  Wm Maxwell,
Jn Jackson,
```

Householders' List, 1740, for 'Turany' (Tiranny) Barony, Tynan Parish.
(PRONI T/808/15258, RCB Library Ms 23, the National Library Ms 4173,
the National Archives NA 1A 46 100 and the Genealogical Office, GO 539.)

The Armagh householders' returns (apart from Mullaghbrack)
are available in the RCB Library (Ms 23). The returns for Derrynoose
and Tynan are available at the National Library (Ms 4173) and
returns for County Armagh are located at the National Archives
(NA 1A 46 100) and the Genealogical Office (GO 539).

1766 RELIGIOUS RETURNS

In March and April 1766 Church of Ireland rectors were instructed
by the government to compile complete returns of all householders
in their respective parishes, showing their religion, as between

Church of Ireland (Episcopalian), Roman Catholic (termed 'Papists' in the returns) and Presbyterians (or Dissenters), and giving an account of any Roman Catholic clergy active in their area. Some of the more diligent rectors listed every townland and every

PETITIONS OF PROTESTANT DISSENTERS

IN OCTOBER AND NOVEMBER 1775

Parliamentary Papers in Record Office, Dublin.

Bundle 28. Nos.1-42 (5.0 - 195 - 11).

No.15. Clare Congregation in Ballymore Parish, Co. Armagh.

John Young	James Lewis
Alexander Patton	Tugwell Black
Samuel Livingstone	Daniel MacKelvey
Jno MtGomery	Robert Cockburn
Charles Meins	John Maffet
Thomas McBurney	Samuel Parker
Thomas Ferris	John Hear
George Craige	David Geddis
Robert Boyd	Thomas Lewis
James Orr	Thomas Greenaway
Robert McKelvey	John Aston
Hugh Wallace	John Moore
James Purdy	William Craige
John Girvin	William Crozier
William McDonnell	David Parker
Thomas Beggs	James Fryer
Archd. Girvin	Thomas Fryer
Alexander English	John Black
Hugh Morrison	William Strong
John Morrison	Robt. McMahon

Petition of Protestant Dissenters, Clare Congregation in Ballymore Parish, 1775 (PRONI T/808/14977 and the Armagh County Museum).

household, but many drew up only numerical totals of the population. All of the original returns were destroyed in the Four Courts in 1922, but extensive transcripts survive for the parishes of Armagh, Ballymore, Creggan, Drumcree, Kilmore, Loughgall and Tartaraghan. Copies are held by the Public Record Office, reference T/808/15264-7 and T/3709, with a transcript version available on the shelves of the Public Search Room.

A full listing of all surviving manuscripts is available on the shelves of the National Archives Reading Room. Some originals and transcripts are available at the Genealogical Office, GO 537 and the National Archives, NAI Parl. Ret 657. The parish returns for Creggan parish were published in the *Louth Archaeological Society Journal*, vol 8 (1934), pp.156–162.

1770 CENSUS OF ARMAGH

The so-called Census of Armagh City includes individual names and occupations. The head of the household is named and it is recorded if they are married. The names of the wives are not recorded although their religion, if different from that of their husband, is included. According to the census the number of families in Armagh were as follows:

Church families	162
Presbyterian	131
Popish	209
Total number of families	502

A manuscript edition with an alphabetical index is available at the Robinson Library, Armagh. An indexed typescript copy is also deposited at the Armagh Museum. A number of manuscript copies are deposited at the Public Record Office of Northern Ireland under the following reference numbers, T/389, T/1228 and T/808/14938, 14977. Copies are also available at the National Library, NL Ms 7370 and at the Family History Centres, SLC film 258621.

ENGLISH STREET

NAME	TRADE	CHILDREN	SERVANTS	RELIGION
Lord Primates	House			
Dr Grueber & w(ife)	Schoolmaster		3 men, 4 maids	EC

Tho McCann & w(ife)		8	5	
Jn Burgess & w(ife)	Attorney	3	2 men, 2 maids	
Hen Bambrick & w(ife)	public house	3		EC
W(ife) Presb ---				
Graham & w(ife)	Cooper			
Wm Hall & w(ife)	public house	2 sons 2 dau		EC
Alex Murphy & w(ife)	" "			
Jm Greaves & w(ife)	" "	1		EC
Lt Townshend & w(ife)	EC	W(ife) Presb		

1775 PETITION OF PROTESTANT DISSENTERS

The petition of Protestant dissenters is simply a list of names of dissenters in either a parish or congregation basis. Armagh parish and Clare congregation in Ballymore parish have survived for County Armagh and are available at the Public Record Office of Northern Ireland, ref T/808/14977. A transcript is available on the shelves of the Public Search Room. Copies can also be found at the Armagh County Museum, Armagh.

THE FLAXSEED PREMIUMS OF 1796

This is a list of 56,017 individuals who benefited from a government initiative to encourage the linen trade, under which they received a loom or one or more spinning wheels depending on the acreage of flax grown. More than half the names relate to Ulster and are arranged by parish within counties.

These awards were made by the Irish Linen Board and in 1796 they published a list of recipients. The only copy of this work known to exist until recently was held in the Linen Hall Library Belfast. Another copy has now been acquired by the Irish Linen Centre in Lisburn Museum.

The Ulster Historical Foundation has computerised this source and it is available on a searchable database on the UHF website. Heritage World has also made it available on CD-ROM. A microfiche copy of the printed volume with an index is available in PRONI (ref. MF|7|1). A copy of the printed list for Co. Armagh (consisting of some 4,000 names) was published in the *Ulster Genealogical and Historical Guild Newsletter* Vol.1 No.7 (1981).

COUNTY OF ARMAGH.

A List of Persons to whom Premiums for sowing Flax-feed in the Year 1796 have been adjudged by the Truftees of the Linen Manufacture.

Purfuant to the Scheme offered by them for encouraging the Growth of Flax throughout the Kingdom, *viz.* " To the Perfon who fhould fow between the 10th " Day of March and the 1ft Day of June 1796, with a fufficient Quantity of " good found Flax-feed, any Quantity of Land, well prepared and fit for the purpofe, " not lefs than 1 Acre—4 Spinning Wheels,——3 Roods 3 Ditto,——2 Roods— " 2 Ditto,——1 Rood—1 Ditto. And to the Perfon who fhould fow in like " Manner any Quantity of like Land, not lefs than 5 Acres, a Loom, or Wheels, " Reels, or Hatchells to the Value of 50 Shillings, and for every 5 Acres over and " above the firft five a like Premium."

⁎ The Claimants for one Rood, who are entitled to one Wheel each, are requefted to apply to the County Infpector Mr. John Neill for their Wheels, there being a fufficient Number ready to diftribute among them: The other Premiums will be difcharged in Rotation as the Wheels can be made, of which due Notice fhall be given.

Every Perfon preferring Reels may have two of them in lieu of a Spinning Wheel.

The Scheme of Premiums offered by the Board for the Year 1796, has had fo extenfive an Effect, that it will require 37,135 Wheels to difcharge the One Rood Claimants; and not lefs than 88,719 Wheels, together with 227 Looms, to difcharge the whole, which neceffarily produces much delay in delivering.

As the higheft Price is paid for the Wheels in order to have them of the beft Fabric, of feafoned Timber, and of full Size; no Claimant is to receive any Wheel deficient in any refpect: They are al to be ftamped with the Board Seal before delivery, and with the Maker's Name.

And in order to render the national benefit propofed by the Truftees as efficacious as poffible, they requeft that any neglect or delay of the Infpector in delivering Wheels of the beft quality and equal excellence to the Pattern depofited with him, be inftantly made known to them by information to any Truftee, or to the Infpector General, or by Letter to their Secretary, at the Linen-Office, Dublin.

N. B. Any Infpector, Deputy Infpector, or Surveyor, or other Perfon acting under him or them, who fhall directly or indirectly receive any Fee, Gratuity, or Reward for the performance of his duty, becomes by fuch offence difqualified by Act of Parliament to hold any Employment under the Linen Board.

Prfh. of ARMAGH.

Name	Linen	Wheels	Name	Wheels	Name	Wheels
Jofeph Oliver	1		Mofes Archer	3	Anne Reed	2
			John Fergufon	3	Samuel Coulter	2
		Wheels.	Thomas Downy	3	Edward Mullan	2
John Wyne		4	Ellen O'Claghan	3	Robert M'Clean	2
William Coufer		4	Daniel Toole	3	James Wilken	2
Robert Donally		4	Thomas Hayes	3	James Barnet	2
David Hamilton		4	Mary Guinnefs	3	Mary Barcly	2
James M'Cullough		4	Patrick Kel'y	3	John Duncan	2
John Thompfon		4	Thomas Carrol	3	Patrick Largey	2
John Toner		4	Dominick Toole	3	Elizabeth Adams	2
Anne Hutchefon		4	Jane Brookes	3	James Grey	2
Patrick and Thomas Traynor		4	William Montgomery	3	Francis Tredden	2
William Lappin		4	Francis Moffit	3	Thomas Magee	2
John Wilkin		4	Samuel Dixon	3	Alexander Feemfter	2
John Magee		4	Samuel Hair	3	John Feemfter	2
John M'Williams		4	Bridget Troden	3	John Frookes	2
John Bryars		4	William Allen	3	James M'Farlin	2
William Davis		4	Edward Brawly	3	Terence Dillon	2
Thomas Pearfon		4	Phelix Conolly	3	Mary Dillon	2
John Oliver		4	Thomas Hafty	3	Edward Donagley	2
Alexander Hannah		4	Patrick Campbel	3	John and James Campbel	2
James Oliver		4	John M'Cracken	3	Patrick Gribben	2
Elizabeth Crawford		4	James Moffet	2	Terence Nugent	2
William Bell		4	James Angel	2	Luke M'Kee	2
James Clarke		4	John Adams	2	John M'Cattin	2
Neal M'Gurk		4	James Magee	2	Michael M'Coney	2
David O'Neal		4	John Raverty	2	Elizabeth Long	2
William Anderfon		4	William Allen	2	Bridei Johnfton	2
Terence Egan		4	Daniel M'Kenna	2	Patrick M'Ferlin	2
Thomas Reed		4	John M'Kenna	2	Patrick Byrne	2
William Stewart		4	Barney Kairos	2	Owen Nugent	2
William Anderfon		4	Jofeph Davidfon	2		
William Rice		4	William Simonton	2	Edward Rocks	2
John Platt		3	John Brooks	2	William Flanagan	2
Arthur M'Cormick		3	Samuel Birch	2	Patrick Rocks	2
John Traynor		3	William Adamfon	2	Robert Marks	2
Patrick Monaghan		3	James Kilpatrick	2	James Marks	2
Martha Cowler		3	Bernard Lappin	2	Thomas Maffet	2
James M'Kenna		3	Hugh Crawford	2	Daniel Cavanagh	2
William Carfon		3	Thomas Moore	2	John Carfon	2
Alexander Dobbin		3	John Quigley	2	John Brownfield	2
Robert M'Kinftry		3	Francis M'Guirk	2	Terence Hughes	2
John Rippit		3	John Wade	2	Hugh Wilfon	2
John Dobbin		3	James Macquy	2	George Hamilton	2
Bernard Donally		3	Patrick M'Ilverna	2	James Todd	2
Eleanor Quigley		3			Thomas Linfey	2
Anne Hutchefon		3			Andrew Simpfon	2

Page from the printed Flaxseed Premiums list, 1796 for County Armagh.

THE SEVENTEENTH AND SIXTEENTH CENTURIES

THE IRISH FIANTS OF THE TUDOR SOVEREIGNS - 1521–1603

Fiants were a documentary series unique to Ireland. These documents preceded the issue of royal grants by letters patent. The term 'fiant' derives from the first word in a normal letters patent 'Fiant literae patentes' meaning 'Let letters patent be made'. The preliminary fiants prepared in Ireland provide far fuller information about individuals than the actual letters patent issued in London. The uniqueness of the information included in the fiants encouraged the staff in the newly established Public Record Office of Ireland to publish calendars of these fiants. Ingeniously they got these calendars published by including them as appendices in the steady stream of annual reports published by the office in the years 1875–90 (reports Nos. 11–13, 15–18 of the Deputy Keeper of Public Records of Ireland). The attention of the scholarly world to the quality of the information available in the fiants was recently aroused by the publication of reprints of these calendars of Irish fiants for the years 1521–1603 by Edmund Burke in 1994. These serve as very adequate substitutes for the original records destroyed in PROI Dublin in 1922.

When Irish chiefs were granted pardons under the 'surrender and regrant' policy they often listed scores of members of their extended families including kern and gallowglasses (mercenary soldiers), horsemen and yeomen, husbandmen, tenants and even occasionally cottiers. Individuals were identified with their full names often with specific locations. In the pardon granted to Tirlagh McHenry O'Neale chief of the Fews in South Armagh a total of 270 names were recorded including a few women (see Appendix 1). Rev. Lawrence Murray publicized this source by issuing an edition of the document in the *County Louth Archaeological Journal* Vol.VIII (1934).

CALENDARS OF PATENT ROLLS OF JAMES I
1603–1625 AND CHARLES I 1625–1633

Irish Patent Rolls were also destroyed in the Public Record Office, Dublin, in 1922. Fortunately, some of the material had been published in calendar form. Printed calendars have survived for the patent rolls of King James I and the early part of the reign of Charles I. These contain the names of the native Irish who received grants of land or were pardoned for transgressions committed during the years 1603–1633. The calendars also include the names of Scots who were given grants of denization to enable them to settle in Ulster. Rev. David Stewart, a Presbyterian minister and very active local historian, extracted from the printed calendars of James I the names of about 1,000 Scots who were granted denization and this list, first published by the Presbyterian Historical Society was reprinted by the Ulster Historical Foundation in their journal *Familia* in 1995 (this issue is now out of print).

The calendar of patent rolls for James I was prepared under the direction of the Irish Record Commission and was partly printed before the Commission was closed down in 1830 and partly afterwards. The Irish Manuscript Commission published a facsimile of the printed calendar c.1970 but this publication is now out of print. Unfortunately no personal and place name index to this calendar has yet been published although one was prepared.

A series of calendars of patent and close rolls (Chancery) Ireland 1513–1633 compiled by J. C. Morrin were published in 1861–63. The indexes to these volumes are quite inadequate and numerous corrections are required in the text.

1612–13 SURVEY OF UNDERTAKERS PLANTED IN ARMAGH

A survey of the Undertakers and Servitors planted in Armagh between 2 February 1612 and April 25, 1613, Hastings Manuscript published by the Historic Manuscripts Commission, vol.4 (1947): 159–82. The following extract is for the Barony of O'Neilland:

> 1,000 "**107(1).** Mr. Matchet hath made a square bawn of timber clefts of good thickness 10 feet in height rampiered within with earth and sods to the height of 6 feet having 2 whole flanks, each side of the bawn containing 40 yards, a house with it of timber work on groundsels a story and a half high, and purposeth a brick house in that place, for

which he hath about 40,000 of brick ready for the kiln. He hath made 8 freeholders, and 4 lessees for years. His wife and family resident there, and his stock on the ground. 2,000 " **108(1).** William Powel his proportion is now in the hands of Richard Rowlestone, who hath set up a windmill and erected there 8 tenements, and hath the frames of 4 others ready to be erected. There are 100,000 bricks ready burnt, and as many more ready for burning, with lime and other provisions lying in readiness for making of a brick house and bawn, whereof the foundation is laid. He hath his full number of freeholders, leaseholders and cottagers with their goods and cattle on the ground. 2,000 "**109.** Sir Anthony Cope hath built a fair house of hewn stone with clay, of great charge, which being brought to perfection a great part of it fell suddenly down, so that the whole must be demolished to the ground and newly raised with lime, which as yet is not taken in hand by his agent there for want of direction. There are no tenants as yet come over, but a certain agreement was showed me whereby a part of that proportion is made over to certain gentlemen in England, who are to bring thither such families as shall plant the same."

ARMAGH MANOR COURT ROLLS, 1625–27

These consist of a series of rolls relating to Courts Leet in the Manors of Armagh, Arboe, Artrea, Donaghmore, County Tyrone and Termonfeckin, County Louth. The Courts Leet were local courts presided over by the local landlord, who was also lord of the manor, or his representative the Seneschal. A list of names representing persons brought before the court as either litigants or jurors was compiled by T. G. F. Paterson and published in *Seanchas Ardmhacha*, Vol. 11, No. 9, 1957, pp.295–322.

MUSTER ROLLS c.1630

Muster rolls are militia lists of the seventeenth and eighteenth centuries. All able-bodied Protestant men between the ages of 16 and 60 were liable for military service. They were armed at their own expense.

The surviving copies of muster rolls contain lists of the principal landlords in Ulster, and the names of the men they could assemble in an emergency. These are arranged by barony. The copy muster rolls 1630-31 are an important source for family historians because they are the first comprehensive list of the English and Scottish emigrants who settled in Ulster during the early seventeenth century. The following copies of muster rolls are available at the Public Record Office of Northern Ireland:

Muster roll for County Armagh, 1631	PRONI, T/934/1
Muster roll for Ulster 1630	PRONI, MIC/339, NLI Pos 206

The muster for County Armagh names 950 men who were fit to bear arms and this list edited by T.G.F. Paterson, was published in *Seanchas Ardmhacha* Vol. 5 No. 2, in an essay in 1970, entitled 'An Unpublished Early 17th Century Census of the Men and Arms on the Estates of the English and Scotch Settlers in Co. Armagh'.

SUBSIDY ROLLS, c.1634

The few surviving copies of subsidy rolls are made up of those who possessed sufficient property to be liable to payment of the subsidies to the monarch. During the seventeenth century subsidy was the chief form of direct taxation. These lists naturally represent the wealthier citizens. They include the amount paid and the status of the person.

Subsidy Rolls have survived for the parish of Shankill giving the personal names and there is also a valuation for Seagoe Parish (T/808/14950).

A Subsidy Roll for the Portadown area is also available for 1634, (PRONI T/281/7, and National Archives, Dublin, NAI M.2471, 2475).

DEPOSITIONS OF 1641

The Depositions of 1641 are the collected accounts of witnesses to the robberies and murders that took place during the rising. Eight Protestant clergymen, led by Henry Jones, Dean of Kilmore, were empowered to take evidence during town commissions in December 1641 and January 1642. In 1652, following Cromwell's subjugation of the country, a High Court of Justice was established to collect evidence for the trials of those who had risen against the settlers.

More than 140 depositions relating to the rising of 1641 in County

Armagh have survived and are deposited in the library of Trinity College, Dublin. Most of the witnesses were English settlers and their occupations ranged from 'gentlemen' to 'tanners', 'tailors' and 'inn keepers'. Nevertheless, they named their attackers or those rumoured to have taken part in the rising and the Depositions do provide rare documentary evidence of the native Irish families who had once dominated the country.

EXTRACT OF 1641 DEPOSITION

> The examination of John Taylor aged about 30 years, being duly sworn saith, that being an inhabitant of Tandragee, at the beginning of the rebellion, was kept there by force in the said town with many more both English and Scots till about May following. 'But upon the march of the British Army towards Newry, the Irish then in and about Tandragee caused all the prisoners to be gathered together, to the constables house of the said town, from which place they were carried away about a mile to the river, and then was stripped naked, knocked on the head, and thrown into the river, all both men and women and children. The chief actors in this bloody massacre was, Colonel Edmond Ogge O'Hanlon, Governor at Tandragee, and his 3 brothers Patt Ogge O'Hanlon, since slain, Ardell Oge O'Hanlon, since died likewise, and Furdorragh O'Hanlon with their soldiers. And that William McToole was, as this examinant heard, one of the actors; the clothes of the murdered being brought to his house, the rest of them, and there was divided...' Taken before us 8 June 1653, George Rawden, Tobias Norrice.

Copies of the 1641 Depositions are available at the PRONI, reference T/2706/8 and MIC/8/1. Depositions relating to County Armagh are also available in a bound transcript edition at the Armagh County Museum.

THE DOWN SURVEY, 1654–55

The Down Survey was carried out between 1654 and 1655 by trained surveyors who measured the land which was plotted on accompanying maps. It is a mapped record of landownership and was largely concerned with the lands which were confiscated after the Cromwellian victory in Ireland. Lands which were already in Protestant hands were not measured or subdivided. A number of copies or fragments of the Down Survey maps can be found at the Public Record Office of Northern Ireland. The most beautiful of these is a volume of late eighteenth century copies which includes a brief description of each denomination and a list of proprietors. The maps for counties Down, Armagh and Tyrone can be found in a single bound volume, reference D/597/4/1–90.

CENSUS OF IRELAND c.1659

This census of Ireland was probably made by Sir William Petty's surveyors. It contains only the names of those with title to land (tituladoes) and the total number of English and Irish resident in each townland. The census is divided up into Parishes/ Places (Townlands)/Numbers of people/Tituladoes' Names/English & Scots/Irish.

The Census was published in 1939 by the Stationery Office Dublin on behalf of the Irish Manuscripts Commission, and edited by Seamus Pender. Included are a breakdown of the figures for each county and an index of both personal names and placenames.

The name of an individual landowner is usually given and generally encompasses a number of townlands. Occasionally, however, where a town has been established a number of Tituladoes are listed. It is interesting to note that the English and Scottish settlers had become so intermingled that they were not distinguished by those who compiled the census. The following extract is for the parish of Shankill, County Armagh, listing the names of the principal inhabitants of the newly established town of Lurgan:

EXTRACT FROM 1659 'CENSUS' FOR COUNTY ARMAGH

PARISHES	NO. OF PEOPLE	TITULADOES' NAMES	ENG & SCOTS	IRISH
Shankell	344	Sr William Bromloe, Knight	242	102
		Fulke Martin Esq		
		William Draper		
		William Jones		
		Alexander Gill		
		Richard Bromloe		
		John Realy		
		John Burne		
		John Barnes		
		Cuth: Harrison &		
		Wrighton Taylor and		
		Lawrence Swarbricke gent		

Copies of the 1659 census are also available at the Public Record Office although these have been incorrectly labelled as Poll Tax Returns. See MIC/15A/76 and T/808/14929. Copies are also available at the National Library of Ireland, Dublin, NLI 16551 and the Family History Centres, SLC film 924648.

HEARTH MONEY ROLLS, c.1660s

Surviving copies of the hearth money rolls of the 1660s are a useful source of information for local historians. They list by townland and parish the names of the householders and the number of hearths on which they were taxed. The tax was levied twice a year, at Lady Day (25 March, the official start of the year until 1752) and Michaelmas (29 September, the feast of Michael the Archangel). During this time the tax was the government's major source of revenue. Its unpopularity led to its abolition in England and Wales after the Glorious Revolution of 1688. In Ireland it continued to be levied until the Act of Union in 1800. Unfortunately the originals were destroyed by fire in 1922 but copies do survive for certain areas in County Armagh and relate to the returns made in the mid-1660s.

Hearth Money Roll, 1664–65	PRONI T/604 GO ms 538 NLI ms 9586/9856 NAI m2745, 2745
The Hearth Money Rolls for County Armagh	*Archivium Hibernicum VIII* (pp 121–202) and in *Seanchas Ardmhacha* III (pp 96–142)
Extract for the Barony of Fews	*Louth Archaeological Journal*, 8 (2), 1934: pp.152–156

The following extract illustrates the sort of information hearth money rolls contain:

BARONY OF ORRIER

DENOMINATION OF LAND	INHABITANTS' NAMES	FIRE HEARTH	SUMS PAYABLE
Brenock	Sr Toby Pointz knt	nine	0.18.0
Aghataran	Hugh Wallace	one	0.02.0
	John Allen	one	0.02.0
Edernagh	Dennis Cawell	one	0.02.0

	Owen McQourte	one	0.02.0
	Owen o Hinan	one	0.02.0
Ballyleck	William McEnkilly	one	0.02.0
	Collowe McEnkilly	one	0.02.0
	Owen McEngarge	one	0.02.0
	Patrick McCramir	one	0.02.0

EXTRACT FROM HEARTH MONEY ROLLS FOR COUNTY ARMAGH

THE FRANCISCAN PETITION LISTS 1670–71

Although the Hearth Money Rolls remain the main genealogical source for the seventeenth century, the Franciscan Petition lists should not be neglected for they contain the names of individuals in County Armagh which are not found in any other archive.

The records themselves relate to a dispute between the Franciscans and the Dominicans which had its origins in the 1640s. During the seventeenth century the Dominicans, as a result of their increasing membership, had come into conflict with the Franciscans about their respective rights over the collection of alms or donations. The majority of the clergy and laity in Ulster supported the Franciscans and elected members of the congregation to represent their views to the Lord Primate Oliver Plunkett.

The Franciscan Petition Lists, therefore, contain the names of the clergy, gentry and parishioners of various townlands and parishes within the Armagh Diocese.

EXTRACT FROM THE PETITION FOR THE PARISH OF CREGGAN

'Here followeth the names of the parishioners of parish of Creggan, by their one consent and humble request drawen, against certaine Dominicans pretending to intrude unjustly upon them, and severall others, commonly begging at their alters to their same and unhability etc. being unable (God help them) to maintaine their one clergy booth secular and regular, as their predecesors did, which is enough for them, I pray God they may doe it.

Manutius Conneus curatus etc.

Pattr: Grome O Quine	Bryan O Quine
Neall McShane	Thorlaugh McGoirk
Edd McShane	John McGoirk
Owen McShane	Pattrick McGille
Caheer McShane	Edmond McShane

Phelim McShane	Thorlough McGoork
Cormuck O Quine	Hugh O Quine
Pattr: O Quine	Pattr: Callaghan
Bryan O Quine	Cormuck Callaghan
Eneas Quine	Thomas Callaghan
Bryan Mc Cardell	Edd Donnelly
James Mc Cardell	Bryan Callaghan.'

The complete list for the Diocese of Armagh has been published by Patrick J. Campbell, in *Seanchas Ardmhacha*, Journal of the Armagh Diocesan Historical Society, vol 15, No 1 (1992).

BOOKS OF SURVEY AND DISTRIBUTION

The Books of Survey and Distribution were compiled around 1680 as the English government needed reliable information on land ownership throughout Ireland to carry out its policy of land re-distribution following the wars of the mid-seventeenth century. The Books of Survey and Distribution are laid out on a barony and parish basis and include a record of land ownership before the Cromwellian and Williamite confiscations as well as the names of the individuals to whom the land was distributed. They were used to impose the acreable rent called the Quit Rent, which was payable yearly on lands granted under the terms of the Acts of Settlement and Explanation. A fire in 1711 in the Surveyor and Auditor General's Office destroyed the office copies of the Books of Survey and Distribution, but fortunately duplicate copies have survived. A set can be found in the Annesley Papers at the Public Record Office of Northern Ireland, (D/1854/1/18). Also see (T/370/A and D).

An extract for Creggan parish has been published in *Louth Archaeological Journal*, vol 8 No. 2 (1934).

PROTESTANTS IN COUNTY ARMAGH ATTAINTED BY JAMES II, 1689

This is simply a list of names, with some places of residence, of those Protestants who were deprived of their lands through conviction for high treason during James II's unsuccessful attempt to win back his throne on the battlefields of Ireland. (T/808/14985 and SLC 1279332.)

MAJOR COLLECTIONS

A number of major collections are available to researchers that include material covering more than one century.

CHURCH RECORDS

Armagh has been the spiritual capital of Ireland for 1,500 years and is the seat of both Protestant and Catholic archbishops. St Patrick called Armagh 'my sweet hill' and persuaded Daire, the local chieftain, to grant him the hilltop site where he built his stone church and where the Anglican cathedral now stands. After the foundation of Patrick's church in 445 A.D. other churches, colleges and schools flourished, making Armagh one of the great centres of learning in Europe.

From the eighth century the abbot-bishops of Armagh pressed their claims as the inheritors of St Patrick's mission, and in 1004 this primacy was recognised by Brian Boru as High King of Ireland.

Nonetheless, Armagh's status as the ecclesiastical capital of Ireland was disputed by Dublin until the 17th century when the area was planted with English and Scottish settlers. The religious foundations at Armagh attracted the Vikings during the ninth century and they frequently attacked and destroyed the monastic settlements in the city before Brian Boru won a decisive battle over them at Clontarf in 1014. Brian, his son and nephew were killed on the battlefield and their bodies are said to be buried on the north side of the Church of Ireland Cathedral.

The monastic settlements in Armagh were frequently at the mercy of opposing Irish forces as the O'Neills established their dominance over their neighbours. The Anglo-Normans during the later twelfth century attacked and plundered Armagh on numerous occasions, and during the sixteenth century and early seventeenth century, the city was sacked by opposing Irish and English forces. With the Plantation of Ulster Armagh re-established itself as the ecclesiastical capital of Ireland and it was the Anglican Primate Richard Robinson, appointed in 1765, who is responsible for many of the fine buildings that can be seen in Armagh today.

The city is now dominated by the Anglican and Roman Catholic Cathedrals. The Church of Ireland Cathedral of St. Patrick has been destroyed and rebuilt at least seventeen times in its long history. The present building is essentially an 1834 restoration of Archbishop Patrick O'Scannail's thirteenth-century church. Dominating a hilltop with its twin spires is St. Patrick's Roman Catholic Cathedral. The foundation stone was laid in 1840 but the Great Famine delayed the work and the building itself was not completed until 1873.

In the centuries that followed the Plantation of Armagh, each of the religious denominations has left its mark on the county. The planters from lowland Scotland brought with them their Protestant religion, largely Presbyterian in character, which often brought them into conflict with their Anglican landlords. Alongside them, and competing for land and jobs, were the native Irish who retained their Roman Catholic religion. Armagh, however, was one of the few counties in Ireland where Catholics remained in the minority. More unusually, it was Church of Ireland members rather than the Presbyterians who were the most numerous Protestant grouping in the county.

The Public Record Office of Northern Ireland has a large collection of church records relating to all denominations in County Armagh. This is an invaluable source for family historians and it is worth checking at your local library for the *Guide to Church Records* published by the Ulster Historical Foundation and PRONI (an updated version is available in PRONI). This lists by civil parish all church records held by the Public Record Office or elsewhere. It is also worth making contact with the minister or elder of the relevant church just in case some additional genealogical material may remain in local custody.

The Public Record Office has published a *Guide to County Sources for County Armagh* which lists the parishes in alphabetical order, with the location of the records for each denomination included in some detail. A list of the parishes of County Armagh and the location of church records is also given in James Ryan's *Sources For Family and Local History*, published in 1988.

CHURCH OF IRELAND RECORDS

From 1537 until 1870 the Church of Ireland was the state church in Ireland. Although committed initially to spreading Protestantism to the native Irish population, its congregations were made up mostly of English and Scottish settlers and officials. Its parishes were units of local government. There was a legal obligation for the Church of Ireland to keep records from 1634, although many rural parishes did not start to keep detailed records until the middle of the eighteenth century. As a result the records of the Church of Ireland generally start much earlier than those of other Protestant denominations and of the Roman Catholic Church. The records of Shankill parish church in Lurgan, for example, include baptisms dating back to 1681, burials to 1675 and vestry minutes dating from 1672.

Parish registers of baptism, marriage and burial are the most important class of parish record available to researchers. They should not be neglected because an ancestor was of another denomination. Before 1782 it was not legal for Presbyterian ministers to perform marriages and until 1844 they could not perform 'mixed marriages'. For this reason many marriages of other denominations, especially those classed as Dissenters, are recorded in the Church of Ireland registers. The *1844 Act for Marriages in Ireland: and for Registering such Marriages* introduced the civil registration of Protestant marriages. These registers were kept in duplicate and a copy returned to the local registrar. From that date the information entered in the Church of Ireland marriage registers is the same as that contained in the records held at the General Register Office.

Baptismal records include the date of baptism, the child's Christian name, the father's name, the mother's Christian name and the name of the officiating clergyman. The majority of Church of Ireland clergymen recorded burials as well as marriages and baptisms. These registers are of interest for families of other denominations because many Catholics and Dissenters were buried in Church of Ireland graveyards, if only for the very practical reason that in some areas the Episcopal Church administered the only cemetery.

THE PARISH VESTRY

In Ireland it was the Church of Ireland that administered the parish. The concept of an Established Church meant that every person in the parish was considered to be a parishioner regardless of denomination, even though he or she did not worship at the local parish church. The vestry meeting held annually on Easter Tuesday was therefore a meeting of all the inhabitants of the parish.

The vestry was an assembly of parishioners who met for the dispatch of parochial business and took its name from its meeting place – the vestry or room in the church in which the priest's vestments were kept. The select vestry was a small committee which could levy taxes for religious purposes – the maintenance of the church and the payment of parish officers such as the sexton and the parish clerk. More important was the general vestry which could raise funds for local services such as poor relief, parish constables, road repair, the organisation of education and the provision of recruits for the army.

Vestry minute books sometimes contain baptism, marriage and burial entries, particularly in the late seventeenth and eighteenth centuries. They often contain items such as the names of the church wardens, of the confirmed, of cess applotters and cess payers, of the poor, the widowed and the orphaned receiving relief, and of overseers of the poor and of the roads. The vestry minute books are not only a useful substitute for parishes which have no surviving registers, but they also include details of individuals who were not baptised, married or buried in the parish but who were of some significance locally.

The money which the churchwardens spent on behalf of the parish was raised largely from the parish cess, a local tax on householders, and to a lesser extent from the sale of seats in the parish church. The applotment, or assessment, of the parish cess, which appears periodically in the church wardens' account books or the vestry minute books, is a valuable record of the local community. Following the abolition of the penal laws, membership of the general vestry was open to all householders in the parish irrespective of their religion, although its proceedings were effectively controlled by the Protestant minority since all officers had to be members of the Church of Ireland.

The records of the transactions of the vestries, essentially vestry minutes and churchwardens' accounts, provide an important and much under-used resource for the local communities and their inhabitants. They complement the basic information which can be obtained from registers of baptisms, marriages and burials by providing additional details of the activities and circumstances of the residents of the parish. Inevitably vestry records are richest for the cities and large towns; vestry records for rural parishes tend to be less rewarding.

Copies of church vestry books are located at the Public Record Office of Northern Ireland. Many of the vestry minute books only cover the last 100–150 years. There are, however, exceptions such as the Parish of Shankill in Lurgan, whose minutes go back to 1672 (ref MIC/1E/33), Derrynoose dating from 1709 (MIC/1/14), Seagoe dating from 1734 (MIC/1/73–75) and Killyman dating from 1756. Most vestry books remain in local custody. It is therefore worthwhile contacting the relevant church.

The main repository for Church of Ireland records is the Library of the Representative Church Body, Braemor Park, Dublin.

However, the Public Record Office of Northern Ireland has copied most of the pre-1900 baptismal and burial registers and pre-1845 marriage registers for the nine counties of Ulster.

Listed below are the Church of Ireland records which are available at the Public Record Office of Northern Ireland, together with the date of the earliest records for each church.

CHURCHES (CIVIL PARISH/TOWNS)	REFERENCES	STARTING DATE
Aghavilly (Lisnadill)	MIC/583/9	1844
Annaghmore (Loughgall)	MIC/583/10–11	1856
Ardmore (or Mointaghs)	MIC/1/79; MIC/583/4; DIO/1/14/9	1789
Armagh	MIC/583/12–14	1750
Balleek (Loughgilly)	MIC/1/66–67	1827
Ballymore (Tandragee)	MIC 583/5, 17, 24; T/2706/8	1783
Ballymoyer (Whitecross)	MIC 583/17, 19; MIC 1/11, MIC/1/113	1820
Camlough (Killevy)	MIC/583/28	1832
Clonfeacle	MIC/583/4	1763
Creggan (Crossmaglen)	MIC/1/11, 112; MIC/583/5	1793
Derrynoose	MIC/1/14; MIC/583/2	1709
Drumbanagher (Killevy)	MIC/1/11; MIC/583/2	1838
Drumcree (Portadown)	MIC/1/21, 42–43	1788
Eglish (Moy)	MIC/1/1A–B; MIC/583/3	1803
Grange	MIC/1/65; T/2540; T/2706/122–149	1780
Keady	MIC/1/51–52; MIC/583/1	1780
Killeavey (Killevy)	T/2432	1879
Killylea (Tynan)	MIC/1/85	1845
Killyman	MIC/583/33–35	1741
Kilmore	MIC/1/8; T/476/1; T/636 pp.73–80; T/2706/10 pp.69–98	1732
Knocknamuckly (Seagoe)	MIC/1/99; DIO/1/14/2	1838
Loughgall	MIC/1/59–60; D/54–56	1706
Loughgilly (Markethill)	MIC/1/66–67	1804
Middletown (Tynan)	MIC/1/13	1812
Milltown (Tartaraghan)	MIC/1/89	1840
Mullaghbrack	MIC/1/83–85	1764

Mullagh	MIC/1/254, 261	1826
Mullavilly (Kilmore)	MIC/1/70; MIC/583/3; T/2706/10	1814
Newtownhamilton	T/1075/15; T/808/14963	1823
Portadown (St.Mark's)	MIC/1/66	1826
Portadown (St.Saviour's)	MIC/583/5; T/2706/10	1858
Seagoe	MIC/1/73–75; T/2588	1672
Shankill	MIC/1/18, 24–25	1672
Tartaraghan	MIC/1/77–78; T/679/26	1824
Tynan	MIC/1/12–13, 18; T/808/15294	1683

CATHOLIC CHURCH RECORDS

In spite of the Penal Laws of the late seventeenth and early eighteenth centuries which removed the rights of Catholics to public office, the ownership of land and careers in the professions, the Catholic Church emerged at the beginning of the nineteenth century in a stronger position than it had been a century earlier. During the eighteenth century the Catholic Church had been able to set up diocesan and parochial structures which replaced the old Gaelic system based largely on family ties.

By the beginning of the eighteenth century the church in Ulster remained poor because so much land had been transferred to Protestant settlers that the Catholic peasantry could support neither priests or proper mass-houses. By the 1760s things were changing for the better. County Armagh was benefiting from the expansion of the linen industry and Catholic tenants and cottiers were now supplementing their income by weaving and spinning yarn. In 1764 the chapter of Armagh welcomed the new wave of church-building in Ulster but asked the Primate, Anthony Blake, to monitor those priests who were neglecting their pastoral duties:

> As much as we rejoice, my Lord, at the success your Grace met with in building mass-houses where none had been before, we equally feel and partake of your Grace's concern at the negligence, as yet, of some parish priests in promoting properly the erecting of chapels in their parishes, which is attended with many bad consequences to our congregation; wherefore we most humbly request that your Grace may be pleased, not to remove or translate for the future, any parish priest whom you will find negligent in that duty, to any better benefice before he leaves some such good monument behind him of his said performance.

By the middle of the nineteenth century a massive church-building programme was taking place and there was a dramatic increase in the numbers of regular clergy. By 1861 nearly half, 48.8%, of the population of County Armagh was Catholic. However the Penal Laws had, for more than a century, militated against regular record-keeping and Roman Catholic registers generally date from a later period than their Protestant counterparts, the majority dating from no earlier than the 1820s. They are almost entirely for baptisms and marriages, though death or funeral entries do occur occasionally (these generally record only the name of the deceased and the date of death). The baptism entries do, however, usually include the names of sponsors and occasionally the names of witnesses.

Roman Catholic parishes are often made up of parts of more than one civil parish and so searching under several parishes is necessary to find all the records of the Roman Catholic parish. Also most Roman Catholic parishes have more than one church. Sometimes only one register was kept for the entire parish, but at other times each church had its own registers. The Public Record Office has microfilm copies of pre-1880 registers for parishes in Ulster. They are to be found under the PRONI reference code MIC/1D. In addition there are some xerox copies under CR/2. The following list contains those records held by PRONI and the National Library of Ireland.

PARISH (CIVIL/CHURCH)	REFERENCES	STARTING DATE
Aghagallon & Ballinderry (Lurgan)	MIC/1D/6, 63	1828
Armagh	MIC/1D/41–42, NLI Pos. 5590–5591	1796
Balleek (Loughgilly)	MIC/1D/9	1846
Ballymacnab (Kilclooney)	MIC/1D/37–38, NLI Pos. 5586	1844
Ballymore & Mullaghbrack (Tandragee)	MIC/1D/37, NLI Pos. 5586	1843
Creggan Lower (Crossmaglen)	MIC/1D/40, NLI Pos. 5589	1845
Creggan Upper	MIC/1D/43, NLI Pos. 5592	1796
Derrynoose (Keady)	MIC/1D/40, NLI Pos. 5589	1835
Dromintee (Killevy)	MIC/1D/41, NLI Pos.5590	1853
Drumcree (Portadown)	MIC/1D/37; CR/2/8, NLI Pos.5586	1844

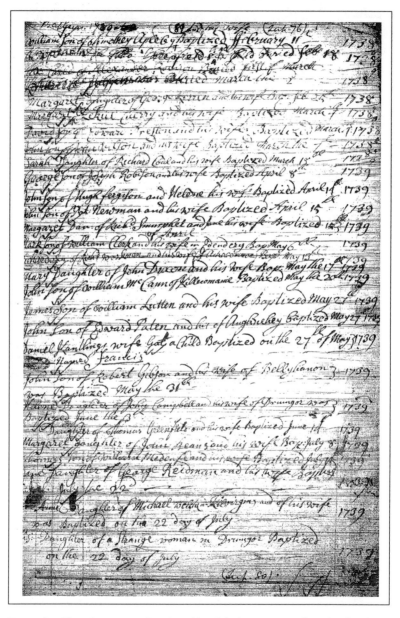

Records of baptisms, marriages and burials for Seagoe Church of Ireland
Parish Church date back to 1672. An index to these records, 1672–1919,
is available in the Public Search Room, PRONI.
Above print from microfilm (MIC/1/74A/1) for some entries in 1738–
39 reproduced with kind permission of the Deputy
Keeper of the Records, PRONI.

Eglish	MIC/1D/36, NLI Pos. 5585	1862
Forkill	MIC/1D/38, NLI Pos. 5587	1844
Inver	MIC/1D/86	1861
Killeavy Lower (Bessbrook)	MIC/1D/39, NLI Pos. 5588	1835
Killeavy Upper (Cloghogue)	MIC/1D/39, NLI Pos. 5588	1832
Kilmore (Rich Hill)	MIC/1D/38, NLI Pos. 5587	1845
Loughgall and Tartaraghan	MIC/1D/38, NLI Pos. 5587	1833
Loughgilly	MIC/1D/38, NLI Pos. 5587	1825
Seagoe	MIC/1D/23–24, NLI Pos. 5498	1836
Shankill (Lurgan)	MIC/1D/23, NLI Pos. 5498	1822
Tynan	MIC/1D/40 NLI, Pos. 5589	1822

PRESBYTERIAN CHURCH RECORDS

During the Reformation, the Church of Scotland became Presbyterian. The Presbyterians rejected the traditional hierarchy of the Church of England in favour of a general assembly, synod, presbytery and kirk session. Its doctrines were strongly influenced by Calvinism. Presbyterianism came to Ireland from Scotland with the first plantation of Ulster during the early seventeenth century. In County Armagh Scots from East Lothian and Midlothian settled in the barony of Fews. However, it is not until after the 1641 rising that a clear picture of the Presbyterian community in the county emerges. Mrs John Goodall, a Scottish woman who resided in County Armagh with her husband during the seventeenth century, left a diary which is preserved in the Advocate's Library, Edinburgh. According to Mrs Goodall, Mr Hope Sherrid, a Puritan minister, was preaching in Armagh and it was he who baptised her second son Sampson.

By the beginning of the eighteenth century Presbyterianism was severely curtailed by the penal laws which made it illegal for Presbyterian ministers to perform marriages of members of their congregation. This prohibition lasted until 1782. It was not until 1845 that they could legally marry a Presbyterian and a member of the Church of Ireland. Marriages of Presbyterians are therefore often recorded in Church of Ireland registers.

In general, Presbyterian registers start much later than those of the Church of Ireland, and early records of Presbyterian baptisms, marriages and burials are often to be found in the registers of the local Church of Ireland parish. Presbyterian registers were organised by church not by parish. Another feature of Presbyterianism is the number of places which have more than one Presbyterian church and are referred to as 1st, 2nd and 3rd. This, together with the fact that congregations tended to split or secede, makes life somewhat difficult for the researcher.

A good place to start your research for Presbyterian ancestors is the Presbyterian Historical Library located at Church House (Room 218), Fisherwick Place, Belfast. The library has many manuscripts relating to Presbyterian families and baptismal and marriage records of some fifty Presbyterian Churches throughout Ireland some of which have been copied by PRONI.

Presbyterian records copied by the Public Record Office of Northern Ireland are available under the PRONI reference codes MIC/1P and CR/3.

CHURCH (CIVIL PARISH)	REFERENCES	STARTING DATE
Ahorey (Kilmore)	MIC/1P/353	1834
Armagh 1st	MIC/1P/4; MIC/637/1; T/636/47–50	1707
Armagh 2nd	MIC/1P/281	1825
Armagh 3rd	MIC/1P/297	1837
Armaghbreague (Keady)	MIC/1P/297	1848
Clare (Ballymore)	MIC/1P/329	1824
Clarkesbridge (Newtownhamilton)	T/2523	1822
Donacloney	MIC/1P/342	1798
Drumminis (Kildarton)	MIC/1P/286	1846
Gilford (Tullylish)	MIC/1P/384	1845
Keady 1st	MIC/1P/296	1819
Knappagh (Eglish)	MIC/1P/402	1839
Lislooney (Tynan)	MIC/1P/401	1836
Loughgall	MIC/1P/287; T/3049/1	1842
Lurgan 1st (Shankill)	MIC/1P/71	1746
Lurgan 2nd & 3rd (The Mall)	MIC/1P/281	1916
Lurgan (Hill Street)	MIC/1P/109	1861
Markethill 1st (Mullaghbrack)	MIC/1P/428; T/2853/3–5	1843
Markethill 2nd (Mullaghbrack)	MIC/1P/429; T/2853/1	1821

Middletown (Tynan)	MIC/1P/212	1829
Mountnorris (Loughgilly)	MIC/1P/29	1804
Newmills	MIC/1P/398	1838
Newtownhamilton 2nd	MIC/1P/443	1823
Portadown 1st	MIC/1P/52	1838
Portadown 2nd	MIC/1P/269	1868
Redrock (Kilclooney)	MIC/1P/285	1807
Richhill (Kilmore)	MIC/10/372	1845
Tandragee(Ballymore)	MIC/1P/258	1835
Tartaraghan	MIC/1P/288	1845
Tullyallen (Loughgilly)	MIC/1P/29	1829
Vinecash (Kilmore)	MIC/1P/348	1838

METHODIST RECORDS

In 1738 John Wesley and his brother Charles started the movement which soon acquired the nickname of Methodism. They made several visits to Ulster and spoke to enthusiastic crowds at Lurgan, Tandragee, Richhill, Charlemont and Armagh. Wesley spoke to especially ardent crowds at Tandragee 'describing one service as having a London congregation, both for number and seriousness.'

However, he described Portadown, only a few miles from Tandragee, as 'a place not troubled with any kind of religion'. The Wesleyan Methodist Society in Ireland dates from the mid-eighteenth century. The majority of its members were members of the Established Church and they remained members of their own churches. Therefore they continued to go to the parish church for the administration of marriages, burials and baptism. In 1816 a split developed between the Primitive Wesleyan Methodists, who retained their links with the Established Church, and the Wesleyan Methodists who allowed their ministers to administer baptisms.

As a result the majority of Methodist baptism registers do not begin until the 1830s and the marriages until1845. There are few, if any Methodist burial registers because Methodist churches simply did not have their own burial grounds. However, an important source for researchers is a large volume of copies of baptism entries for some eighty Methodist churches throughout Ireland which is among the administrative records of the Methodist Church in Ireland and is available in PRONI on microfilm (MIC/429/1).

It contains baptisms from 1815 to early 1850s and these occasionally pre-date existing baptismal registers for the church.

Also of interest is the petition from the Primitive Wesleyan Methodist Society community on the Verner estate to Colonel Verner M.P., requesting the use of the meeting house at Derrylee, Co. Armagh. This is available at the Public Record Office of Northern Ireland, D/1127/1, as are the following records:

CHURCH (CIVIL PARISH)	DATES	REFERENCES
Armagh	1845–1985	MIC/1E/3, MIC/429/1/p.433
Ballinacor (Seagoe)	1845–1950	MIC/1E/33
Bannfoot (Montiaghs)	1819–1950	MIC/1E/33
Bluestone (Seagoe)	1819–1950	MIC/1E/33
Inver	1860–1982	MIC/1E/34
Lurgan, High Street (Shankill)	1819–1959	MIC/1E/33
Lurgan, Queen Street	1823–1986	MIC/ 1E/21A/1 MIC/ 429/1/p.439
Markethill (Mullaghbrack)	1866–1918	MIC/ 1E/4
Portadown (Thomas Street)	1830–1904	MIC/ 1E/8
[Primitive Methodists]	1847–1901	MIC/ 1E/8
[Primitive Wesleyan Methodists]	1871–9	MIC/ 1E/8
Richhill (Kilmore)	1886–1931	MIC /1E/6
Tandragee & Fivemilehill (Ballymore)	1819–1981	MIC /1E/5, MIC/ 429/1/p.477

Methodist Records for the Newry circuit were published in *Seanchas Ardmhacha*, 1977, vol 7, No 2.

THE RELIGIOUS SOCIETY OF FRIENDS

The Religious Society of Friends, also known as 'Quakers' or 'Friends', originated in the north-west of England during the mid-seventeenth century. The Quaker movement was brought to Ireland by William Edmundson when he established a business in Dublin in 1652. A few years later he moved north to Lurgan, Co. Armagh and the first meeting was held at Edmundson's house. By 1675 meetings were being held at the houses of Robert Hoope, Mark

Wright, Thomas Calvert, Francis Robson and Roger Webb. By the end of the century the Quakers were firmly established in the town and according to the surviving minutes a meeting house was built 'upon a tenement called Madden's tenement on the South end of the town of Lurgan upon a copyhold lease from Brownlowe Esq., in the name of Robert Hoope being for this meetings use'. A Lurgan record notes the origins of twenty families who emigrated to Ulster during the seventeenth century; one is from Scotland, nine from Yorkshire, four from Cumberland, two from Lancashire, two from Northumberland and one each from Westmoreland and Durham.

Although the meeting at Ballyhagan near Kilmore was one of the earliest established in Ireland, the minutes only survive from 1705. The current meeting house in Richhill replaced the old meeting house in 1793.

From the beginning the Quakers were among the best record-keepers. Monthly meetings contain registers of birth, marryings and deaths, minutes of meetings, accounts of sufferings and charity papers. As a result Quaker records contain a great deal of information about local affairs. Such detailed record-keeping has enabled Craigavon Borough Council to restore to its former glory the old Quaker burial ground at Lynastown near Lurgan. The first burial was of William Lynas who died on 20 June 1658. Most of the early Quaker families from Lurgan are buried at Lynastown and the meticulous Quaker record-keeping has ensured that the full details of the 200 interments have been preserved; they have been reprinted in full on a sign mounted at the graveyard. This is particularly useful because until the eighteenth century Quakers did not have headstones to mark the position of graves.

The Quaker Library is located at The Friends Meeting House, Lisburn, County Antrim, and contains records for Ulster meetings dating from the seventeenth century. Most of these records have been copied by the Public Record Office of Northern Ireland (MIC/16). The records for Lurgan Meeting House include births, deaths and marriages dating from 1632.

Ballyhagen	1680–1834	MIC /16/39
Lurgan	1632–1979	MIC/ 16; C.R./8/1
Richhill & Grange	1793–1960	MIC /16/39–42

BAPTIST RECORDS

Baptist Church records remain in local custody or with the Baptist Union of Ireland, 117 Lisburn Road, Belfast. Family historians should either contact the Public Record Office or check the local directory for the location and number of the relevant church.

CONGREGATIONAL CHURCH

Although the Congregationalists came to Ireland as early as the seventeenth century, few records exist before the 1880s. An exception to this rule are those of Richhill Congregational Church with baptismal records from 1846, marriages from 1850 and lists of members and minutes from c.1848. These records are deposited in the Public Record Office of Northern Ireland (CR/7/7).

REFORMED PRESBYTERIAN CHURCH

The Reformed Presbyterian Church consisted of those who wished to follow more closely the Covenants of 1638 and 1642. The records of the Reformed Presbyterian Church of Ballenon are deposited in the Public Record Office of Northern Ireland including baptisms 1860–1877, marriages 1851–65 and deaths 1850–68 (MIC/1C/16).

MARRIAGE LICENCE BONDS

During the seventeenth and eighteenth centuries, when it was illegal for 'dissenting' ministers to perform marriages, some Roman Catholic and Presbyterians chose to be married in the Church of Ireland. To do so they would ask the minister to publish banns or purchase a licence from the bishop of the diocese. Before the licence was granted the couple had to enter a bond at a diocesan court. These bonds included the names of the bride and groom and their ages and place of residence. Sadly most of the bonds and licences were destroyed in the Public Record Office, Dublin, in 1922, but indexes to many of them have survived. These indexes contain the names of the bridegroom and bride and the date of the bond.

EXTRACT FROM THE DIOCESE OF ARMAGH:

Ardrey	Jane and John Dawson	1765
Ardrey	Mary and John Leech	1791
Ardry	Margaret and Mark Duffy	1829
Ardry	Margaret and John Mullen	1827
Ardry	Rachael and Thomas Henderson	1827
Ards	Marianne and Richard Kearns	1830
Armour	James and Margaret Patrick	1780
Armstrong	Adam and Eleanor Lawden	1817
Armstrong	Andrew and Mary Johnston	1794
Armstrong	Andrew and Jean Robinson	1784
Armstrong	Andrew and Ann Story	1744
Armstrong	Ann and Edward Carroll	1778
Armstrong	Anne and William Holly	1844
Armstrong	Anne and David Willey	1816

The indexes for the dioceses of Armagh are available on microfilm at the Public Record Office of Northern Ireland under the following references:

MIC/5B/1	A to Greenaway, part 1, 1727 to 1845
2	A to Greenaway, part 2, 1727 to 1845
2	Greenaway to Miller, 1727 to 1845
3	Miller to Young, 1727 to 1845

SCHOOL RECORDS

In the early years of the nineteenth century the education system in Ireland was in a chaotic and disorganised state. There were some charter schools for the education of the poor, which were established by royal charter in 1733, receiving grants from the Irish parliament, and built by private subscription. There was also a great number of pay or hedge schools for Catholic families who objected to the proselytising character of the charter schools. These were usually set up by itinerant schoolmasters who were paid according to the size of the school. They were sometimes, as their name suggests, held in the open air, but more commonly they were established in a local barn or cabin. The Society for the Education of the Poor in Ireland, better known as the Kildare Place Society, was founded in 1811 and aimed to provide a system of interdenominational education. The Established Church remained suspicious of these attempts to remove its influence over the education system, and ironically, the Roman Catholic clergy remained suspicious of what they continued to see as a proselytising organisation. Nevertheless, Sir Charles Coote, who published the *Statistical Survey of the County Armagh* in 1804, found that: 'The youth of this county have the advantages of a better education than in most parts of Ireland; this is evident from the superior civilisation and manners of the people.'

Few records have survived from the eighteenth and early nineteenth centuries. The most important of these for County Armagh are the records for Lurgan Free School, established in the 1780s for the education of poor children from all denominations in Shankill parish, which have survived in the Brownlow estate archive (ref D/1928/S). The following extract, dating from 11 September 1786, illustrates the quality of these records:

CHILD'S NAME	PARENT'S NAME	DENOMINATION	RESIDENCE	AGE	PROGRESS
James Lynes	William & Jane	Papists	BallyBlough	9	Spelling mono syl
David Smart	Archibald & Elizbeth	Presbyter	Lurgan	8	Spelling mono syl
Ralph Smart	Do	Do	Do	6	Beginning Letters
John McCarten	Dennis & Mary	Papists	Do	13	Spelling mono syl
John Morgan	John & -------	Do	Stonewall		Beginning Letters
Robert McMahon	John & Margaret	Church	BallyBlough	12	Spelling mono syl
Thos Bullock	Charles & Ann	Do	Back Lane	6	Beginning Letters

The establishment of a state-run system of elementary non-denominational education took place as early as 1831 under the direction of Lord Stanley the lord lieutenant. The national schools which resulted were built with the aid of the Commissioners of National Education and local trustees. According to the *Second Report of the Commissioners of National Education*, there were twenty-seven national schools attended by 1,625 pupils in the county by 1835. This number increased considerably during the nineteenth century until by1903 one commentator found that the Armagh circuit 'is overcrowded with school-houses, a very large number of which could accommodate fifty per cent. more than the present average attendance; and although the Compulsory Education Act is now in operation almost throughout the entire area of the circuit, I am of the opinion that many of these schools could be usefully dispensed with'.

It is worth pointing out that although by the end of the nineteenth century free elementary schooling was provided for all children, the number attending schools in many areas was sparse. Despite the fact that the Acts of 1876 and 1880 prohibited the employment of children under 10 years old and children up to 13 were required to attend school, the *Reports of the Commission for Education* make it clear that many children made only infrequent attendance at school. In his general report into the Armagh Circuit on 1903 Mr Murphy commented that: 'The character of the attendance remains practically unchanged. The same causes are at work in town and in country and the same unsatisfactory results are noticeable. In rural districts the pupils attend for the most part very irregularly. This is due to the demand for child labour, and partly to a seeming inability on the part of parents to appreciate the injustice they do to their children, when they keep them from school without sufficient reason.'

Despite their limitations, school records are an important source for family historians. At their best they can help to make up for the loss of the nineteenth-century census records. If you do not know the school that your ancestor attended, the first step is to find the location of schools in the area where he or she lived. This can be done using commercial street directories that list schools from the middle of the nineteenth century. Ordnance Survey maps and the Ordnance Survey Memoirs may also provide useful information.

Many of the surviving records for County Armagh schools are held at the PRONI. Of particular interest are the registers which record the full name of the pupil, date of birth (or age of entry), religion, father's address and occupation, details of attendance and academic progress. A space is also provided in the registers for general comments which might detail previous schools the child attended, where the child went to work after leaving school or if he/she emigrated. Most have an index at the front which greatly eases searching. These records can be found under the reference SCH. It is worth checking your local library for a copy of a *Guide to Education Records*, published by the Public Record Office. This includes an alphabetical listing of schools for Northern Ireland

and a breakdown of the material held on deposit.

Since they provide the age of pupils, school registers will facilitate a search for baptismal records or birth certificates. Most of the schools in the North, particularly in the early part of the century, were cross-denominational with the religion of the child listed as RC (Roman Catholic), P (Presbyterian) and EC (Established Church or Church of Ireland).

ALPHABETICAL LIST OF COUNTY ARMAGH PRIMARY,
PUBLIC ELEMENTARY AND NATIONAL SCHOOLS
FOR WHICH PRONI HOLDS RECORDS:

(For civil parishes see Appendix 6)

Aghacommon	SCH/1292
Aghavilly	SCH/228
Ahorey	SCH/1505
Annaghmore	SCH/1055
Armagh (Armstrong)	SCH/886
Armagh Boys	SCH/1541
Armagh (Callan Street)	SCH/493
Armagh (College Street)	SCH/21
Armagh (Gosford Place)	SCH/40
Armagh (Mall)	SCH/337
Armagh (Mount St. Catherine's Convent)	SCH/560
Armagh (St. Patrick's Infants)	SCH/1551
Armaghbreague	SCH/458
Aughnagurgan	SCH/109
Ballinacorr (Kearn)	SCH/714
Ballinliss (St. Josephs)	SCH/1493
Ballyargan	SCH/423, 1543
Ballylane	SCH/518
Ballymoyer (St. Malachy's)	SCH/1497
Ballytyrone	SCH/14
Ballywilly (Ballyhegan)	SCH/1532
Balteagh	SCH/430
Battlehill	SCH/640
Bessbrook	SCH/460
Blackwatertown	SCH/439
Blackwatertown (Boys)	SCH/1533
Blackwatertown (Girls)	SCH/1534

Bluestone SCH/641

Breagh SCH/447

Cabra SCH/881

Camlough (Lislea Boys and Girls,

later St. Malachy's) SCH/1486

Camly McCullagh SCH/456

Carnagh SCH/436

Carrickgologhly SCH/454

Cassells SCH/434

Cavanbellaghy SCH/464

Cladymore SCH/519

Clintyclay SCH/1523

Cloncore SCH/467

Clonmain SCH/475

Cloughogue SCH/1556

Cohara SCH/448

Collone SCH/887

Cope, the (Loughgall No.2) SCH/514

Corcrain Boys (Portadown) SCH/1489

Corkley SCH/453

Corlust SCH/435

Cortamlet SCH/1051

Crossdall SCH/441

Crossmore Monastery SCH/1500

Cross Roads SCH/428

Darkley SCH/891

Derrycarne (Derrykerrin) SCH/784

Derrycughan SCH/426

Derryhale SCH/893

Derrylard SCH/468

Derrynoose (Boys) SCH/1546

Derrynoose (Girls) SCH/1547

Derryvane SCH/226

Drelincourt SCH/492

Dromantee SCH/107

Drumbanagher SCH/516

Drumgoose SCH/437

Drumsallen SCH/1399

Edenderry SCH/880

Edgarstown No.1 SCH/1022

Edgarstown No.2 SCH/117

Eglish SCH/1483

Esky SCH/490

Essawary SCH/461

Foley SCH/1400

Forkhill (St. Oliver Plunkett's) SCH/1501

Glenanne SCH/476

Gortshalgan SCH/642

Granemore SCH/802

Grange SCH/914

Grangemore SCH/494

Grange O'Neiland SCH/443

Grove SCH/449

Halftown (St Teresa's) SCH/779

Hardy Memorial (Richhill No.1) SCH/919

Jerretspass SCH/431

Jonesboro (Boys) SCH/1560

Keady SCH/455

Keady Convent, F3 (St. Clare's) SCH/1528

Keady, Technical School SCH/520

Killean (Girls) SCH/1492

Killylea SCH/1054

Kilmonarty SCH/193

Kilmore SCH/432

Kinnego SCH/280

Knockavannon SCH/452

Lisadian SCH/75

Lisdrumchor SCH/181

Lislea Murphy (formerly Lislea No. 1) SCH/470

Lislea No. 2 SCH/1542

Lissummon SCH/1574

Loughgall No. 1 SCH/1499

Lurgan (Ardmore) SCH/491

Lurgan (Carrick) SCH/489

Lurgan (Church Place Convent) SCH/1293

Lurgan (Edward Street Convent) SCH/1294

Lurgan (Edward Street Convent SCH/1296
Evening School)

Lurgan (Hill Street)	SCH/485
Lurgan (John Street)	SCH/486
Lurgan	SCH/472
Lurgan (Lurgan Industrial)	SCH/1297
Lurgan (Lurgan Model)	SCH/482
Lurgan (North Street)	SCH/483
Lurgan (Queen's Place)	SCH/474
Lurgan (Queen's Street)	SCH/473
Lurgan (St. Peter's)	SCH/1290
Lurgan (Tullygally)	SCH/487
Lurgan (Victoria Nursery)	SCH/446
Lurgan (Victoria Street)	SCH/484
Lurgan (William Street Monastery)	SCH/1295
Madden No. 1 (St. Joseph's)	SCH/1510
Madden No.2	SCH/471
Maghery	SCH/1517
Maghon	SCH/225
Markethill	SCH/427
Middletown Convent	SCH/1498
Middletown No. 1 (Boys)	SCH/1495
Middletown No. 2	SCH/214
Milford	SCH/915
Milltown	SCH/469
Mountnorris	SCH/462
Mullaghmore	SCH/463
Mullaghglass	SCH/792
Mullavilly	SCH/424
Mullavilly No. 1	SCH/1544
Mullavilly No. 2	SCH/916
Newtownhamilton	SCH/1552
Outleckan	SCH/451
Portadown (Academy)	SCH/444
Portadown (Boys)	SCH/1490
Portadown (Church St.)	SCH/1025
Portadown Convent (Presentation Convent)	SCH/1481
Portadown (Curran Street Junior)	SCH/1488
Portadown (Hart Memorial)	SCH/1027

Portadown (Park Road)   SCH/488
Portadown (Portadown or Church St)   SCH/227
Portadown (St. Columba's Boys)   SCH/1487
Portadown (Thomas St)   SCH/440
Poyntzpass   SCH/512
Poyntapass No. 1   SCH/1482
Raws (Glassdrummond)   SCH/1494
Richhill No. 1 (see Hardy Memorial)
Richhill No. 2   SCH/920
Richmount   SCH/495
St. Mary's, Granemore   SCH/802
St. Teresa's, Halftown   SCH/779
Salter's Grange (Hockley)   SCH/913
Silverbridge   SCH/1555
Tamnamore   SCH/974
Tandragee (Clare)   SCH/477
Tandragee (St. James)   SCH/429
Tandragee   SCH/425
Taniokey   SCH/515
Tannaghmore   SCH/785
Tartaraghan No. 1   SCH/465
Tartaraghan No. 2   SCH/466
Ternagreevagh   SCH/270
Townsend   SCH/445
Tullygally   SCH/487
Tullysaran   SCH/1524
Tullymore   SCH/1491
Turmoyra   SCH/433
Tynan (Lislooney)   SCH/51
Wastelands   SCH/69

ESTATE RECORDS

Ulster, like the rest of Ireland, was a predominantly rural society
until the middle of the nineteenth century. At the same time Ulster,
reflecting its colonial beginnings, remained a province of large
landed estates. The importance of the major landowners to the
development of the surrounding countryside was acknowledged

by Mr and Mrs Hall who toured Ireland shortly before the Great Famine: 'The principal proprietor of Tanderagee is Lord Manderville, who, with his neighbours, Lords Farnham and Roden, Colonel Blacker and the Marquis of Downshire, have contributed largely to the present cheering condition of the county of Armagh. Lord Manderville has established no fewer than sixteen district schools on his estate in this neighbourhood, for the support of which he devotes £1000 per annum, out of an income which is by no means large'.

During the seventeenth century the traditional Gaelic system of land ownership was replaced by English and Scottish landlords. They were required by the Crown to settle British colonists on their estates and throughout the seventeenth century many English and Scots found Ulster a more convenient source of cheap land than the American colonies. For much of that century they migrated into County Armagh. Initially many Irish freeholders adapted to the new system of land tenure because it gave them greater independence and security than that which had existed under their traditional chiefs. The rising of 1641 and the Williamite campaigns of the early 1690s, however, led to a major transfer of land to British settlers, with Irish tenants being reduced to the status of sub-tenants in the more heavily colonised areas or being absorbed into the new society as is shown by the survival of Gaelic and anglicised names in the records of Protestant congregations.

Details of the undertakers and servitors who helped establish the plantation in County Armagh and the progress of each by 1612–13 can be found in the *Hastings Manuscript* published by the Historical Manuscripts Commission in 1947. Unfortunately tenants are not named.

> Upon James Creage (Craig) his portion I found nobody that could inform me of his purposes. He hath caused a mill to be built, and some pieces of timber to be brought in place for building. I had speech with a dozen Scottish men, then newly arrived, who affirmed that they were sent thither to inhabit on that proportion, but had not as yet any estates passed to them.

SURVEY OF UNDERTAKERS PLANTED IN ARMAGH, HASTINGS MANUSCRIPT 1947

Although during the Plantation and subsequent land settlements landlords were granted extensive powers under royal patents, they were forced by economic circumstances to lease their lands for rents to tenants. In order to encourage colonists to settle on their estates they had to attract them with leases on good terms. A lease guaranteed security of tenure so that the tenant had the incentive to improve the productivity of his land. Many tenants also sublet their holdings to subtenants and this was particularly profitable where a dense population created a strong demand for land.

The success of the linen industry in County Armagh brought healthy incomes into the hands of many small farmers and weavers and attracted fresh migrations into the county. With the increasing population the struggle to obtain leases direct from landlords intensified and forced up rents. Those who could not afford leases held small portions of lands as cottiers paying rents to more substantial tenants. By the middle of the eighteenth century this competition for land was to lead to bitter sectarian fighting in County Armagh between the Peep of Day Boys, who later formed themselves into Orange Clubs, and their Catholic neighbours who formed a revival organisation known as the Defenders.

In south Armagh the local landowner Johnston of the Fews was determined to retain a firm grip on the local population. He established the village of Johnston Fews which he hoped would meet with the same success as many of the similar foundations of his neighbours. Four fairs were granted to the village and in 1740 it was described as a 'very small village in the middle of wild country called the Fews, notorious for robbers'. However by the beginning of the nineteenth century it consisted of no more than six houses. The Johnston family's attempts to bring law and order to the district, which included the building of Fews Barracks, resulted in the famous couplet about them:

> Jesus of Nazareth, King of the Jews,
> Protect us from Johnston, the King of the Fews.

Most estates were built up slowly by purchase and marriage. With the increase in wealth and land came responsibility for the manor, the development of the local economy through the introduction of markets and fairs, and a dominant role in the rise of local towns and villages. Unlike most other European countries where towns had been established by medieval times, many of the villages and towns in Ulster were established on estates. Towns such as Markethill, Richhill, Lurgan and Tandragee resulted from the ambitions of the local landlord. In Lurgan, for example, the Brownlows sought to promote the linen industry through the development of a market town on their estate. Within the Brownlow archive are rentals, leases and title deeds relating to tenements or properties for the town of Lurgan. The Manchester estate records contain similar material for Portadown and Tandragee and the records for the Gosford Estate include a map of Hamiltonsbawn showing tenant's houses c. 1850.

The impact of the Great Famine and agrarian and political unrest during the middle of the nineteenth century resulted in the break-up of the great estates as government-assisted schemes enabled tenants to buy the land from the local landlord. This culminated in the Irish Land Act of 1903 (better known as Wyndham's Act) which offered the landlords an incentive to sell out their entire estates. The purchase terms were also made easier for the tenant with the repayment period being extended to 68½ years.

Estate papers are an invaluable source for family historians. They include leases, rentals, deeds, maps and correspondence covering every aspect of life on the estate.

A lease was granted by a landlord to a tenant and this gave him the right to occupy the property for a specific period of time. Two copies of the lease were usually prepared. The original lease was signed by the landlord and kept by the tenant. The counterpart was signed by the tenant and kept by the landlord. A lease was usually for a term of years 1, 21, 50 or 99 years.

In Ulster, as in the western half of England, leases were usually for three lives: the lease expired when all the three persons named in the lease died. The lease was stated to continue for twenty-ninety years or, if earlier, until the death of the last named person. In a lease for lives the names of relatives are often included. The lease could be renewed at the fall of each life by inserting a new name on payment of a renewal fine. The three-life lease was therefore in reality a perpetuity as long as the tenant wished to renew it. The maximum term of a Roman Catholic lease was 31 years until the 1778 Act altered this.

Before beginning a detailed search through leases or title deeds it is worth tracking down any lists of tenants in leasebooks which may, for various reasons, have been compiled by the landlord. The Gosford Papers included a Return of Freeholders on the estate dating from around 1840 (D/1606/14/1). There is also a list of tenants holding leases on the De Salis estate at Tandragee, 1722–87 (D/720). More unusually the Duke of Manchester lists the names of the 'able-bodied poor' on his estates at Tandragee and the surrounding townlands c. 1835 (D/1248/O/14). The Brownlow estate papers include an extensive series of electoral registers (D/1928/F/1).

Maps and plans form an important element in most estate collections. These show the property of the landlord who employed a surveyor to illustrate the extent of his land and the more important features on his estate. Maps come in all shapes and sizes and can be coloured or roughly etched in black and white. Often there are blank spaces where the land does not belong to the employer. Surveys may include the names of tenants and the extent of their holdings. Included are many place-names that have long disappeared and the location of vanished mills, woodland, paths and houses. They illustrate the method of agriculture employed in a particular area and the size of fields and holdings.

Rentals allow local historians to trace individual tenants and over a period of time show how one plot of land or property changed hands. They show the terms under which individuals held their land. In a lease for lives the names of relatives are often included. Title deeds, although more cumbersome to use, include any document that has been used to prove ownership to the property.

The majority of estate records for County Armagh are deposited at the Public Record Office of Northern Ireland. The quality of these records will vary from estate to estate. For example, a vast quantity of three-life leases has survived for the Brownlow estate. In 1804, Sir Charles Coote commented on the highly concentrated nature of the tenantry on the estate: 'This manor (Brownlow-derry), which is the estate of William Brownlow, Esq. is all leased in so small divisions, as to average less than five acres, and a great number so low as three; all the farms are leased for three lives; excepting in the town of Lurgan, there is not a perpetuity on the whole.' He was also struck by the extensive exploitation of the local bogs: 'The fuel here is turf, which is more abundant than in most other parts of the country; yet it is not cheap, but yields large sums to the occupying proprietors. I have already noticed one tenant on Mr. Brownlow's estate, who realizes above £1000 per annum on turf bog only.' It is hardly surprising therefore that the fourteen moss rentals dating from 1827 provide a great deal of genealogical information for the family historian.

However, these are only a few items in the rich variety of material to be found in the estate archives. Rentals, leases and rent rolls, manor court records; militia records; business records; charity records; grand jury records, tell us much about the daily lives of ancestors living and working on a big estate. Another interesting item within the Brownlow archive are Ejectment Books dating from the 1830's. Each Ejectment Book includes the names of tenants, the townland, the amount each tenant owed and whether or not they were ejected from their tenancy. Few such items have survived for Northern Ireland. A good place for researchers interested in the Lurgan area to start is to consult *Settlement and Survival On An Ulster Estate*, edited by R. G. Gillespie and published by PRONI in 1988, which reproduces the Brownlow Leasebook originally compiled between 1667 and 1711. It is indexed and documents the names and landscape of Brownlow's estate during the late seventeenth and early eighteenth centuries.

The quality of the landed estate collections for County Armagh can be seen in the papers relating to the archdiocese of Armagh, which date from the thirteenth century. The Church of Ireland was an important landowner in its own right and this was noted by one traveller who journeyed through County Armagh during the 1790s. 'The revenues of the Archbishop amount to eight or nine thousand pounds sterling per annum, but it is known that the estates belonging to the seat bring in to those who have farmed them £150,000...If the Archbishop had such an income, it might well excite the jealousy of the Government, as well as the discontent of the rent-farmers, who regard these estates as heritages belonging to their families, thus, prudently, the leases are renewed every year at the same price, plus a considerable pot-de-vin.'

The archive of the Primacy of Armagh includes archbishops' registers of correspondence dating from the thirteenth century; rent rolls, leases, maps and surveys relating to church lands; and

visitation returns and papers dating from the early seventeenth
century. These have been deposited at the Public Record Office,
(DIO4). A typescript copy of the rentals preserved in the
Archbishop's Registry for the seventeenth and early eighteenth
century has been made by the former curator of Armagh Museum,
Mr T.F.G. Paterson. This volume, which is indexed, includes rentals
covering the period 1615–1624, a survey of 1676 and extracts of
the leases belonging to the see of Armagh, 1722–1746. A copy of
this manuscript can be found at the Irish Studies Library, Armagh.

The principal landowners in the Markethill area were the
Achesons, later Earls of Gosford. During the early part of the
eighteenth century Sir Arthur Acheson, who was married to the
daughter of the Right Honourable Philip Savage, a Chancellor of
the Exchequer in the Irish Parliament, was a close friend of Jonathan
Swift, author of *Gulliver's Travel's*. Swift paid three visits to Markethill,
staying from three to eight months at a time, between 1728 and
1730. Swift commented that County Armagh 'excepting it's cursed
roads, and want of downs to ride, is the best part I have seen of
Ireland'. His verdict on Markethill was that it was 'situated in the
midst of a fertile country, the extensive demesne and splendid castle
of Gosford, the property of Viscount Gosford, adding greatly to
its beauty'. In Swift's poem, *The Revolution at Market-Hill*, there are
references to those of a much lower social rank on the Gosford
Estate. Those featured include Hannah, Lady Acheson's waiting
maid, Sir Arthur's butler, Peggy Dixon, the Achesons' housekeeper
and Lorimer their agent. The poem, written at a time when Swift's
relations with the Achesons had cooled somewhat, contains an
unflattering description of Sir Arthur and the emphasis is on the
social divisions of the time. He refers to the tenantry on the Gosford
estate as follows:

> ...what the wretches most resent,
> To be his slaves must pay the rent;
> Attend him daily as their chief
> Decant his wine, and carve his beef.

The records of the Gosford estates, which consist of more than
30,000 documents, are deposited at the Public Record Office of
Northern Ireland. These include a great deal of material relating to

the original estate at Markethill. Included are leases, rentals and account books for more than thirty townlands for the Markethill estate, together with a further sixty townlands spread over the former Graham estate at Markethill and the former Richardson estate at Richhill. The earliest leases and rentals date from the late eighteenth century. The reference number is D/1606. PRONI also published in 1976 the *General Report on the Gosford Estates in County Armagh 1821 by William Creig*. With an introduction by F.M.L. Thompson and D. Tierney, this publication gives a fascinating insight into life on the Gosford estates during the reign of George IV.

Jonathan Swift was also on friendly terms with Robert Cope, whose estate included the town of Loughgall. Swift wrote that : 'I am grown so peevish, that I can bear no other countryplace in this Kingdom (than Loughgall); I quarrel everywhere else and sour the people I go to as well as myself....The worst of it is, that if you grow weary of me (and I wonder why you do not), I have no other retreat'. Records to the Cope estate at Drumilly and Loughgall are deposited at PRONI, reference D/1345. These include leases, deeds and wills as well as Irish land commission sale papers.

The Manchester estates were in the Portadown and Tandragee areas. They embrace more than thirty-five townlands. They include rentals for the Kernan and Ballymore estates dating from 1715 and for the complete estates from the 1830s. The reference number is D/1248. Sir Charles Coote, who visited in the area in the early nineteenth century, was struck by the number of families living on the estate: 'The farms on this estate are very small, the population immense. The average size of farms is under four acres, and the proportion of inhabitants nearly seven to a house; they hold their tenures under one life only.' This passage serves to remind us that although an ancestor may have lived on one of the major estates, they may not be named if they were a subtenant or if they were a member of the family rather than head of the household. Family historians faced with this situation should seek out the relevant church records where each member of the family may be represented in the baptismal or marriage records.

The following table is a guide to the estate records for County Armagh which are deposited at the Public Record Office of Northern Ireland. The table includes only those references which are of genealogical interest:

ESTATE AND LOCATION	REFERENCES	DATE OF EARLIEST RECORD
Alexander Estate, Forkill and Portadown	D/935; D/2395/2	1861
Armstrong Estate, Killylea	T/1144/2-7; T/1206/1, T/1307/1; D/1670 /9/1-3; D/2727	1736
Atkinson Estate, Crowhill and Loughgall	T/1213/18; D/712/ 1-77; D/799/4; D/959/2; D/1382; D/1815/2-5	1675
Bacon Estate, Richhill	D/1606/6C/1-6 and 7B/1-45	1822
Brownlow Estate, Lurgan	D/1928; T/2069; T/2485/2/1-7	1610
Blacker Estate, Portadown	D/959; D/1252; MIC/74 c. 1667	
McGeough–Bond Estate, Drumsill	D/288; T/3012/2/2	1678
Burges Estate, Moy and Armagh	T/1007; T/1147/1-7; D/1252; D/1594	1685
Caledon Estate, Caledon	D/266/337; D/2433	1639
Chambre Estate, Newry	T/529/1-22; D/294	1611
Charlemont Estate, Moy and Armagh	T/1175/2; T/1176/1-6; T/1208/1; D/266/378 /1-102; D/1644/1-30; D/1670/2/1-4; D/2363 /1-16	c. 1750
Close Estate, Drumbanagher	T/1175/2; T/1301; D/670; D/935	1784
Clarke Estate, Loughgall	T/2431	1794
Cope Estate	D/935	1687
Dartrey Estate, Blackwatertown	D/526; D/1670/3/1-2	c.1800
De Salis Estate, Tandragee	D/763/1-6; D/1253	1733
Fforde Estate, Lurgan	D/1252	1863
Gosford Estate, Markethill	D/1606; T/1233/1	1750
Hall Estate, Mullaghglass	T/2821/1-3; D/2090/2-7 D/1540/1-2	1613
Irwin Estate, Keady	D/1515; D/268; D 2523	1750
Kilmorey Estate, Newry	D/2638	1755

Manchester Estate, Portadown and Tandragee	D/1248; D/935	1669
Molyneaux Estate	MIC/80/3; MIC/215	1696
Castledillon	T/2521/1	
Obre Estate, Clontylew	D/1719/1-6; D/1134 c.1790s	
Richardson Estate, Moyallen	D/1252; D/2628	c.1700
Verner Estate, Moy	D/236/51-455, 483-486 509; D/849/29	1751
Wallace Estate, Portadown	D/2223/11/1, 30	c.1800

Estate records relating to County Armagh are also available in original and microfilm in various Dublin archives. The following records are held at the National Library, Dublin:

Brownlow estate rentals	1636, 1659, 1667–77	NLI Pos 207
Richard Johnstone rentals	1731	NLI Pos 1014
Rental of the estate of Michael Obins	1770–71	NLI Ms4736
A list of freeholders on the estates of the Earl of Charlemont, arranged alphabetically within each Barony	1820	NLI Ms 3784
Rentals for Charlemont estate	1798–1802	NLI Ms 2702
Rent Rolls of the Viscount Cremorne's estate in County Armagh	c.1780s –1850s	NLI Ms 3183– Ms 3189
Rental of the estates of 2nd Baron Cremorne in the counties of Monaghan and Armagh	1846	NLI Ms1648
Rent roll of the estates of Lord Dartrey in counties Louth and Armagh	1777 & 1779	NLI Ms 3283

The following estates which are of interest to the family historian interested in County Armagh are held at the National Archives, Dublin:

Records of the Chambre family, Hawthorn Hill 1714–1867. These include a list of landed proprietors in County Armagh (189 names); list of sheriffs of County Armagh, 1714–1846; lists of Grand Jury Spring and Summer 1829; list of proprietors eligible for office of High Sheriff

returned at the Summer Assize 1829; names of tenants 1841–42; wage book 1846–1863	M 7035
Rental of property in County and City of Armagh for the George family, 1863	M 5537
Documents relating to the property of the See of Armagh including details on tenants, nineteenth century	M 5378
Rent rolls of the estate of James Johnston 1791–1802, containing tenants' names. There are also a number of rentals dating from the 1850s and early 1860s. Of particular interest is a rental dating from 1860 which includes tenants' names for Knappagh on the Johnston estate	M 3502–21
Valuation of property held by John E Livingston, Armagh City, 27 May 1871, with list of sub-tenants	M 5378
Rental and accounts of the estate of Rev Wm Moore 1850–72	M 2977
Rentals for the Moore Estate, 1848, 1850, 1851, 1872	M 2977
Rentals 1834–1870, for the Winder family, relating to properties in and near Armagh City	M 5863
Reference Genealogical information on the O'Callaghan family, Tullydonnell 1803	M 5714

There are a number of ways to locate the landlord for a particular area. Many of the great family estates were broken up in the latter years of the nineteenth century under the Land Acts. Before this happened a list of landowners was compiled, 1871–1876, by Government order and printed in *the Return of Owners of Land of One Acre and Upwards, in the Several Counties, Counties of Cities, and Counties of Towns in Ireland, to which is added A Summary For Each Province and for All of Ireland (Presented to both Houses of Parliament by Command of Her Majesty)*. The area measured covered more than 20 million acres and the number of owners of one or more acre was 32,614. An owner was defined as anyone who held title to the property outright or held a lease of more than 99 years, or a lease with the right of perpetual renewal. The names of owners are listed alphabetically by province and county with their addresses, the extent of their property and its valuation. Copies can be found at all of the major archives and libraries including the Public Record Office of Northern Ireland, the Irish Studies Library, Armagh and the Linen Hall Library and Central Library, Belfast.

It is also worth consulting the printed Griffith's Valuation Books, where the landlord's name normally appears in the column headed 'lessor'. These are available in most major public libraries and on the shelves of the Public Search Room of the Public Record Office in Belfast and at many of the larger libraries.

Burke's Peerage, Landed Gentry and Irish Family Records and *Cokayne's Complete Peerage and Complete Baronage* contain a great deal of information on the gentry and titled families. Volumes on the histories of single families have also been published and these are available at most major libraries including the Linen Hall Library and Central Library, Belfast.

The principal landowners in County Armagh are as follows:

LOCATION	OWNER	ACRES
Armagh	Estate of the archbishopric	
Charlemont	Charlemont	20, 695
Forkill	Alexander	8, 324
Keady	Trinity College	
Killylea	Armstrong	2,280
Loughgall	Cope	9, 367
Lurgan	Brownlow	15,166
Markethill	Acheson (Gosford)	12,177
Portadown & Tandragee	Manchester	12,298
Richhill	Bacon (Richardson)	5,816
Tandragee	De Salis	3,663

THE MANOR COURT

The manor was an important unit of local administration in England from the middle ages. Unfortunately, few records have survived in Ulster and these are generally limited to the more important judicial functions of the manorial system. Nevertheless, the duties and obligations of tenants or classes of tenants can be ascertained from these records.

The right to hold manorial courts, i.e. the court-baron, the court-leet, and the court of piepowder, was granted to landowners during the plantation. Manorial lords held by right periodical courts and tenants were expected to attend. The sort of information recorded illustrates the organisation of the manor itself, and includes disputes over customs, the regulation of the agricultural activity of the manor and dues and services required by the landlord. Manor court records also give a great deal of information on the regulation and development of markets and fairs. The form of the court-baron which existed in Ulster until the mid-nineteenth century was the 'freeholders' court' which met every three weeks to try actions for debt, trespasses, etc., under forty shillings.

The court-leet was summoned twice a year by the steward or seneschal of the manor and everyone who owed suit to the lord's court was bound to attend. It dealt with a wide range of matters affecting the welfare of the manor boundaries, annoyances and nuisances, the condition of roads, streams and drains, false weights and measures, the regulation of the markets, the licensing of ale houses, the assizes of bread and ale. The court-leet was able to levy fines and to commit a person to the pillory or the stocks, but it could not imprison anyone. Unfortunately few examples of manor court and court-leet records have survived. However, manorial records can be found in the Brownlow archive, deposited at PRONI, under the following references:

Estate Court Book for Manor of Brownlowsderry, listing the jury, overseers and grievances   1776–1847   D/1928/J/1

Estate Court Book for Manor of Richmount, listing the jury, overseers and grievances   1816–34   D/1928/J/2

Seneschals Court Book for Manor of Richmount, listing the names of parties, witnesses and decisions   1827–31   D/1928/J/3

Seneschal's Court Book for Manor of Brownlowsderry, giving names of plaintiffs, defendants and witnesses   1827–37   D/1928/J/4

Manor Court manuscript copy out-letter book   1839–47   D/1928/J/5

The following books are to be found in the Gosford archive (ref D/1606) also deposited at PRONI:

Manor Court Book for the Manor of Drumorgan and Hamilton's Bawn   1838–48   D/1606/13/1

Manor Court Book for Balleek Manor   1842–7   D/1606/13/2

Armagh Manor Court Rolls, 1625–27, listing jurors attending sessions, those fined for non-attendance and plaintiffs and defendants in various cases, have been published in *Seanchas Ardmhacha*. The original Rolls are deposited at the Robinson Library, Armagh. Extracts from the manorial records for the Manor of Ballymore in 1847 can be found in *Armagh Miscellanea* volume VIII, deposited at the Armagh County Museum. Also of interest is a return of tenants' names for the manor court of Armagh which was held by the Archbishop of Armagh in 1714, a copy of which is deposited at the PRONI, (T/729/1–3).

The court-leet book for the manor of Brownlow's Derry is a good example of the wide variety of genealogical information which this type of volume can contain. There are lists of jurors who met each May and November. One of their duties was to appoint individuals to various positions of responsibility and who were charged with enforcing the powers of the court-leet during the year. These included the 'Overseers for Regulating the size of Bread'; the 'Regulators of the Flesh Market, and such Wares and Commodities as are or may be exposed to Sale in the Town of Lurgan'; the appointment of Scavengers and local constables.

COURT-LEET BOOK FOR THE MANOR OF BROWNLOW'S DERRY, NOVEMBER 1776

> We present William Emerson of Lurgan to be Constable for the ensuing year of that part of Lurgan next to the Church, and We also present Wm Emerson and John Crooks to be Appraisers for the Said district. We present James Livingston of Lurgan to be Constable for the ensuing year for that part of Lurgan next Ballyblough and We also present Jas. Livingston and David McComson [sic] to be Appraisers for the Said district.

ENCUMBERED ESTATES

During the Great Famine many landlords, already burdened with debt and facing crippling poor law payments with income badly affected by the non-payment of rents were forced to sell their estates, often heavily mortgaged. Under the 1849 Act an Encumbered Estates Court was established with authority to sell estates on the application of the owner or encumbrancer (one who had a claim on the estate). After the sale the court distributed the money among the creditors and granted clear title to the new

owners. The function of the court was assumed by the Landed
Estates Court in 1853. During the 1850s more than five million
acres, almost a quarter of the land in Ireland, passed into the hands
of new landlords, many of whom were wealthy speculators.

There is a fairly complete set of Irish Encumbered Estates Court
Rental covering the whole of Ireland available in the Public Record
Office of Northern Ireland, in bound volumes. These rentals or
'brochures' were issued before the sale of a property and therefore
contain very detailed information on each estate in order to attract
potential buyers. They are divided into counties, townlands and
tenements, and list the names of the parties involved and the dates.
Included are rentals, surveys of the estate giving tenants' names,
location of tenancy or property, and details of tenancy including
those named on the three-life renewable leases, the most common
form of lease in Ulster during the eighteenth century. Those named
often include close relatives although Mrs Isabella Kean, a widow
who lived on King's Street, Newry, in 1859, named as her three
lives 'Queen Adelaide, since deceased, the present Duke of
Cambridge, and the Princess Augusta of Cambridge'.

The following extract, for properties in Portadown, is taken from
the printed rental for the property of William Lutton Cooke whose
estate was sold on 22 October 1859:

DENOMINATIONS	NAMES OF TENANTS	YEARLY RENT	GALE DAYS	TENURE OF EACH TENANT
1 House in John-Street	William Martin	16:0:0	1 May & 1 Nov	Tenant from year to year
2 Ditto	Terence McKenna	4:6:4	Saturday in each week	Tenant from week to week
3 Ditto	James Lappin	4:6:4	Saturday in each week	Tenant from week to week
4 Ditto	Margaret Mathews	4:6:4	Saturday in each week	Tenant from week to week

The Encumbered Estate archive is deposited at the Public Record
Office of Northern Ireland, D/1201. This volumes including
material on County Armagh are:

County Armagh	D/1201/1
Counties Armagh, Clare, Carlow, Down, Galway, Kilkenny, Meath, Limerick, and Tipperary	D/1201/2
Counties Down, Armagh, Antrim, Tyrone, Londonderry, Fermanagh, Cavan, Tipperary	D/1201/22

A townland index to Encumbered Estates Court Rentals is also available on microfilm, in PRONI (MIC/80/2.)

LAND REGISTRY

The Irish Land Commission was established by William Gladstone in 1881. Its most important function was to set 'fair' rents where disputes existed between tenants and their landlords. The Land Commission also advanced loans to tenants who wished to become owners of the farms they had often leased for generations from the local landowner. By the turn of the century the Land Commission had helped to bring about the end of the great landed estates in Ireland and replaced them with a new class of farmer/owners.

The Land Registry archive, one of the largest held at the Public Record Office of Northern Ireland, contains a variety of papers which chronicle the changes in the ownership and occupancy of land in Ireland brought about by the Irish Land Commission. Included are title deeds, testamentary papers, including wills, and schedules of arrears which list those tenants still owing back rent. There are individual agreements between the landlord and tenant over the sale of land. For example, a bundle of more than twenty such agreements can be found in one box of material from the estate of the Rt Hon William Grey Ellison Macartney MP. On 1 March 1907 both he and Mrs Georgina Anne Elizabeth Dunbar-Buller agreed to sell their tenant, Anne McManus of Leish, County Armagh, the land she currently occupied amounting to just over 11 acres, for the sum of £169. The tenant applied to the Irish Land Commission for an advance of the agreed price which was to be repaid at the rate of 5.9.10 a year.

There are three indexes which can be used to identify documents in this massive archive. The most useful is the alphabetical index. This lists the material by name of estate and in each case the relevant county is also included. However this is only a rough guide because most of the larger estates spread into more than one county. A record number and box number are given. For example, Cecil Fane De Salis, County Armagh is box number **1426** and record number NI 00057. Most estates are given the prefix **LR/1** and the box number is used to complete the reference. Therefore the records of Cecil Fane De Salis would be **LR/1/1426**. The relevant calendar should then be consulted on the shelves of the Public Record Office which will give a brief description of its contents.

Just to complicate matters further the records of the larger estates, such as the Manchester estate, Tandragee, are listed in a separate calendar. These records are given the extra prefix **L**. The material relating to W. G. Ellison Macartney looked at earlier, for example, has the box number **0048L**, indicating that it can also be found in the separate calendar for the large estates.

Another way for the family historian to access the records of the Land Commission is through the pages of the local newspapers. The sittings of the Land Courts were reported in considerable detail. These include the cases of individual tenants who placed their cases before the Commissioners.

DUKE OF MANCHESTER'S ESTATE

> Isaac Clayton, tenant
> Area 4a 1r 21p; rent £11; valuation, £9 5s. The tenant stated that he had been residing on the farm since 1827. There was a lease at that time. In the year 1840 the lease had expired, when his rent was raised to £5 7s 6d. There was a further increase in the year 1861, which amounted to £13 1s 8d. Two years afterwards he went to the agent and informed him that he would give up the farm, as he was not able to pay such an exorbitant rent. He asked some remuneration for his improvements. He was ordered out of the office. When the agent saw that he was determined to give up the farm the rent was reduced to £11, and has remained at that figure up to the present time. A fair rent would be 18s an acre. – Meredith Smith, valuator, said that he had made a field to field valuation of the farm, and he was of opinion that 18s an acre would be a fair rent'. *Portadown and Lurgan News*, 28 September 1882

The Commissioners' decisions are often followed by a list of tenants with the old rent and the new judicial rent given. Lists such as these can provide evidence that an ancestor lived on a particular estate towards the end of the nineteenth century.

Because so few newspapers are indexed it is important to know something of the major land acts before approaching the microfilm collections to be found at one of the main libraries.

1870 LANDLORD AND TENANT (IRELAND) ACT

This act sought to compensate tenants for improvements made by them to their holding or for any disturbance to their occupancy. Tenants could borrow up to two-thirds of the price which they could repay at 5 per cent over 35 years.

1881 LAND LAW (IRELAND) ACT

This act established the Land Commission and the Land Court; the object was paid rent, free sale and fixity of tenure.

1882 AMENDING ACT

This act empowered the Land Commission to cancel arrears of rent due by tenants of less than £30.

1885 PURCHASE OF LAND (IRELAND) ACT

Under the terms of this act tenants were allowed to borrow the full amount of the purchase price to be repaid over 49 years at 4 per cent. Between 1885 and 1888 more than 25,000 tenants purchased their holdings.

1887 LAND ACT

This was an amendment to the 1881 Act extending the terms to leaseholders.

1896 LAND ACT

This amended the 1891 Land Act and empowered the Land Court to sell bankrupt estates to tenants.

1903 LAND ACT

This act offered the landlords a 12 per cent bonus in addition to the agreed price if they agreed to sell out their entire estate. This act, more than any other, brought about the transfer of estates from the landlord to the tenantry.

REGISTRY OF DEEDS

The Irish Registry of Deeds, founded in 1708, is an invaluable source for family historians and is particularly useful when tracing ancestors from the eighteenth century. One of its main functions was to ensure the enforcement of legislation which prevented Catholics from buying or taking long leases on land. Up until the 1780s, Catholics could not invest in mortgages or take leases on land for a longer period than 31 years.

Registration was not compulsory. The percentage of landowners who registered their deeds varied from place to place but the majority tended to avoid registration, with the landlords of County Armagh among the worst offenders. It should also be pointed out that if your ancestor was a labourer, servant or a weaver who was a sub-tenant with a small farm there is little chance of their being recorded, particularly during the eighteenth century.

The sorts of material registered are leases, mortgages, marriage settlements and wills. This can provide the researcher with names, addresses and occupations of the parties involved as well as the names of those who acted as witness. During registration, which often took place years after the original transaction, a copy of the deed called a memorial was made. The details of the memorial were then copied onto parchment and bound in large volumes and these are what you will be working on should you visit the Registry of Deeds.

Two indexes are available to the researcher: the first is an index of grantors. The format of this has changed over the years. Before 1832 the Index gives the surname and christian name of the grantor, (the first party) the surname of the grantee and the reference number. There is no indication of the location of the property concerned. After 1832 the index is more detailed and includes the county in which the property is located.

The lands index is arranged in volumes by county or city until 1828. After that date the entries are recorded alphabetically only with regard to the initial letter. Also after 1828, the lands index is subdivided by barony so that is necessary to know which barony the relevant townland is located.

The index of grantors and the lands index are both available on microfilm at the National Library and at the Public Record Office of Northern Ireland. PRONI has copies of the Memorial Books themselves (some 2,000 reels, see MIC/7 and MIC/311).

The original records are deposited at the Registry of Deeds, King's Inns, Henrietta Street, Dublin. For those researchers with limited time or experience it may well be worth engaging the services of a professional researcher to tackle these records.

SOLICITORS' RECORDS

Solicitors' records are an invaluable source for estate records. Many of the estate collections held by PRONI were deposited by local solicitor's firms. Records from the Brownlow estate, for example, were held by Watson and Neill, Solicitors, Lurgan. PRONI also holds a number of solicitor's archives which often include title deeds, testamentary papers, copy wills, rentals, valuations, in short every kind of document produced by a major estate. Many such collections are deposited at the Public Record Office of Northern Ireland.

Carleton, Atkinson & Sloan, solicitors, Portadown, contain records which provide a valuable insight into the development of Portadown, Tandragee and the neighbouring countryside. Papers from the Wakefield, Richardson, Blacker and Fforde estates are represented. Items of interest include rentals relating to the town of Portadown and surrounding townlands such as Kinnego, Derrymacash, Derryadd and Raughlan towards the end of the nineteenth century. More unusual is a survey of the townland of 'Bocommery' [Bocombra], part of the estate of Jonathan Richardson. This lists land held from 1804 by undertenants, a class rarely represented in estate records. (D/1252).

The records of Fisher and Fisher, solicitors, Newry, County Down, include Irish Land Commission papers relating to the

Manchester, Cope and Close estates, County Armagh and rentals of the Alexander estate, Forkill, County Armagh 1878–79 (D/935).

The records of Joshua Peel & Son include title deeds and leases for various estates at Armagh, Keady, Richhill, Charlemont, Markethill, Hamiltonsbawn and Blackwatertown (D/889).

In order to discover if the records of a particular solicitor's firm are deposited at PRONI see the Subject Index (available on computer at the reception area or in printed form in the Public Search Room) under the heading *Legal System: Solicitors and attorneys.*

MISCELLANEOUS SOURCES

VOTERS, POLL AND FREEHOLDERS' RECORDS

Poll books and freeholders' registers are lists of people entitled to vote or of people actually voting at elections. They are normally arranged on a barony and county basis. Until the late nineteenth century the qualification for voting was generally linked to the tenure of land and only a small minority of men had the right to vote, those aged 21 or over, who held freehold land with an annual value of forty shillings or more. In Ireland, from 1727 to 1793, only Protestants with a freehold worth at least 40s. per year had a vote. Between 1793 and 1829 both Protestants and Roman Catholics with 40s. freeholds had the franchise although a Catholic was still unable to become a member of parliament. The more forty-shilling freeholders a landlord had on his land, the greater his influence during an election. When examined before the Devon Commission in 1884, Colonel William Blacker, a landowner and

agent on the Gosford estate, pointed out that landlords' desire to
gain an element of political advantage over their neighbours had
helped to change the landscape of County Armagh. He told the
Commission that: 'The general size of the farms in the district
varies very much. A few years ago, when the 40s. freeholder system
prevailed, several large properties were cut up into ribbons to make
40s. freeholders. There is now a backing out of that system; but
upon my own property it prevails less than anywhere else.'

In 1828, Daniel O'Connell, who led the fight for Catholic
Emancipation, won a by-election in County Clare. The fight for
the right to sit in Parliament had gained unparalleled support
throughout the country and resulted in the Catholic Relief Act of
1829. Catholics were now allowed to sit in parliament and to hold
government posts, except those of Lord Chancellor, Lord
Lieutenant and Regent. However, at the same time as the Relief
Act, the qualification for the vote was changed from forty shillings
to £10. This reduced the number of voters in Ireland from about
191,000 to 26,000.

As the century proceeded the right to vote was extended by a
series of acts in 1832, 1867 and 1884. By 1884 the majority of
male householders over 21 were entitled to vote. Women did not
obtain the vote in general elections until 1918 and even then it was
limited to those over thirty who were householders or the wives
of householders. It was as late as 1928 that the vote was granted
to women over twenty-one.

Elections in County Armagh, as in much of Ireland, were often
controversial. They were often the scene of intense rivalry between
neighbouring landlords and, of course, were frequently the occasion
of intense sectarian rivalry between rival mobs. A statue of one of
Portadown's most famous adopted sons takes a prominent place
in front of St Mark's Church. It is a likeness of Colonel Edward
Saunderson, Unionist MP for North Armagh and leader of the
party until his death in 1906. He is shown standing contemptuously
on the first home rule bill introduced into the House of Commons
in 1886. During that same year Cavan-born Saunderson stood
against the Nationalist candidate, James Williamson, and described
the events which led up to a riot between the rival factions in
Portadown. Saunderson spoke to his followers in front of St Mark's

Church, while his rival held a meeting a few hundred yards away. In a letter to his wife dated 8 July 1886, Saunderson writes, 'We were dragged by the people in a huge break to the Church where I spouted. Then off we went, still dragged, all round the town down near where my opponent was holding forth. A line of Police separated us from him so all the people would do was to vent their rage in yells of an awful description. Some, however, found out a way of turning the police and gained a point of vantage where they could shell the rebel meeting with stones. This they did. The Police charged them but the people drove the police back with great slaughter. Military were telegraphed for to Armagh but by the time they arrived it was all over'. In fact casualties were limited to 16 policemen and two district inspectors wounded.

Poll books and electoral registers are of obvious value to family historians despite the limited numbers who were entitled to vote. Poll books are the books in which are recorded the votes cast at parliamentary elections. They contain the name and address of the voter and often the address of the 'freehold' which entitled the voter to his vote. These records predate 1868, the last election before the Ballot Act. In 1872 Gladstone's Ballot Act established secret voting. This enabled tenant farmers to register their votes without having to take account of the political views of their landlord. This had an immediate impact in Ireland where it enabled a strong Irish Home Rule party to be formed at Westminster.

Poll books and freeholders' registers for County Armagh are:

1738	Armagh Freeholders	NL Pos. 206
1753	Armagh Poll Book giving the names and addresses of freeholders	NA M 4878 GO MS 443 PRONI T/808/ 14949 LDS film 1279237
1747–1802	List of freeholders from the Portadown Distict	PRONI D/2394/3/5 and T/281/5
1753–1845	Electoral Registers for all of County Armagh, Brownlow Estate Archive	PRONI D/1928/F/1– 103
1792–1802	List of registered freeholders from the Portadown district	PRONI T/281/6
1813–1832	Armagh Freeholders	NL Ir 94116 a 1, Ir 352 p2 PRONI ARM/5/2/1–17

1813–1856	Freeholders' lists for various baronies in County Armagh	PRONI MIC/15D/9
1821–31	Armagh freeholders	PRONI T /862
1830	Return of freeholders on the Gosford estate	PRONI D/1606/14/1
1830–39	Freeholders' register, County Armagh	PRONI T/808/14934
1851–52	Register of voters for County Armagh	PRONI T/808/14927
1859	List of voters in Armagh Borough	PRONI T/524/69
1871–72	Register of voters for County Armagh	PRONI T/2883
1918–39	Electoral registers for the Armagh	PRONI ARM/5/3/2/ PRONI D/2394/3/5 1A–22D
1927–49	Electoral registers for the Tandragee district	PRONI LA/70/F/1

The voters' poll book, 1753, for Armagh, provides an interesting insight into eighteenth-century Irish society. It is more than a list of names for it includes the reasons why certain individuals were not allowed to vote:

OBJECTIONS

No 59   Rich Crump – as being married to a Papist
65a   Adam Bell – not polled as he was not registered until 3 May 1753
86   James Osborn – for being a minor
94   James Ogle – Do
98   Robert Jones – for being seen at Mass and giving offerings to the Priest
126   Tho. Chambers – objected to by the Sheriffs for not being registered in the Clerk of Peace Book
139   Arch McCartney – for having a lease for 3 lives or 31 years
160   Tho. Rynon – for being a minor and an apprentice
166   Wm Compton – for having sold his freehold in Dromogher to Sir Capel Molyneux
208   Jon Watt – for having made over his freehold to his son
220   John William – for having sold to Jas. Shannon
287   Wm Simons – for being married to a Papist
308   Silas Hamilton – for being a Rioter

WILLS AND TESTAMENTARY RECORDS

Once the date of death of a particular ancestor has been discovered, it is worth while finding out if they left a will. Wills contain not only the name, address and occupation of the testator, but also can include details of the larger family network, such as cousins, nephews etc. Many wills also include the addresses and occupations of the beneficiaries, witnesses and executors. Perhaps only 5 per cent of the total population made wills which were probated.

WILLS BEFORE 1857

Up until 1857 the Church of Ireland was responsible for all testamentary affairs. Ecclesiastical or consistorial courts in each diocese were responsible for granting probate and conferring on the executors the power to administer estates. Each court was responsible for wills and administrations in its own diocese. However, when the estate included property worth more than £5 in another diocese, responsibility for the will or administration passed to the Prerogative Court under the authority of the Archbishop of Armagh.

Unfortunately most original wills before 1858 were destroyed in Dublin in 1922. However, manuscript indexes to these destroyed wills do exist and are available on the shelves of the Search Room at the Public Record Office of Northern Ireland and the National Archives, Dublin and some of these have been published. They are useful for genealogical searching; for although the original will cannot now be produced, the index contains some information about individual persons and the date that their will was proved. These indexes relate to a diocese and not to a county. For those wishing to trace ancestors in County Armagh the diocese of Armagh (Cos Armagh and Louth, the east part of County Tyrone and south County Londonderry) is the most obvious starting point. The jurisdiction of the consistory court of Armagh included all parishes in County Armagh with the exceptions of Magheralin, Montiaghs, Seagoe and Shankill. These parishes fell within the consistory court of the diocese of Dromore, and the parish of Newry within the consistory court of Newry and Mourne.

Four volumes containing indexes to the diocese of Armagh, c.1635–1857, are also available on the shelves of the public search

COUNTY OF ARMAGH.

A LIST of APPLICATIONS to REGISTER, and to REGISTER ANEW, as VOTERS for the COUNTY OF ARMAGH:

BARONY OF ARMAGH.

No.	Name, Description, and Residence of Applicant.	In what Right Claiming.	Description of Property, with Name of Barony, &c. &c.	Yearly value.
				£.
1	Alexander, Mathew, Naul, farmer	Leaseholder	Houses and land, Naul, Barony of Armagh	10
2	Alderdice, David, Charlemont, victualler	Freeholder	do Corr & Dunavally do	—
3	Anderson, Thomas, Armagh		House and Offices, Armagh do	—
4	Alexander, John, jun., Naul, farmer	Leaseholder	House and lands, Naul do	10
5	Alexander, John, sen., do do	do	do do do	—
6	Alexander, Mathew, do do	do	do do do	—
7	Armstrong, Adam, Drumgar do	do	do Drumgar do	—
8	Anderson, Joseph, Drum do	do	do Drum do	—
9	Anderson, Robert, do do	do	do do do	—
10	Armstrong, George, Ravenhill do	do	do Ravenhill do	—
11	Agnew, Robert, Lisdrumbrocas do	do	do Lisdrumbrocas do	—
12	Agnew, Hugh, do do	do	do do do	—
13	Agnew, Thomas, do do	do	do do do	—
14	Armstrong, John Tew, Dublin, attorney	do	do Derryhaw do	20
15	Armstrong, Adam, Drumgar, farmer	do	do Drumgar do	10
16	Alexander, John, jun., Naul, do	do	do Naul do	—
17	Alexander, John, sen., do do	do	do do do	—
18	Alexander, Mat., do. & Killylea do	do	do Naul and Killylea do	—
19	Armstrong, Andrew, jun., Brootally do	do	do Brootally do	—
20	Anderson, Joseph, Drum do	do	do Drum do	—
21	Anderson, Robert, do do	do	do do do	—
22	Armstrong, James, Brootally do	do	do Brootally do	—
23	Brown, James, Carnagh do	do	do Carnagh do	—
24	Baird, John, Curryhughes do	do	do Curryhughes do	—
25	Baxter, R., Armagh, carpenter & bldr.	do	do Beresford row do	20
26	Blevins, William, Cavanacaw, farmer	do	do Armagh do	—
27	Blevins, John, do do	do	do Cavanacaw do	10
28	Blair, James, Tassagh do	do	do T.mallog, Mowillan, D.large do	20
29	Blair, John, do do	do	Houses and lands, Tullynamalloge do	10
30	Blakely, Robert, do	Freeholder	do Tassagh do	—
31	Bradley, George, Corclea do	do	do Corclea & Aughnagurgan do	—
32	Byers, William, Charlemont do	do	do Corr and Dunavalley do	—
33	Bean, William, Corclea do	do	do Corclea do	—
34	Blackstock, Thomas, do do	do	do do do	—
35	Baird, Alexander, Naul do	Leaseholder	do Naul do	—
36	Briers, John, Grangemore do	Freeholder	do Grangemore do	—
37	Briers, Joseph, do do	do	do do do	—
38	Blackstock, John, Aughnagurgan do	do	do Aughnagurgan do	—
39	Briers, Robert, Grangemore do	do	do Grangemore do	—
40	Boyd, James, Balleer, linen merchant	do	do Tassagh do	—
41	Bole, James, Naul, farmer	Leaseholder	do Naul do	—
42	Burnett, Robert, do do	do	do do do	—
43	Baird, Alexander, do do	do	do do do	—
44	Bole, James, Drumgar do	do	do Drumgar do	—
45	Busby, Archibald, College hall do	do	do College hall do	—
46	Bell, Thomas, do do	do	do do do	—
47	Brown, John, Lisdrumbrocas do	do	do Lisdrumbrocas do	—
48	Bell, James, Manooney do	do	do Manooney do	—
49	Bole, James, Drumgar do	do	do Drumgar do	—
50	Barry, Andrew, Curmeen do	do	do Curmeen do	—
51	Brown, William, do do	do	do do do	—
52	Burnett, Robert, Naul do	do	do Naul do	—
53	Bole, James, do do	do	do do do	—
54	Barry, William, Curmeen do	do	do Curmeen do	—
55	Baird, Alexander, Drum do	do	do Drum and Naul do	—
56	Busby, Archibald, College hall do	do	do College hall do	—
57	Bell, Thomas, do do	do	do do do	—
58	Campbell, Alexander, Carnagh do	do	do Carnagh do	—
59	Cowser, John, Curryhughes do	do	do Curryhughes do	—
60	Cross, Richard, Carrickaness do	do	do Kilcreevy do	20
61	Caldwell, Robert, Drumkeen, gent.	do	do Armagh do	—
62	Crothers, John, B. watertown, merchant	do	do Ballycullen do	—
63	Corrigan, Robert, Keenaghan, farmer	Freeholder	do Charlemont do	10
64	Caldwell, Robert, Armagh, grocer	Leaseholder	do Armagh do	20
65	Caldwell, John, Tullyelmer, gentleman	Freeholder	do Tullyelmer do	—
66	Cardwell, William, do do	do	do do do	—
67	Carswell, Aw., Aughnagurgan, farmer	do	do Aughnagurgan do	10
68	Cartmill, Fras., Grangeblundels do	do	do Grangeblundels do	—
69	Clarke, Andrew, Corclea do	do	do Corclea do	—
70	Clarke, John, Corr & Donavally do	do	do Corr and Donavally do	—
71	Conroy, Patrick, Grangemore do	do	do Grangemore do	—
72	Connelly, James, Aughnagurgan do	do	do Aughnagurgan do	—
73	Conry, John, Grangemore do	do	do Grangemore do	—
74	Clarke, James, Corclea do	do	do Corclea do	—

No.	Name, Description, of Applic
175	Gray, Alexander, Derna
176	Gray, Samuel, Lisagally
177	Gamble, Joseph, do
178	Geough, Alexander, do
179	Geough, Richard, do
180	Gray, Mathew, Derryhaw
181	Gillespie, James, Manoo
182	Gordon, Benjamin, Kill
183	Gillespie, Robert, Kenne
184	Gray, James, do
185	Grocett, Andrew, Naull
186	Gillespie, William, do
187	Gibson, Joseph, Golan,
188	Gibson, James, do
189	Greer, Robert, Drumgar
190	Greer, Robert, Tullycal
191	Greer, Joseph, Killylea,
192	Gillespie, George, Colle
193	Gillespie, Robert, d
194	Gillespie, James, d
195	Gray, Alexander, Derry
196	Hughes, James, Beltarn,
197	Henry, George, Ballyhra
198	Harris, Hugh, jun Ashfe
199	Hamilton, Alex, Linnag
200	Hill, Robert, Dunlarge,
201	Hill, William, do
202	Hughes, Michael, Carnag
203	Hall, William, Curryhug
204	Henderson, John, Fernal
205	Hughes, Patrick, Armag
206	Humphries, Richard, do
207	Hayes, James, Mahery,
208	Hanson, Thomas, Cloghf
209	Hinchey, Samuel, Tyrea
210	Houston, Alexander, Ty
211	Houston, Robert,
212	Hughes, Peter, Grangeb
213	Hughes, Patrick, Armag
214	Hutcheson, Leland, Ball
215	Hanson, John, Brootally
216	Hanna, James, Blackwat
217	Hanson, David, Balteagh
218	Hillock, William, Drum
219	Hall, Andrew, College h
220	Hamilton, Alexander, Lis
221	Hamilton, Jas, sen, Colle
222	Hamilton, James, jun,
223	Hanson, James, Balteagh
224	Hanson, Edward, do
225	Hanson, David, do
226	Hewitt, Thomas, Lisagal
227	Huston, James, do
228	Hewitt, George, do
229	Hillock, William, Drump
230	Hazleton, Simon, Killyle
231	Houston, William, d
232	Hall, Richard, do
233	Henderson, William, Des
234	Hall, George, Curmeen,
235	Hall, Johnston, do
236	Herron, James, Golan,
237	Herron, William, do
238	Hall, Andrew, College h
239	Hamilton, James, College
240	Hamilton, Alexander, G
241	Hamilton, James, College
242	Jackson, John R. Tullygl
243	Ireland, Gilbert, Carnagl
244	Irwin, Alexander, Grang
245	Jackson, Very Rev James
	degny, dean,
246	Jackson, John, Armagh,
247	Johnston, Mathew, Middl
248	Jones, Rev J. Derrynoos
249	Johnston, James, Derryh
250	Irwin, Robert, Balteagh,
251	Irwin, David, do
252	Johnston, Robert, Derryl
253	Johnston, James, d

ARMAGH—*Continued.*   BARONY OF ARMAGH—*Contin...*

...nt Right ...aiming.	Description of Property, with Name of Barony, &c. &c.	Yearly value.	No.	Name, Description, and Residence of Applicant.	In what Right Claiming.	Description of Proper...
		£.				
...eholder	Houses and lands Dernalea, Barony of Armagh	10	353	M'Cullogh, John, Drumderg, farmer	Leaseholder	Houses and lands, Drum
do	do Lisagully do	—	354	M'Kinstry, John, Armagh, esquire	do	do Clea a...
do	do do do	—	355	M'Erath, John, Fernaloy, farmer	do	do Fernal
do	do do do	—	356	M'Call, Jones, Drumnacanver, farmer	do	do Drum...
do	do do do	—	357	M'Call, Nathaniel, Lisglin, do	do	do Drum...
do	do Derryhaw do	—	358	M'Call, John, Drumnacanver, do	do	do Drum...
do	do Manooney do	—	359	M'Cracken, Robt., Drumgreenagh, do	do	do Drum
do	do Killylea do	—	360	M'Mullan, John, Fernaloy, do	do	do Ferna
do	do Kennedies do	—	361	M'Crum, William, Carnaganon, do	do	do Carna
do	do do do	—	362	M'Crum, John, do do	do	do d...
do	do Naul do	—	363	M'Williams, Wm., Armagh, gentleman	Freeholder	Tenements, Armagh
do	do do do	—	364	M'Donnell, Archd., do builder	Leaseholder	Building ground and h...
do	do Golan do	—	365	M'Clelland, Joseph, Newry, gentleman	Freeholder	Houses and lands, Ang
do	do do do	—	366	M'Clelland, Joseph, do tanner	do	do do
do	do Tullycallidy do	—	367	M'Cardle, Terence, Corran, farmer	do	do Grand
do	do do do	—	368	M'Kee, William, Corclea, farmer	do	do Corcl
...n)	do Killylea do	—	369	M'Mullan, David, do do	do	do do
do	do College hall do	—	370	M'Clelland, Aaron, do do	do	do Corcl
do	do do do	—	371	M'Mullan, Joseph, Aughnacloy, do	do	do Augh
do "	do Derryhaw do	—	372	M'Kee, William, Aughnagurgan, do	do	do Augh
do	do Beltaru do	—	373	M'Mahon, George, Tassagh, do	do	do Tassa
do	do Drumacanovor do	—	374	M'Mahon, John, do	do	do do d
...harge	do Cavnagnole do	—	375	M'Kee, Joseph, do gentleman	do	do do
...older	do College hall do	—	376	M'Clave, Samuel, do farmer	do	do d
...holder	do Dunlarge do	—	377	M'Clure, Daniel C., Tandragee, gent.	do	do Tand
o	do do do	—	378	M'Kelvey, David, Drumgar, farmer	Leaseholder	do Drum
o	do Carnagh do	—	379	M'Keone, Hugh, do do	do	do do
o	do Curryhughes do	—	380	M'Kelvey, David, do do	do	do do
o	do Fernaloy do	—	381	M'Call, John, do do	do	do do
o	do do do	—	382	M'Aree, James, Manooney, do	do	do Mano
o	do do do	—	383	M'Cune, James, Armagh, gentleman	Freeholder	Houses, lands, and pre
o	do Mahery do	—	384	M'Clelland John, Lisagally, farmer	Leaseholder	Houses and land, Lisga
o	do Cloghfin do	—	385	M'Cormick, William, Derryhaw, do	do	do Derr
o	do Tyrearly do	—	386	M'Mahon, John do	do	do d
...holder	do Tyrearly do	...	387	M'Aree, James, Manooney, do	do	do Mano
o	do do do	...	388	M'Call, John, Drumgar, do	do	do Drun
o	do Grangeblundels do	...	389	M'Kelvey, David, do	do	do d
...older	do Armagh do	...	390	M'Keone Hugh, do	do	do d
o	do Alistragh do	20	391	M'Cullogh, Robt., Kilcreeyyitra, do	do	do Kilcr
o	do Brootalty do	10	392	M'Cormick, John, Golon, do	do	do Golo
o	do Blackwatertown do	...	393	M'Night, James, Drum, do	do	do Drun
o	do Balteagh do	...	394	M'Cartney, Rev. James, Dublin, clerk	Freeholder	do Augh
o	do Drumgar do	...	395	M'Night, James, Drum, farmer	Leaseholder	do Drum
o	do College hall do	...	396	M'Call, John, Derryhaw, do	do	do Derry
o	do Limnagore do	...	397	Norton, William, Tamlet, do	do	do Tamle
o	do College hall do	...	398	Nugent, Hugh, Aughmagorgan, do	Freeholder	do Augh
o	do do do	...	399	Nugent, Lawrence, do do	do	do d
o	do Balteagh do	...	400	Nugent, Edward, do do	do	do d
o	do do do	...	401	Nugent, Patrick, do do	do	do d
o	do do do	...	402	Nugent, Neal, do do	do	do d
o	do Lisagally do	...	403	Nugent, Edward, do do	do	do d
o	do do do	...	404	Norwood, John, Naul, do	Leaseholder	do Naul,
o	do do do	...	405	Norwood, Robert, do do	do	do do
o	do Drumgar do	...	406	Norwood, John, do do	do	do do
o	do Killylea do	...	407	Norwood, Robert, do do	do	do do
o	do do do	...	408	Olpherts, Rev. Richard, Charleston, Clk	Freeholder	do Arma
o	do Derryhaw do	...	409	O'Neal, Felix, Granemore, farmer	do	po Grane
o	do Curneen do	...	410	O'Neal, James, do do	do	do do
o	do do do	...	411	O'Neal, Neal, do do do	do	do d
o	do Golan do	...	412	Pringle, Michael, Aughnacloy, farmer	do	do Augh
o	do do do	...	413	Porter, Hans, Corclea, do	do	do Corcl
o	do College hall do	...	414	Pointer, Robert, Balteagh, do	Leaseholder	do Balte
o	do do do	...	415	Peebles, William, Derryhaw, do	do	do Derry
o	do do do	...	416	Peebles, James, do do	do	do d
o	do do do	...	417	Pearson, John, Killilea, do	do	do Killil
o	do do do	...	418	Petticrew, Matthew, Golon, do	do	do Golon
o	do Tullyglush do	...	419	Price, John Balteagh, do	do	do Balte
o	do Camagh do	...	420	Russel, John, Legahony, do	Freeholder	do Augh
o	do Grangemore do	...	421	Robinson, Andrew, Tassagh, do	do	do Tassa
			422	Reid, James, Blackwatertown, mercht	Leaseholder	do Black
...older	do Mullyloughran do	50	423	Reid, David, Balteagh, farmer	do	do Balte
...holder	Houses and land, Bellaghey, do	20	424	Reid, Robert, do do	do	do d
...o	do Derryhaw, do	...	425	Robinson, Samuel, jun, Dernalea, do	do	Dern
...older	Rector of Derrynoose, Derrynoose, do	50	426	Reid, Robert, Derryhaw, do	do	Derry
...holder	Houses and land, Derryhaw, do	20	427	Robinson William Dernalea, do	do	Dern...
o	do Balteagh, do	10	428	Robinson, Samuel, do	do	do do
o	do do do	...	429	Robinson, Ben. do	do	Houses and land, Golo
o	do Derryhaw, do	...	430	Reynolds, Thos., Golon do	do	Dert
...o	do do do	...	431	Robinson, Robt., Dernalea do	do	do Dert
...s	do do do	...	432	Robinson, Jas., Lisdrombrocus do	do	do Lisd

List of Electors for the Barony of 'Tureny' (Tiranny), published in
The Newry Commercial Telegraph, 3 October 1839.

room at PRONI. They are listed alphabetically according to the testator's name as can be seen in this example taken from one of the volumes:

TESTATOR'S NAME	RESIDENCE	YEAR OF PROBATE
Stringer Francis	Tassa	1848
Stringer John	Brackagh	1735
Stringer Mary	Armagh	1765
Stringer Ralph	Bracka	1768
Stringer Thomas	Bracka	1719
Stringer William	Armagh	1765

Researchers at PRONI should not neglect the card index for pre-1858 wills which is available in the Public Search Room. These are listed alphabetically according to surname and relate to wills or extracts from wills which are scattered throughout PRONI collections. Included are thousands of copies and abstracts of wills in the Tenison Groves collection.

WILLS 1858–1900

The testamentary authority of the Church of Ireland was abolished by the Probate Act of 1857 and such matters were brought under civil jurisdiction. Most of the nine county province of Ulster was covered by District Probate Registries established at Armagh, Belfast and Londonderry. These local registries made transcripts of the wills they proved before sending the original wills to PROI, Dublin and these will books for most of Ulster 1858–1900 are now deposited in PRONI. These serve as a substitute for the original wills destroyed in PROI Dublin in 1922. The will books are available on microfilm in PRONI (MIC 15/C) and each will book contains an alphabetical index.

There is no comprehensive index to these post-1858 wills and grants. However, there are bound annual indexes called 'calendars' on the shelves of the reception room. These calendars are a great convenience to genealogists because they include the name, address and occupation of the deceased person, date of death, names and addresses of executors, value of estate and the place and date of probate. Each calendar covers a single year and the entries are in alphabetical order. Even if you have only an approximate date for the death of an ancestor it is worth looking through a number of volumes in the hope of spotting an entry giving details of their will.

When using these calendars it should be noted that the official date of a will is the 'date of probate', that is, the date when it was officially proved in the probate Registry of the High Court. This date of probate is normally a few months after a person died; however, there are occasionally unaccounted-for lapses of time which occur between death and probate, particularly where probate was in the Prerogative Court.

A consolidated index to the calendars, 1858–1877, is available in the National Archives, Dublin and at PRONI. UHF has completed this consolidated index of the Irish will calendars 1878-1900 adding dates of death and county of origin.

MILITIA RECORDS

The militia was a local defence force usually raised when the country was under threat from foreign invasion. The force was almost exclusively recruited from the poorer classes and was susceptible to political propaganda; during the late eighteenth century it was repeatedly infiltrated by United Irishmen. Members were also prone to lose discipline when sent to disturbed areas for policing duties. As a result the Irish militia were frequently sent to other parts of the United Kingdom to serve. During the American War of Independence militia from Ireland had been sent overseas and this caused a great deal of popular hostility to serving in the force.

Local constables were empowered to draw up lists of all the able-bodied men in their area. A ballot was then held to decide which of these men were to be called upon to serve or else pay for a replacement. Peers, clergymen, articled clerks, apprentices, and those who had served previously were among those who were exempt. Also, any man selected by the ballot to serve could be excused service if he could provide a suitable substitute. Volunteers frequently prevented the raising of men by compulsion. The local gentry who provided the militia high command used their considerable influence to keep their militia regiments well supplied by volunteer recruits.

```
MILITIA OFFICERS in the County of ARMAGH 1761

Independent Troops of Dragoons arrayed in 1756
Capt   Lord Viscount Charlemont
Lt   Thomas Seaver      Cornet   George Bannerman

Capt   Sir Archibald Acheson, Bart.
Lt   John Johnston      Cornet   Wm English

Capt   Richard Jackson
Lt   James McCullogh      Cornet   Thos Rowe

Capt   Henry Wm Moore
Lt   Charles Courtney      Cornet   Edward Corry

Capt   Wm Richardson
Lt   Thos Roe      Cornet   James Nugent

Capt   Wm Brownlowe      First Lt   James Forde
Second Lt   David Maziere   Cornet John Camack

Capt   John Maxwell

Capt   Sir Capel Molyneux, Bart.
Lt   Leland Hutchinson   Cornet   Leonard Dobbin

Capt   George Gordon
Lt   George Hamilton      Cornet   Wm Henry

Capt   Thos Townly Dawson
Lt   Thos McCann      Cornet   George Hutchinson

Capt   John Cope
Lt   Alexander Hayes      Cornet   Thos Farlow
```

Militia Offiers for County Armagh, 1761. (Published army and militia
lists are available at the Linen Hall Library, Belfast Central Library
and the Irish Studies Library, Armagh.)

YEOMANRY RECORDS

The yeomanry were formed in September 1796 under the threat
of imminent invasion from France. The local gentry and magistrates
throughout Ireland were empowered to raise infantry companies
and cavalry troops in order to maintain a military presence in the
absence of troops and militia if called upon to intercept any
invasion. The government paid, clothed and armed this volunteer
force and their main function was to free the regular army and
militia from their local peacekeeping activities.

Service was usually two days per week and members were expected to turn out during emergencies. They were formed into small local units which, in times of emergency, could be formed into battalions. Despite the intentions of the government it became a largely Protestant force in Ulster, and after the Union of 1800 with Great Britain it remained a powerful symbol of Protestant determination to retain control of law and order in the north. The formation of the County Constabulary and a decade later the Irish Constabulary removed the need for such a peacekeeping force, but the yeomanry lingered on until it was officially disbanded in 1834.

The names of those local grandees who commanded local militia and yeomanry regiments were published during the eighteenth and nineteenth centuries. These will be available at major libraries such as the Linen Hall and Central libraries in Belfast or the local Irish Studies Library, Armagh. On the shelves of the Linen Hall Library, for example, there are more than 200 volumes of army, navy and militia lists giving local and national information.

A number of yeomanry and militia lists including the names of the rank and file have survived and are available at the Public Record Office of Northern Ireland.

The most generally useful are listed below:

Militia officers, 1761	T/808/15235
Militia lists by parish in the barony of O'Neilland West, 1793–5	D/1928/Y/1
Militia pay lists and muster rolls, 1799–1800	T/1115/2A–C
List of officers of Armagh militia, 1808	T/561
Crowhill yeomanry pay list, c 1820	T/2701
Ardress yeomanry Book, c 1796	D/296
Churchill yeomanry Book, c 1796	D/321/1
Muster rolls, Armagh militia, 1793–1797	D/183

LOCAL GOVERNMENT RECORDS

With the conquest of Ulster completed by the beginning of the seventeenth century, and the establishment of landlords and administrators sanctioned by the Crown, came the need to put the

```
        YEOMANRY OFFICERS  1804  ARMAGH     9.

    Corps         Rank      Officers      Date

    Crewhill      C    Joseph Atkinson   31 Oct 1796
                  L    Francis White     15 Aug 1801
                       Richard Robinson  29 Nov 1803
                       Walter Atkinson      do
                       Robert Atkinson      do

    Crier         C    John Ogle         31 Oct 1796
    Upper              Charles Atkinson   7 May 1801
    Cavalry       L    Richard M'Dougal  31 Oct 1796
                       Henry M'Neil         do

    Keady         C    Fra Earl of Charlemont
                                         31 Oct 1796
                       Arthur Neville    18 Aug 1803
                  L    John Simpson         do
                       James Mathews     29 Nov
                       Joseph Holmes        do

    Killevy       C    Jonathan Seaver   31 Oct 1796
                       James Hamilton     8 Sept1801
                  L    Thomas Seaver     21 Jun 1803
                       John Biggs        13 Nov
                       Robert Hamilton   17 do
                       John White           do

    Lurgau        C    William Brownlow  31 Oct 1796
                       Henry M'Veigh     21 Jun   98
                  L    T. Morris         20 Jul 1803
                       William Burke        do
                       J.  Trench           do
                       Robert Ellis         do

    Markethill    C    Hon. A. Acheson   31 Oct 1796
    Cavalry            James Dawson       9 Feb 1804
                  L    William Barker    15 May 1804
                       Andrew Frew          do

    Mullyglass    C    George Atkinson    8 Sep 1801
                  L    Wood Gibson       29 Sep
                       William Duff         do
                       Absalom Best         do
```

Yeomanry Officers for County Armagh, 1804. (Published army and yeomanry lists are available at the Linen Hall Library, Belfast Central Library and the Irish Studies Library, Armagh.)

government of the newly acquired territories on a proper footing. The development of local government in Ulster was naturally enough based on the English model, but it was soon adapted to meet the particular requirements of the colonists. Manor courts, grand juries, boards of guardians and town commissioners as well as urban and district councils all form part of the development of local government in Ulster.

GRAND JURY RECORDS

By the beginning of the nineteenth century the grand jury was the most important local body in Ireland. It had the power to raise money through the collection of county rates, known as 'county cess', and had responsibility for the repair of roads and bridges and the upkeep of local institutions such as hospitals and lunatic asylums. Grand juries were appointed yearly by the county High Sheriff and had an important judicial function in that their members were to preside at the assizes and examine bills of indictment relating to criminal matters.

A major legacy of the grand jury system are the attractive court and sessions houses which are a feature of many Irish towns. The excellent road system in Ulster is another legacy of the work carried out by grand juries. The first great wave of road building in Ireland took place in the 1720s. This was paid for by tolls levied on passing traffic. However, the traffic was not extensive enough to cover the costs and so in 1765 the grand juries were empowered to levy a county cess for road building. In many parts of Ulster, as the roads were built the local population moved to live beside them. These were generally the landless labourers who moved in the hope of employment.

The grand jury itself met at the time of the assizes. Between one assize and another the raising of the money and the arrangements for carrying out the work were left to a staff of permanent officials. The jurors themselves were selected by the high sheriff from the leading property owners in the county and one's place on the panel was a matter of great importance to those chosen. The composition of each panel depended on the character of the sheriff who, if he wished to secure the passage of a certain measure, could fill the grand jury with his supporters. The grand juries remained almost exclusively Protestant and often were chosen from a limited group of well-connected families. Catholics were forbidden to serve until 1793.

The resolutions passed by grand juries and an outline of the business carried out when they met can be found in local newspapers. Grand Jury presentments are the chief records of the county administration prior to 1898. These and grand warrants contain information about work ordered to be done by the grand jury on roads, bridges and jails and constabulary duties in the counties. Bound volumes of these can be frequently found in major libraries as well as at the Public Record Office of Northern Ireland. Unfortunately they are not indexed. Nevertheless, they include the names of the grand juries, those officials who carried out the day-to-day administration such as the county surveyors, coroners, prison governors, session house keepers and managers of the local industrial schools. The presentments contained information on those labourers involved in maintaining the road system. This is an important source for a class of people not found in the tithe applotment books and the early valuation records. The following extract is typical of the information contained in the general presentments:

ARMAGH GENERAL ASSIZES HELD AT ARMAGH
ON 12 MARCH 1890

840 3 years – 1st class – Bridge street, Portadown, including footpath – To Robert M'Clatchey, for keeping in repair 136 perches, road from Portadown to Lurgan, between the crown of Portadown bridge and the town boundary in Bridge-street, Portadown, at 7s per perch, £47,12s yearly, to be kept in good shape and repair with whin stone, 2nd levy, one-third 841 3 years – 2nd class – Ballynacorr road – To John Humphries, for keeping in repair 588 perches, road from Lurgan to Stewartstown, between Mr. Irwin's corner in Ballynacorr and Mr. Fford's smith shop in Derrymacash, at 1s 6d per perch, £44 2s yearly, 150 cube yards, whin stone, and 50 cube yards gravel, each year, 2nd levy, one-third, 842 3 years – 2nd class – Ballynery Road – To Henry Abraham, for keeping in repair 505 perches, road from Lurgan to Strewartstown, between Wolf's island in Derrymacash and Edward O'Neill's in Ballynery, at 1s 6d per perch, £37 17s 6d yearly, 200 cubic yards, with stone, each year, 2nd levy, one third...

The most useful grand jury records for County Armagh deposited at the Public Record Office of Northern Ireland are:

Presentments	1758–1899	ARM/4/1
Presentments	1790	D/288/112
Grand Jury Lists	1735–97	T/647

TOWN COMMISSIONERS

Although some town commissioners had already been established under an act of 1828, most came into existence under the Town Improvement (Ireland) Act, 1854. The commissioners were responsible for the provision of lighting, cleaning services and water supply for all towns with a population of more than 1,500. Later town commissioners were given powers to establish and regulate markets, and promote housing schemes.

Those town commissioner records which have survived for County Armagh can be found in the Local Authority Records deposited at the Public Record Office of Northern Ireland. They include minute books and some rate books which are an obvious source for those interested in family history:

Keady Commissioners	Minute Books	1894–1901	LA/40/2BA/1–2
Portadown Commissioners	Minute Books	1828–1901	LA/64/2BA/1–13
Tandragee Commissioners	Minute Books	1863–1899	LA/70/2BA/1
Lurgan Town Commissioners	Rate Book and	1843–1855	LA/51/5BA/1,
	Minute Books	1839–1900	LA/51/2BA/1–11

THE BOARDS OF GUARDIANS RECORDS

During the nineteenth century the Irish Poor Law was the British Government's main instrument of social policy. The aim of this policy was to establish a system of indoor relief through a series of workhouses into which the destitute could be interned out of sight behind the workhouse walls. However, the Great Famine radically altered the system as laid down in 1838, establishing as it did the principle of outdoor relief, which ensured that the Poor Law would become the foundation of both northern and southern Ireland's social services. The Poor Law system remained largely intact in Northern Ireland until 1948 by which time the health and welfare functions of the boards of guardians were transferred to local health authorities and county councils.

Ireland was divided into one hundred and thirty-seven unions, based on market towns where a workhouse was built. In County Armagh workhouses were established at Lurgan, opened February 1841, and Armagh, opened January 1842. Lurgan workhouse served a population of 71,000 and had accommodation for 1, 512 inmates. The population within the radius of Armagh workhouse was more than 110,000 with accommodation for 1,300 inmates.

Because each union was generally composed of the country within a ten mile radius of the workhouses, many unions crossed county boundaries. Newry workhouse, for example, although in County Down crossed into County Armagh. Lurgan Union stretched into counties Armagh, Down and Antrim and Armagh Union encompassed areas in both counties Armagh and Tyrone.

The boards of guardians, were elected by the rate-payers of each union, together with ex-officio members who Justices of the Peace, and not disqualified by being 'a stipendiary magistrate or assistant barrister, or a person in Holy Orders or a regular Minister of any religious denomination'. Lists of guardians elected each year can be found in the minute books. Also included are details of the day-to-day running of the workhouse including information on problem inmates and those employed in the workhouse as teachers, nurses, chaplains etc. Each workhouse kept a very detailed register of those admitted to the workhouse including the name, religion and townland in which the pauper lived.

The harshness of the conditions within the workhouse can also be seen in the records. This can be seen in the case of certain destitute women taken from the minute book of Armagh Board of Guardians and dated 31 Oct 1846:

'A number of women whose husbands had deserted them viz. Sarah Winchester, Elizabeth Copland, Anne McDonald, Mary Clarke, Margaret Gibson, Jane Thompson and Bridget Fallon were brought before the Board and on refusing to swear information against their husbands they were ordered to be discharged from the workhouse on Monday next.' A punishment book was kept by the Master of the workhouse who was empowered to punish any pauper for a whole range of misdemeanours which included 'Making any noise when silence is ordered'; 'Not duly cleansing his person' and 'Playing at cards or any game of chance'. Punishments authorised for Armagh workhouse for 8 November 1845 included 'Maria McQuaid; disturbing the ward and swearing; to break stones for a week' and 'John Brown, Robert Minday, Thomas Martin and John Hamilton; abusing their new shoes; to go without shoes for a week and to be flogged'.

The poor law system was barely in operation before the catastrophe of the Great Famine hit Ireland. In the middle of September 1845 the maturing potato crop began to rot over much of Ireland. In Ulster, where the poor law system was established more quickly than anywhere else in Ireland, the workhouses began to fill up for the first time since they had opened their doors.

Fever, as usual, followed in the wake of the famine and relief committees were empowered to provide temporary hospitals, to ventilate and cleanse cabins and to procure the proper burial of the dead. By 1847 almost every person admitted into workhouses was a patient suffering from dysentery, fever or in the early stages of disease. There were casualties among the boards of guardians also, including the chairman of Lurgan board of guardians, Lord Lurgan, who died from the fever in 1847. The death rate in Lurgan workhouse was so appalling that at the end of January 1847 the Poor Law Commissioners demanded an explanation. Dr. Bell, the medical officer, wrote in reply:

> Many diseases are now prevalent in the country, and the great majority of new admissions are, when brought into the house, at the point of death, in a moribund state. Many have been known to die on the road, and others on being raised from their beds to come to the workhouse have died before they could be put into the cart, and numbers have died in less than 24 hours subsequent to their admission...many dying persons are sent for admission merely that coffins may be obtained for them at the expense of the Union.

The number of deaths in Lurgan workhouse had risen sharply during the month of January 1847, rising from 18 for the week ending 2 January to 95 by the end of the month. In a letter of 19

February 1847 to Lord Lurgan, chairman of the board of guardians, the Protestant chaplain, the Rev. W.P. Oulton, blamed the 'dreadful mortality which has swept our workhouse' largely on the poor quality of food given the inmates; the bread was 'very dark-coloured, not sufficiently baked, probably that it might weigh the heavier, and it was sour'. The broth was made of unsound beef which, according to wardmaster Lutton, 'was so offensive, when cutting it up after being boiled he could hardly stand over it'.

As a means of reducing the numbers of destitute persons and lessening the burden of the crippling poor rate on the landowners, the government gave its wholehearted supported to assisted emigration schemes. The Poor Relief Acts of 1838, 1843, 1847 and 1849 empowered the boards of guardians to raise such sums 'not exceeding the proceeds of one shilling in the pound' of the annual poor rate to 'assist poor persons who would otherwise have to be accommodated in the workhouse' to emigrate, preferably to the British colonies. The Colonial Land and Emigration Commission was set up in England in 1840, under the control of the British Colonial Office, to organise and supervise emigration from both Britain and Ireland. The availability of emigration was constantly brought to the attention of the boards of guardians in circular letters issued by the Poor Law Commissioners. A representative of the Emigration Commission visited workhouses in Ireland to inspect and select persons for emigration, and those chosen were offered a free passage and supplied before departure with clothing and a little money to support themselves on arrival.

The Board of Guardian records are deposited at the Public Record Office of Northern Ireland. Those with a particular reference to County Armagh are:

Armagh	County Armagh	BG/2
Lurgan	County Armagh	BG/22
Newry	County Down and County Armagh	BG/24

Also of interest is the 'Castleblayney Poor Law Rate Book', (covering Newtownhamilton, and parts of the parishes of Creggan and Forkill) published in the *Clogher Record*, 5 (1) 1963.

COUNTY COUNCILS

County councils were established in 1899, superseding the grand juries and taking on many of the functions held by the boards of guardians. By the early part of the twentieth century there was a steady growth in the powers of the county councils as they acquired housing and planning powers. They were responsible for elementary and secondary education. The county councils divided the county into districts for the management by a district committee of public health, housing, roads and water supply.

After 1945, local government responsibilities in the fields of social services, education, social work and housing expanded considerably. Legislation, 1946–49, established county health and welfare authorities for their areas and provided for the transfer to them of the relevant functions of the board's of guardians, as well as those of borough, urban and rural councils.

The most important records for the local historian are the minutes and other records of the council itself and of its committees and the accounts. Local newspapers will also provide relevant information as will the publications produced by the councils. They include local directories, year books and diaries. Local Authority Records for County Armagh are deposited at PRONI.

1899-1973	Armagh County Council	LA.2
1899-1973	Armagh Rural District Council	LA.9
1813-1973	Armagh Urban District Council	LA.10
1899-1967	Banbridge No. 2 [later Tandragee] Rural District Council	LA.69
1901-1922	Crossmaglen Rural District Council Castleblaney Rural District Council	LA.82
1894-1973	Keady Urban District Council	LA.40
1893-1973	Lurgan Borough Council	LA.51
1898-1973	Lurgan Rural District Council	LA.52
1899-1973	Newry No. 2 Rural District Council	LA.57
1828-1973	Portadown Borough Council	LA.64
1850-1973	Tandragee Urban District Council	LA.70

PRINTED SOURCES

LOCAL HISTORY JOURNALS

There are a number of local history journals published in County Armagh and these can be a very helpful source for family historians. They can be found in local libraries and are worth checking, as articles on specific parishes or townlands often include lists of names from documents such as subsidy rolls, hearth money rolls or census returns. The journal *Seanchas Ardmhacha*, published by the Armagh Diocesan Historical Society, is particularly useful from this point of view. For example in *Seanchas Ardmhacha*, vol 2, No 2 (1957), an article on the Armagh Manor Court Rolls, 1625–1627, by T.G.F. Paterson, includes lists of litigants in alphabetical order as well as lists of juries. The appendix includes fiants from the reign of Elizabeth I, patent rolls from the reign of James I, some depositions from 1641, and a précis of Irish surnames from the census of 1659. The journals for County Armagh are:

Review, the journal of the Craigavon Historical Society
Seanchas Ardmhacha, published by the Armagh Diocesan Historical
    Society
The Journal of the Poyntzpass History Society.
Seanchas Dhroim Mor, published by the Dromore Diocesan Historical
    Society.

PARISH AND COUNTY HISTORIES

It is worth checking published accounts of particular parishes and
eighteenth and nineteenth century histories of the county. These
often contain details on particular families or lists of those who
held clerical or secular office within the county. *The History of Tynan
Parish, County Armagh and Other Papers*, by Thomas Hughes and
published in 1910, for example, contains genealogical information
on many of the prominent families in the parish from before the
Plantation. Also included is a breakdown of land ownership in the
parish by townland. The value of these pre-1922 publications is
that they often reprint material that was lost in the almost complete
destruction of the Public Record Office, Dublin archive, in that
year. In a section of the book in which he lists grants and grantees,
he writes, 'We have the first mention of an English planter in 1615,
when we find Robert Cowell tenant for a term of sixty years of
four balliboes, at £20 a year. This tenant got the best portion of
the church lands, while the old Irish tenants were driven into Mount
Irwin and Dillay. He was a pensioner, this planter; for he
surrendered the daily pension of 8s Irish on May 16th, 1615, at
Tynan, and on the 20th May a like sum was granted to Liew. R.
Cowell.'

Parish and county histories will also provide the family historian
with a great deal of background material. It seems a pity to limit
oneself to a list of names and dates when a great deal of colour
can be added from details of life in the town or parish at the
relevant point in history. In his *Statistical Survey of the County of
Armagh* published in 1804, Sir Charles Coote describes the customs,
the habits and the working practices of the local people. Such passages
must always be viewed with caution as all writers are subject to their
own prejudices. The following extract on the spending habits of both
sexes in County Armagh is, shall we say, a touch masculine in outlook:

Women's wear, of cotton, will amount to about 3l., with cloak, petticoat, shoes, stockings, &c. If drugget is substituted for cotton, the cost will be about one-third less, and the article more durable. In general, the women are better clad than the men, and make a gayer appearance on holidays. Their earnings are generally spent on finery, as the man's labour procures them provisions.

GUIDES AND TRADE DIRECTORIES

Guides, trade directories and almanacs are an invaluable source. The first trade directory was published in 1751 but it was not until the early nineteenth century that a range of country-wide and local directories began to appear. Ulster street directories contain a great deal of information on the gentry, clergy, the professional classes, merchants etc. Once again those from more humble backgrounds such as tenant farmers, labourers and servants are excluded.

During the nineteenth century a number of provincial directories were produced. These directories include information on even the smallest of market towns and ports in Ireland. Beginning with a description of the town and surrounding countryside, the names and addresses of the local butchers, pawnbrokers, and coach builders are given, as well as the various places of worship, with the names of the local ministers, and the location of local schools.

Street directories can be useful if you wish to find out which church or school your ancestor attended. The names and addresses of the local member of parliament, magistrates, poor law guardians and town commissioners are also included in many street directories. Those directories with special reference to County Armagh are as follows:

1819

Thomas Bradshaw's General Directory of Newry, Armagh, Dungannon, Portadown, Tandragee, Lurgan, Waringstown, Banbridge, Warrenpoint, Rosstrevor, Kilkeel and Rathfryland, c1819, which includes an alphabetical list of traders but does not include local gentry.

1820

Pigot's Commercial Directory of Ireland. The towns of Ireland are listed alphabetically, supplying the names of the nobility etc., and the traders of each town including Armagh.

1824

Pigot's Commercial Directory includes lists of traders, nobility, gentry and clergy for Armagh, Blackwatertown, Lurgan, Portadown and Tandragee.

1841 AND 1842

Mathew Martin's Belfast Directory includes an alphabetical list of traders, merchants and gentry and residents of the principal streets for Armagh, Lurgan, Portadown and Waringstown.

1846

Slater's Directory of Ireland, arranged by province; trade lists for each town and village within the provinces are included. There are lists of nobility, gentry and clergy; however, the principal farmers are not included. Includes Armagh, Blackwatertown, Loughgall, Lurgan, Portadown and Tandragee.

1852

Henderson's Belfast and Province of Ulster Directory includes a street-by-street listing and an alphabetical list of the 'principal inhabitants' for Armagh, Blackwatertown, Lurgan and Portadown.

1856

Slater's Commercial Directory includes lists of nobility, gentry, clergy and traders in Armagh, Keady, Middletown, Richhill, Tynan, Markethill, Blackwatertown, Loughgall, Lurgan, Portadown and Tandragee.

1865

R. Wynne's Business Directory includes Armagh, Lurgan and Portadown.

1870

Slater's Directory of Ireland includes lists of traders, nobility and clergy for Armagh, Crossmaglen, Lurgan, Newtownhamilton, Portadown and Tandragee.

1877

Henderson's Belfast and Province of Ulster Directory includes Armagh, Blackwatertown, Keady, Lurgan, Moira, Portadown, Richhill and Tandragee.

1881

Slater's Commercial Directory contains lists of traders, clergy, nobility and farmers in Armagh, Crossmaglen, Lurgan, Newtownhamilton, Portadown and Tandragee.

1883

Farrell's County Armagh Directory & Almanac contains street directories for Armagh and alphabetical lists for the towns of Lurgan, Portadown, Richhill and Tandragee.

1888

George Henry Bassett's Guide and Directory of County Armagh, 1888 contains comprehensive lists for all major towns and villages in the county.

1894

Slater's Royal Directory of Ireland includes lists of traders, farmers, police, teachers and private residents in the towns, villages and parishes of County Armagh.

ORDNANCE SURVEY MEMOIRS 1830s

Ordnance Survey Memoirs also provide a great deal of background information on the character and habits of the people who lived in Ireland during the early part of the nineteenth century. In 1824 a House of Commons committee recommended a townland survey of Ireland, with maps at the scale of six inches to one statute mile, to facilitate a uniform valuation for local taxation. The survey was directed by Colonel Thomas Colby, who had available to him officers of the Royal Engineers and three companies of sappers and miners. In addition to this, civil assistants were recruited to help with sketching, drawing and engraving maps, and eventually, in the 1830s, the writing of the Memoirs.

The Memoirs were written descriptions intended to accompany the maps, containing information which could not be fitted on to them. They are a unique source for the history of the northern half of Ireland before the Great Famine as they document the landscape and situation, buildings and antiquities, land-holdings and population, employment and livelihood of the parishes. The surveyors recorded the habits of the people, their food, drink, dress and customs. Details of ruined churches, prehistoric monuments and standing stones were also included.

The Ordnance Survey Memoirs contains valuable information on ancient forts, settlements and graveyards. The following extract is taken from the memoir for the parish of Tartaraghan, County Armagh, compiled by Thomas McIlroy and dated 15 December 1837:

ANCIENT GRAVEYARDS

There is a very old graveyard in the townland of Eglish near the Glebe House, which is still made use of. It is generally believed that there was formerly an abbey near it, but there is no vestige of it remaining. There is another graveyard of the same description at Maghery and close to the shore of Lough Neagh which is also still made use of, and almost exclusively by Roman Catholics. Campbell is the prevailing name of persons buried there. The ruins of a small chapel in a very dilapidated state are standing within the burial ground. The townlands of Eglish and Maghery are both abbeylands and tithe free. The townland of Crankill is also tithe free, probably from the same cause.

The memoirs also contain a great deal of information on local schools, churches and landed estates as well as descriptions of the towns and villages. The section headed 'Habits of the People' can often contain valuable information for the family historian. In the memoir for the parish of Kilmore, for example, the following account is given of the local people:

> Food and dress are the same as in the surrounding country, and the
> poorest endeavour to appear clean on Sunday. Their fuel is in general
> turf, which is brought principally from Drumcree and Tartaraghan
> parishes. The prevailing names are Hutchison in Cloghan townland,
> Williamson in Creenagh and Adams in townlands of Bracchagh
> and Ballylisk. There are no prevailing customs, and the language of
> the people is in general tolerably good English with a Scotch accent,
> as is usual in the north.

The Ordnance Survey memoirs have been published in 40 volumes
by the Institute of Irish Studies at The Queen's University of Belfast.
The first volume in the series covers all the parishes in County
Armagh. All volumes in the series can be purchased via the online
bookstore on the Ulster Historical Foundation website.

The Public Record Office of Northern Ireland holds microfilm
copies of the original Ordnance Survey memoirs (held in the Royal
Irish Academy, Dublin). The references for Co Armagh are MIC/
6C. The originals are held in the Royal Irish Academy.

NEWSPAPERS

The first newspapers were published in the seventeenth century.
However, it was not until the eighteenth century that the larger
towns in Ireland began to publish their own newspapers. These
early newspapers can prove disappointing for local historians
because they concentrated mainly on national and international news.
Local news only began to feature later in the eighteenth century.
They are useful, nevertheless, because they include advertisements,
obituaries, market prices and properties to let.

By the early nineteenth century newspapers had become the most
important medium of public opinion and information and local
newspapers began increasingly to cover local issues. Births, deaths
and marriages are included more frequently but, like obituaries,
these usually relate only to the higher echelons of society. The minutes
of the boards of guardians were also published in considerable
detail, as were the proceedings of local court cases. More usefully
for family historians, local papers occasionally published articles
by local historians and these were often accompanied by a list of

inhabitants. For example, in 1935, the *Portadown Times* published a list of houses and occupiers in Portadown from 1835.

Local newspapers can be consulted in public libraries. They are often available only on microfilm and have only very rarely been indexed. They are, nevertheless, important sources and should not be neglected. The Irish Studies Library at Armagh is the most important source of newspapers relating to County Armagh. The most important newspapers are as follows:

Armagh Guardian, first published in 1844
Armagh Guardian, 1844–1982
Armagh Standard, 1879–1909
Lurgan Gazette, 1861–74
Lurgan Mail, 1890–current
Lurgan Times and Portadown Recorder, 1877–1915
Portadown Weekly News (later *Portadown and Lurgan News*), 1872–90
Ulster Gazette, 1844–current
Portadown Times, 1923–current

EMIGRATION RECORDS

AMERICA AND CANADA

Emigration from County Armagh is dominated by the mass migration during the mid-nineteenth century which occurred as the result of a significant slump in the linen industry and the devastation caused by the Great Famine. These emigrants were mostly Catholic and often of the more disadvantaged element in the county. Nevertheless, emigration had already taken place on a large scale during the previous century . These emigrants were for the most part Protestant, and in particular Presbyterian. During the early part of the eighteenth century, many of these emigrants could not afford the passage-money and had to work their way out as indentured servants. However, as the century wore on there was a marked rise in the affluence and social status of the average emigrant.

The main cause of eighteenth-century emigration was not primarily economic, although in times of depression such as the late 1720s and 1770s there were substantial increases in the number of emigrants. The main cause of emigration at this time was the attraction of the American colonies for those who were eager to improve their prospects – younger sons in particular.

America was also seen as a land where freedom of religion was guaranteed. In Ireland the government and church were hostile to the advancement of those who were not part of the Established Church.

Throughout the eighteenth century, Pennsylvania drew the majority of the Ulster emigrants. There is little doubt that their earlier experiences of frontier life in the Ulster plantation moulded the Ulster emigrants for similar experiences of frontier life in America. James Logan, himself born in Moira, County Armagh, during his time as the Colonial Secretary of Pennsylvania, was worried about the aggressive movements of Indian tribes on the borders of Quaker and German settlements. He wrote William Penn saying that he 'thought it might be prudent to plant a settlement of such men as those who had so bravely defended Londonderry, and Enniskillen as a frontier in case of any disturbance...these people if kindly used, will be orderly...and easily dealt with'. By 1730 Logan stated that five North of Ireland families gave more trouble than 50 of any other people. They were 'troublesome settlers to the government and hard neighbours to the Indians'. He deplored their 'audacious and disorderly' squatting on frontier lands.

Emigration had a number of beneficial effects. It reduced pressure on land and provided work for the numerous ship-owners and their agents engaged in promoting it. By the beginning of the nineteenth century the government had come to appreciate the beneficial effects which emigration would have upon the Irish economy, and by the outbreak of the Great Famine, the government was providing some funds for assisted emigration. Nineteenth-century emigrants, especially after 1845, were for the most part Catholic. They came mostly from the poorest part of the country, the west, and their emigration was caused by the harsh economic conditions. These emigrants settled, to a large extent, in the eastern cities of America and the number who took up farming was small in proportion to German and Scandinavian emigrants.

An extensive collection of emigrant letters has been deposited at the Public Record Office of Northern Ireland. These letters document the experience of emigrants as they braved the harsh conditions on board emigrant ships, and often contain a mixture of family gossip and the latest news from across the Atlantic. One such County Armagh emigrant was Thomas McGinity who followed his sister to the United States. Once established in his adoptive country he wrote home to Newtownhamilton with news of his adventures and of his sister and her new husband: 'I take this favourable opportunity of writing to youse to let youse know that I and John arrived safely thank God after a passage of 30 days. I never had better health than that which I had at sea. We had two deaths aboard of which were children [sic] and 4 of whom we left as Quarentine. When we came in to town I went to look for my sister. I went to the person with whom she lived and they told me she was married and living out in the country both she and her husband. I went out of the city and found them about 80 miles up the north over from New York. He is a clean young man, an Irishman from the County Cavan, his name is Edw. Riley...' (24 Oct 1847, T/3539/2). Once he had settled in Pittsburgh, Thomas encouraged friends and relatives to follow his example. 'Now if you see that you cannot do to your wishes in Ireland', he declared in a letter to his brother John in Newtownhamilton, 'come out here by all means while you have the means, you have all my experience and knowledge on which you can rely with confidence which, limited as it may be, would cost you considerable experience to find out. I can show you the towns in the county where a Catholic Church is to be found, tell you where to settle....' (10 Feb 1850, T/3595/5).

Many Ulster families settled in Canada, others moved on to the United States via Canadian ports. It was cheaper to travel to Quebec from the port of Londonderry than to go from Belfast or Liverpool to Boston or New York. The voyage was also usually shorter. One such emigrant was Isaac Topley who wrote home from Montreal to his family at Markethill in County Armagh. In one letter, postmarked February 1850, with Famine still rife back home, he declared, 'the winter here is very pleasant. I can work with my coat off all day, the winter is getting something like home, the snow is not more than 2 or 3 inches deep this winter as yet, everyday is like a Christmas here for eating and drinking there is so many thing(s) on the table we do not know what to eat...' (PRONI, T/2149/1).

Isaac's brother Abraham, writing to their brother-in-law James Boardman at Tandragee a few years later, passed on news of their sister Elizabeth. He also told them that he was thinking of getting married: 'I was thinking of looking for a woman as the people is advising me to marry. I believe I could get one...she [has] fifty acres of good land and has the deed in her own name but she has four children. She is from Comber below Belfast the people advise me not to take her on the account of her having a family, so I think I will not heed it now nor never with the same...'(PRONI T/2149/2).

Emigrant letters were often published in the local press. During the Franco-Prussian War of 1870 a letter was published in the *Armagh Guardian* from one A. Styleman Herring from 'our peaceful colony of Canada', reporting on the progress of those who had emigrated from Ireland. He found 'the country prosperous, with every facility for emigrants to advance in life'. He found that although there were a few who disparaged emigration 'most are content and happy'. He continued: 'I have travelled much in Canada, and am convinced that this is an especially good country for a poor man – Any industrious, sober, and persevering person after seven years work generally acquires a good position, and has money in the bank.' He encouraged the Canadian government to work even harder to promote emigration. 'To the patrons of emigration, I would urge them to proceed in this blessed work, collect funds to send out many more respectable but poor people, who have scarce any work to support life with. None starve here. There are no workhouses or stone yards, and most of the inhabitants seem happy, contented, and prosperous.'

THE RECORDS

Some passenger lists have survived for the ships bringing emigrants to America and Canada. These list emigrants from certain parishes in County Armagh. Copies of the following lists are available at the Public Record Office of Northern Ireland:

List of emigrants to America and Scotland,
Derrynoose Church of Ireland records,   MIC/1/14
1840–1855   and T/679/10

Register of Girls' Friendly Society members who
emigrated from County Armagh, 1890–1921   D/648/9

Passenger lists are another valuable source of emigration records. Of course these records do not relate exclusively to County Armagh. The most important of these are:

List of passengers from Warrenpoint and Newry
to Philadelphia and New York, 1791–2   T /711/1

Passenger Lists – Philadelphia, 1800–82   MIC/333/1

Passenger Lists – Baltimore, 1890–92   MIC /333/2

Passenger Lists – Boston, 1871–91   MIC/ 333/3

Passenger Lists – New York, 1826–27, 1840–2
and 1850–2   MIC /333/4

Passengers from various origins arriving mainly
in New York, 1802–14   T/1011

Passenger Lists from Belfast, Cork, Limerick,
Londonderry, Newry, Sligo, Warrenpoint to
USA, 1803–06   T/3262

Passenger Lists from Ireland to America,
1804–06 (index available in Deputy Keeper's
Report 1929)   T/521/1

Passenger Books of J&J Cooke, Shipping
Agents. Sailings from Londonderry to
Philadelphia, Quebec, St John's, New   D/2892/1/1–14
Brunswick, 1847–71   (see also MIC 13).

List of names of petitioners for naturalisation,
Laurens County, South Carolina, 1806–1825   T/3538

Typescript list of passengers to America from
County Londonderry 1815–16   T/2964

Passenger Lists of Vessels Arriving at Boston 1820–1891. Extracts from passenger lists available on microfilm at PRONI.

Passenger Lists of Vessels Arriving at New York 1820–1821. Extracts from passenger lists compiled by Public Search Room at PRONI.

RECOMMENDED READING

Numerous passenger lists have been published. These include: *The Famine Immigrants: Lists of Irish Immigrants Arriving at the Port of New York 1846–1851* (seven volumes edited by A. Glazier, published 1983) which contains data from the original ship manifest schedules, deposited by the National Immigration Archives in the Balch Institute in Philadelphia.

Irish Passenger Lists 1847–1871, compiled under the direction of Brian Mitchell, (Baltimore, 1988), contains lists of passengers sailing from Londonderry to America on ships of the J&J Cooke Line and the McCorkell Line.

Lists of Emigrants to America 1635–1776 contains lists of passengers, including Irish emigrants, who departed from English ports.

Emigrants from Ireland, 1847–1852: State-Aided Emigration Schemes from Crown Lands in Ireland, by Eilish Ellis (Baltimore, 1977). Originally published as 'State-Aided Emigrant Schemes from Crown Lands in Ireland c.1850', *Analecta Hibernica*, No. 22 (1960).

Passenger Arrivals at the Port of Philadelphia 1800–1819, General Editor Michael H. Tepper (Baltimore, 1986).

Passenger Lists From Ireland, Dominick Hackett and Charles Montague Early, (Baltimore, 1965).

Scotch-Irish Migration to South Carolina, 1872 (Rev. William Martin And His Five Shiploads of Settlers) Jean Stephenson (Strasburg, Virginia, 1971).

Immigration Of The Irish Quakers Into Pennsylvania 1682–1750, Albert Cook Myers, (Pennsylvania, 1902).

Emigrants From Ireland To America 1735–1743, Francis McDowell (Baltimore, 1992).

Passenger and Immigration Lists Index: A Guide to Published Arrival Records of about 500,0000 Passengers who came to the United States and Canada in the seventeenth and eighteenth centuries, edited by P. William Filby with Mary K. Meyer (Arizona, 1981).

Of particular interest to researchers interested in emigration to Canada are the passenger lists, the most important of which are listed below:

Three volumes of passenger lists, February
1847–1849, February 1850–August 1857, March
1858–July 1867, of J&J Cooke, shipping agents,
Londonderry. The Canadian destinations are
Quebec and St John, New Brunswick, with
details also being given for Philadelphia and
New Orleans   D2892/1/1–3

Typed transcripts, compiled in 1984, of notices
which appeared in Canadian local newspapers,
mostly the *New Brunswick Courier*, 1830–46, and
the *Toronto Irish Canadian*, 1869. The notices include
queries as to the whereabouts of various persons
who had emigrated from Ulster to Canada
and the United States   D/3000/82

Passenger list, 11 May 1847, issued by A.C.
Buchanan, Chief Agent for Emigration at
Quebec, giving the date of sailing, the names of
the ships involved, their point of departure and
the number of passengers carried   T/3168

RECOMMENDED READING

Irish Migrants in the Canadas, Bruce S Elliot (Belfast 1988).
Irish Emigration and Canadian Settlement: Patterns, Links & Letters,
Cecil J. Houston and William J. Smyth (Belfast & Toronto, 1990).

AUSTRALIA

By comparison with the immense emigration to America and
Canada during the Great Famine, emigration to Australia was
generally a trickle until the discovery of gold in 1851. Nearly 100,000
Irish emigrants came during the 1850s, more than double the rate
of the previous decade and a half. A similar flood of emigrants
occurred during the 1860s as a result of the Civil War in America.

Those emigrants who arranged their travel to Australia were

generally better off than those who left Ireland for North America. Few Irish emigrants could afford the full fare of about £17. Australia, therefore, attracted a significant proportion of emigrants with the resources to set themselves up in business or on the land in the expanding agricultural hinterland of the coastal settlements.

There were, however, government-assisted schemes especially for families of liberated convicts. The Irish convicts and their families used these schemes far more extensively than the English, Scots and Welsh so much so that there was complaint about the 'Tipperarifying' of Australia. There was also a special scheme for the emigration of female orphan paupers from Irish workhouses to Australia during the Great Famine. Labour had become extremely scarce in Australia around the time of the Famine in Ireland and the colonists in New South Wales and Western Australia pressed the Colonial Office to secure more settlers. Arrangements were made with the Colonial Land and Emigration Commissioners for a scheme of assisted emigration and the first 5,000 adults were sent in 1847. At the same time every Australian colony offered financial encouragement for emigration. These ranged from land guarantees to free passages.

As a means of reducing the numbers of destitute persons, and lessening the burden of the crippling poor rate on the landowners, the Government gave its wholehearted support to assisted emigration schemes. The Poor Relief Acts of 1838, 1843, 1847 and 1849 empowered the boards of guardians to raise such sums 'not exceeding the proceeds of one shilling in the pound' on the annual poor rate to 'assist poor persons who would otherwise have to be accommodated in the workhouse' to emigrate, preferably to the British colonies. The Colonial Land and Emigration Commission was set up in England in 1840, under the control of the British Colonial Office, to organise and supervise emigration from both Britain and Ireland. The representative of the Emigration Commission visited every workhouse in Ireland to inspect and select persons for emigration and those chosen were offered a free passage and supplied before departure with clothing and a little money to support themselves on arrival.

Between 1848 and 1850 some 4000 female orphans were sent to Australia by the boards of guardians. The scheme was introduced to alleviate the male-female imbalance in the Australian population and the problem of female orphans in the workhouse during the famine. By 1852 it has been estimated that there was a total of 62,000 orphans in the workhouses.

An earlier source of free passage at government expense was convict transportation. Between 1791 and 1868 more than 36,000 Irish offenders were removed to Australia. Men, women and children were transported, sometimes for the most trivial offences. Boys of twelve and under were sent to the penal colonies for pilfering and women, often with infants or small children, for 'being vagabonds'.

Convict settlements were a feature of Australian society for nearly a century until the transportation system was progressively withdrawn from 1840 onwards. In that year New South Wales was removed from the system. It was followed by Tasmania in 1852 and Western Australia in 1867. The main reason for this was that the Australian colonists came to regard the convict system as a stigma on those who had chosen to emigrate, as well as criticism in both Britain and Australia because of the inevitable brutality of certain aspects of the convict system.

THE RECORDS

There are a number of records deposited at the Public Record Office of Northern Ireland which relate to Australia. These include:

Indexes to male convicts transported to New South Wales, 1830–1845	MIC/468
Indexes to male convicts transported to Western Australia 1850–1842	MIC/648
Passenger List, 1840, Victoria, Australia	T/3036
Register of Girls' Friendly Society – sponsored emigrants from various counties in Ireland, 1890–1921	D/648/9
Indexes to births, deaths and marriages in New South Wales, Australia, 1787–1899	M.F.4

A list of Armagh convicts in Australia, 1800–1806, has been published by Anne-Marie Whitaker in *Seanchas Ardmhacha*, Journal of the Armagh Diocesan Historical Society, vol 16, No 1 (1994). Details include occupation, name of wife, subsequent career in Australia and date of death. Trevor McClaughlin of Macquarie University, Sydney published an article on the emigration of Irish female orphan paupers to Australia c.1848–1850 in *Familia* 1987 and a list of the girls sent from Armagh workhouse in *Guild Interest List*, No 11 (1988).

RECOMMENDED READING:

Letters from Irish Australia, 1825–1929, Patrick O'Farrell (Belfast & Sydney, 1984).
Oceans of Consolation: Personal Accounts of Irish Migration to Australia, David Fitzpatrick, (Cork, 1994).
Irish Families In Australia & New Zealand, (4 volumes) compiled by Hubert William Coffey and Marjorie Jean Morgan.
Barefoot & Pregnant?:Irish Famine Orphans in Australia, Trevor McClaughlin, (Melbourne 1991).

ULSTER-AMERICAN FOLK PARK

A comprehensive database of emigration material is available at the Centre for Emigration Studies, based at the Ulster-America Folk Park, near Omagh. The database includes ship passenger lists, emigrant letters and diaries of emigrants, death and marriage records of former emigrants and births of children of Irish parentage. Researchers can type in an individual or family name and can print out the results of their enquiries.

MISCELLANEOUS COLLECTIONS

The Public Record Office of Northern Ireland has in its custody records compiled by scholars and family historians which are of enormous interest to genealogists. Pedigrees for families from many different parts of Ireland are available. Most notable of these are pedigrees extracted from wills proved in the Prerogative Court of Ireland between the 16th and 18th centuries compiled by or for Sir Bernard Burke, Ulster King of Arms. This collection comprises 42 large volumes of pedigree charts (T/559).

Also of interest are the Groves Manuscripts which contain a great deal of valuable material for genealogists. Tenison Groves, a genealogist and record searcher for more than 40 years, compiled a collection of many thousands of transcripts, abstracts, notes etc., which he made from records in the Public Record Office in Dublin before the destruction in 1922. The Groves Manuscripts include extensive material relating to County Armagh such as the names of the chief inhabitants of Armagh during the seventeenth century including grand jurors, Justices of the Peace and army officers. Also of interest is a list of Protestant refugees from County Armagh who fled to England during the Williamite wars. (T/808/14988). Groves made abstracts and transcripts of thousands of wills and there is a fairly complete personal name index in PRONI to this massive collection particularly for pre-1858 wills.

Ten volumes of transcripts of Irish genealogical material from the manuscript collections of the Society of Genealogists, London, 1569–1841, are also held by PRONI, (T/581).

Canon Leslie's manuscripts include extracts from the Armagh registry, clergy succession lists, extracts of about 700 wills and genealogical notes of numerous families, 1607–19th century, (T/1057).

Another item of interest is the 'Raeburn Manuscript Book'. Robert Pillow, the compiler of these notes, collected a great deal of material relating to Armagh including an important collection of tombstone inscription books now deposited at the Armagh Library. The Raeburn Manuscript includes much genealogical material on prominent County Armagh families. Other items of interest are a list of parish priests registered at the General Sessions, Lurgan, dating from 1704, Lists of Grand Jurors, Armagh, 1731–75; 1801–1821 and High Sheriffs, 1714–1830. (PRONI T/636).

During his time at the Armagh County Museum, T.G.F. Paterson compiled twenty-five volumes of Armagh Miscellanea, which he deposited at the Museum. These volumes contain a wide variety of genealogical material relating to County Armagh including hearth money rolls, extracts from records of various landed estates, militia lists, street directories, Armagh Dissenters, 1775, and lists of surgeons, 1767–1924, at the county infirmary. For a more complete list see *Harvest Home: A Selection from the writings of T.G.F. Paterson*, edited by E. Estyn

Evans, published 1975. Copies of ten volumes of 'Armachiana' were also deposited at PRONI. Included is a list of early eighteenth century tenants in the neighbourhood of Tandragee, probably compiled for election purposes from the estates of St. John, Cope, Brownlow, Acheson, Caulfield, Richardson and Molyneux. (T/2706.)

Researchers should also consult the personal names index in the Public Search Room which contains many references to pedigrees and genealogical papers relating to various family names in County Armagh.

A CONCLUSION

Searching your family history is not simply a matter of looking at old records. Once you have found the farm or townland where your ancestors lived or the location of their burials, visit the places if you can. If you are lucky some of the old houses and buildings mentioned in the records may have survived. Visiting the houses, townlands or villages gives you a better idea of the world your ancestors inhabited. The worst that can happen is that you will get a chance to see parts of the lovely Ulster countryside which fall outside the usual tourist haunts.

No book can hope to give a complete record of all the material relating to a particular county. It is my hope that this book can point you in the right direction and fill in the historical background which would have affected the lives of your ancestors. Remember, by the time you have looked through the records, visited the relevant locations and documented your findings, *you* will be the expert...

All that is left for me to do is wish you success.

BIBLIOGRAPHY AND SOURCES

BARDON, Jonathan *A History of Ulster* (Belfast, 1992)

BEGLEY, D.F. (ed.) *Irish Genealogy: A Record Finder* (Dublin, 1981)

CARLETON, S.T. *Heads and Hearths: the Hearth Money Rolls and Poll Tax Returns for Co. Antrim, 1660–69*, (Belfast)

CLARE, Rev. W. *A Simple Guide to Irish Genealogy* (London, 1938)

CONNOLLY, S.J. (ed.) *The Oxford Companion To Irish History*, (Oxford, 1998)

CRAWFORD, W.H. and TRAINOR, B. *Aspects of Irish Social History, 1750–1800* (Belfast, 1969)

CRAWFORD, W.H. 'The Significance of Landed Estates in Ulster 1600–1820', in *Irish Economic and Social History, XVII* (1990)

CRAWFORD, W.H. 'The Ulster Irish in the Eighteenth Century', in *Ulster Folklife*, Vol 28, 1982

DE BREFFNY, Brian *Irish Family Names: Arms, Origins and Locations* (Dublin, 1982)

DICKSON, R.J. *Ulster Emigration To Colonial America 1718–1775*, (Belfast, 1966)

FABRICANT, Carol *Swift's Landscape* (John Hopkins University Press, London, 1982)

FALLEY, M.D. *Irish and Scotch-Irish Ancestral Research* (Virginia, 1962)

GILLESPIE, R.G. (ed.) *Settlement And Survival On An Ulster Estate* (Belfast, 1988)

GILLESPIE, R.G. and O'SULLIVAN, Harold (eds.) *The Borderlands: Essays On The History of the Ulster-Leinster Border* (Belfast, 1989)

GREEN, E.R.R. (ed.) *Essays in Scotch-Irish History* (Belfast, 1969)

GRENHAM, J. *Tracing Your Irish Ancestors* (Dublin, 1992)

HAYWARD, Richard *In Praise of Ulster* (Belfast, 1938)

HERBER, Mark D. *Ancestor Trails: The Complete Guide To British Genealogy and Family History* (Sutton Publishing Limited, 1997)

HEY, David   *The Oxford Companion to Local And Family
                    History* (Oxford, 1996)
KINEALY, Christine *Tracing Your Irish Roots* (Belfast, 1991)
KINEALY, Christine and   *The Famine In Ulster* (Belfast, 1997)
PARKHILL, Trevor (eds.)

LUCEY, M.   'Rateable Valuation in Ireland', in
                    Administration, Spring 1964, vol 12, no.1
Mac CONGHAIL, Maire   *Tracing Your Irish Ancestors* (Glasgow, 1997)
and GORRY, Paul
McCARTHY, T.   *The Irish Roots Guide* (Dublin, 1991)
Mac CUARTA, Brian (ed.)   *Ulster 1641: Aspects of the Rising* (Belfast,
                    1993)
MacLYSAGHT, E.   *Irish Families: Their Names, Arms and Origins*
                    (Dublin, 1957)
MacLYSAGHT, E.   'Seventeenth Century Hearth Money Rolls'
                    in *Analecta Hibernica*, No. 24 (1967)
MacATASNEY, G.   *The Famine In Lurgan and Portadown* (Dublin,
                    1997)
MAXWELL, I.   *Tracing Your Ancestors In Northern Ireland*
                    (Edinburgh, 1997)
NEILL, K.   *How To Trace Family History In Northern
                    Ireland* (Belfast, 1986)
NOLAN, W.   *Tracing the Past* (Dublin, 1982)
NOLAN, W. (ed.)   *The Shaping of Ireland: The Geographical
                    Perspective* (Dublin, 1986)
O'NEILL, Robert K. *Ulster Libraries, Archives & Ancestral Heritage
                    Centres: A Visitor's Guide* (Belfast, 1987)
PHAIR, P.B.   'Guide to the Registry of Deeds' in *Analecta
                    Hibernica* no 23 (1996).
QUINN, S.E.   *Trace Your Irish Ancestors* (Wicklow, 1989)
ROBINSON, Philip   *The Plantation of Ulster* (Belfast, 1994)
RYAN, J.G.   *Irish Records: Sources for Family and Local
                    History* (Salt Lake City, 1988)
RYAN, J.G.   *Irish Church Records* (Dublin, 1992)
THOMPSON, F.M.L. and   *General Report On The Gosford Estates
TIERNEY, D. (eds.) In County Armagh 1821* by William Greig,
                    (Belfast, 1976)

APPENDIX 1

6662 (5380.) Pardon to Tirlagh m'Henry O Neale, chief of the
Fues in the province of Ulster, Sara ny Neale his wife, Henry
O Neale, Arte O Neale, [
                                    ], Henry, Brian, and Neale O Neale, sons of Donell
m'Phelim roe, Con, Brian, Henry, and Patrick O Neale, [
                                            ] O Neale m'Brian ballagh,
Con O Neale m'Phelim, and Henry O Neale, of the Fues afore-
said, gentlemen, Arte O Neale, Breen O Neale, Phelem roe
O Neale, Neale O Ncale m'Con, [   ] O Neale m' [
        ] M'Eghire [   ] M'Eghire, horseman,
Brian M'Eghir, husb., Aghie M'Eghire, and Patr. roe M'Eghire,
yeomen, Coolie O Quyn, husb., Kaele O Quyne m'Edm.,
horseman, Hugh O Quyn, [priest], Edm. [   ] O Q[uyn],
Kaele m'Art O Quyn, husb., Patr. O Quyn, husb., Doncho
O Quyn, yeoman, Patr. gromy O Quyn, husb., Hugh and Patr.
O Quyne, yeomen, Kale O Quyne, husb., Glassney and One
M'Shane, horsemen, He[   ], yeoman, Phelim M'Shane,
horseman, Neale M'Shane, yeoman, Art m'Shane M'One, husb.,
James m'Shane M'One, and Rorie M'Shane, horsemen, Arte
m'Tohile ro M'Shane, Brian m'Torilagh M'Shane, and Brian oge
M'Shane, husbandmen, [   ] Shane, horseman, Rorie M'Shane
[   ], Torylagh M'Shane, yeoman, Kahire M'Shane, horseman,
Henry M'Shane, yeoman, Henry Rawane M'Shane, husb.,
Glessny M'Shane, yeoman, Patr. M'Shane, husb., John Shenle,
horseman, Patr. [   ], Feriagh M'Cardle, husb.,
Patr. m'Coolie carragh M'Cardle, horseman, Coolie carragh
m'Philip duffe, husb., One M'Cardle, horseman, Patr. ballagh
M'Cardle, yeoman, Philip M'Cardle, husb., Conoghe M'Cardle,
and Donoghe oge M'Cardle, horsemen, Feragh M'Cardle, yeoman,
Patr. M'Cardle, priest, Patr. M'Cardle, husb., Torylagh bane
M'Cardle, yeoman, Henry M'Cardle, husb., Edm. bane M'Cardle,
yeoman, James M'Cardle m'Coolie more, horseman, Brian, Tori-
lagh, Coolie, and Shane M'Cardle, yeomen, Shane m'Cormack
carragh M'Cardle, and Torilagh M'Cardle, husbandmen, Frances
Lewis, woman, Art M'Murchie m'One, Redmund M'Murchie,
Kilty M'Murchie, One buy more M'Murchie, Phelim duffe
M'Murchie, Donchie M'Murchie M'Cerberegh, and Patr. M'Murchie, husbandmen, Manus M'Murchie, yeoman, One beddy
M'Murchie, horseman, Torilagh M'Murchie, husb., Brian
M'Murchie, horseman, Art and Donogh M'Murchie, husbandmen, Donill M'Murchie m'Patr., and Donill M'Murchie m'Edm.,
yeomen, Donchie M'Murchie m'One, husb., Patr. bane M'Mur-
chie, Patr. M'Murchie, and Donchie duff M'Murchie, yeomen,
Patr. m'[N]eale m'Many M'Murchy, husb., Many and Phelim
m'Nele M'Murchie, One M'Murchie m'James, Patr. m'Cormack

and Donill M'Murchie, tenants, Moris, Torilagh, Cormack, and
James M'Evire, husbandmen, Moris, James oge, and Shane
M'Cowane, yeomen, Rorie M'Cowan, husb., Torilagh M'Cowane,
yeoman, Patr. O Brengan, horseman, Brian, Donill, and Art
O Brengan, husbandmen, Patrick M'Garway, Donill M'Gawry,
Brian, Torilagh, One, Mlaghlin, One, and Donell M'Garway,
tenants, Nele and Donill O Lowhan, husbandmen, Mortagh and
Donill O Lowhan, yeomen, Patrick, Mlaghlin, Brian, and Manus
O Hullig, husbandmen, Patr. O Hanraghtie, Hugh O Han-
raghtie m'Evicker, Hugh O Hanraghtie m'Phelim, One, Pat-
rick, Donill, and Phelim O Hanraghty, tenants, James and
Donill O Hanraghty, Patr. O Hanraghty, and Gilleduff O Lurkan,
yeomen, Nele O Kellychan, tenant, Brian O Kellichan, yeoman,
One and Patr. O Kellichan, One O Kellichan m'Shane, Rorie
O Kellie, Brian O Kellie, junior, and Brian O Kellie, senior,
tenants, Torilagh O Corry, Patr. O Corrie, Many O Corry, One
O Corrie, Many O Hanlon, tenant, Shane, Brian, Hugh, and
Glessny O Hanlon, tenants, Art, Brian, and Many M'Gloskie,
kerns, Patr. M'Eldony, yeomen, Rorie and Brian M'Eldony,
horsemen, Hugh M'Eldonie, yeoman, Shane, Brian, Tohile, and
Rich. O Bwyle, James boy M'Coime, Donchie M'Coine, Art
M'Coine, Patrick, Gorry, and Patrick O Hire, Mlaghlen and
Patrick M'Elyre, One oge M'Elane, Elin M'Elane, Kayle and
Hugh M'Conwayle, kerns, Redmund M'Conill, Alexander,
Gilleseoge, and Brian M'Conile, tenants, Art M'Glaskir, Brian and
Many M'Gloskir, kerns, Cormock M'Enemy, Brian oge M'Enemy,
Brian M'Enemy, husbandmen, Manus Cahan, Dorby Cohan, Gorry
Cahan, horsemen, Mlaghlin O Cawortie, Patr. O Murygan, Hugh
O Haghie, Patr. O Duffedie, Rorie M'Gwygine, Nele M'Towchie,
Feagh M'Cronila, Donill O Culline, Hugh M'Eveighe, Hugh
O Hanaghane, Nele O Lurkane, Rorie M'Sirry, Rorie M'Cawill,
Art M'Henry, Brian M'Many, Patr. O Tohile, Shane O Kenan,
Patr. M'Eghile, Donchie M'Eghile, Donchan O Daly, Donell
O Dolan, Phelim reagh M'Conwell, One M'Conway, Murtagh
M'Conway, Brian oge M'Girraty, Patr. modder M'Gerrety,
Sowrly M'Conill, Patr. O Mollan, Terrilagh Ekeslan, One
O Cumar, Tho. O Shele, Teige and Hugh O Ferrall, Donchie
O Fearnmy, Hugh M'Evard, One M'Etanny, Tho. M'Evard, Rich.
O Cahan, Donill M'Echeran, Tirlagh M'Echerane, Coole
O Crawle, Tho. O Bwyle, Patr. O Towill m'Donogh, Phelim
O Tohill, Patr. M'Gwerke, Patr. M'Rorie, Phelim and Shane
M'Elrowhe, Edmund and Philip O Mulish, Teige Moynagh, Shane
M'Wylline, Hugh M'Echalle, James buy O Calane, Mlaghlen
duffe, Patr. M'Gillernewe, Conoghor M'Creverty, Patr. O Conry,
Anne Geoghan alias Fitz Garrald, One oge O Haghie, Murcho
O Casie, Patr. O Karewlan, Hugh M'Elchrive, Morris Leynagh,
Edm. O Brian, Patr. M'Cunny, Henry O Brian, Shane duff
M'Coddane, James Leynagh, Cormock O Kellechan, Manus
O Lennan, Nele M'Kinny, One M'Cawell, Teige O Kessidie,
Finolly ny Cahir, in the Fues, in the province of Ulster, Stephen
Dowdall, of Dundalk, merchant, and Anne Dowdall, his wife.

Provisions *as in* 6629.—*Date destroyed.*—*Lord Deputy's warrant*
dated 24 June 1602.

The Irish Fiants of the Tudor Sovereigns, 1521–1603
EDMUND BURKE PUBLISHER, DUBLIN, 1994

SUBSIDY ROLLS 1634 – SHANKILL PARISH

Killmarertie	Walter Hide	£5	6/8.	
	Henry Fowler	£5	6/8	
	Nicholas Grace	£6	8/–	
Bartriloome	John Carter		5	6/8e
Tawna	William Workman 6	8/–		
	Morris Olliffe	£3	4/–	
Artabratgh	Mrs. Warener	£3	4/–	
	Humphrey Atp ?	3	4/–	
Tawna	John Walton		3	4/–
Bartrilorn	Arthtur Boyes	3	4/–	
	Wm Cooper	10	13/4	
Ballywaran	Walner ?roene Deele	3	4/–	
	Owen McCourt	3	4/–	
Dromakelly	Owen O'Counollan	3	4/–	
	Henrie O'Counollan	3	4/–	
Dromasouth	Bryan McCann	3	4/–	
Mehan	Thos. Workman	£13	16/8	
Tawmagh	Steph Matohett	£8	10/8	

Fines 17 Jas I   –

Cutherd Smythe of Legacorry kept a tavern, fined for exposing & selling
drink without Licence.

APPENDIX 2

REPOSITORIES

ARMAGH ANCESTRY
Location: 42 English Street
Armagh
BT61 7BA
Telephone (028) 37 521802
Email ancestry@acdc.btinternet.com
Website www.armagh.gov.uk

Armagh Ancestry was established in 1992 by Armagh City & District Council to provide a genealogical research service for County Armagh and to compile a database of the main sources. To date the Centre has on computer: the County Armagh Catholic Registers pre-1900; the County Armagh Civil Marriages, covering all denomination pre-1922; a large proportion of the Civil Births pre-1922; a number of Presbyterian Registers pre-1900. There is also a range of sources ranging from the first 'census' of Fews 1602 to the 1796 Flax Growers List, County Armagh. The centre has a small genealogical library which is open to the public for consultation, and offers a professional genealogical research service for a fee. Armagh Ancestry also provides a PRONI Outreach Service. Any visitor can freely access information on the resources held by PRONI relevant to their own family research, making a visit to PRONI much more productive.

ARMAGH COUNTY MUSEUM
The Mall East
Armagh
BT61 9BE
Telephone (028) 37 523070

The Museum's library houses more than 10,000 volumes as well as original manuscripts, the majority of which relate to County Armagh. The papers of T.G.F. Paterson include a great deal of genealogical material including the 1770 census of Armagh, the 1775 Dissenter's Petitions and copies of hearth money rolls.

ARMAGH PUBLIC LIBRARY
Abbey Street
Armagh
BT61 7DY
Telephone (028) 37 523142
Fax (028) 37 524177

The Armagh Public Library, also known as the Robinson Library, is a private non-circulating library and is open to the public. The library houses more than 20,000 volumes including the Archbishop's personal collection of books on early Irish history and heraldry. The manuscript collection has many items of Irish interest and includes land and tithe records.

CENTRAL LIBRARY
Royal Avenue
Belfast
BT1 1EA
Telephone (028) 90 243233
Fax (028) 90 332819
Email info@libraries.belfast-elb.gov.uk
Website www.belb.org.uk

The Central Library, Belfast, houses more than 900,000 volumes including significant holdings of periodicals, manuscripts and microfilms. The Irish Collection and its newspaper collection are the largest in Northern Ireland.

HERITAGE WORLD
The Heritage
Pomeroy Road
Donaghmore
County Tyrone
BT70 3HG
Telephone (028) 87 761306
Email wok@heritagewld.com
Website www.heritagewld.com

Heritage World offers a genealogical service for Counties Tyrone and Fermanagh. However, many of its indexes and holdings relate to County Armagh. These include indexes to the 1901 census; the tithe applotment books 1823–1838; wills and administrations for all of Ireland 1858–1880 and transcripts of gravestone inscriptions. The centre has a small genealogical library which is open to the public for consultation, and offers a professional genealogical research service for a fee.

IRISH STUDIES LIBRARY
    Southern Education and Library Board Headquarters
    1 Markethill Road
    Armagh
    Telephone (028) 37 525353

The Irish Studies Library houses a collection of more than 20,000 volumes and 3,800 microfilms as well as a small collection of manuscript material. There is an extensive collection of material relating to County Armagh including local newspapers, journals, parish histories and trade directories and also some 200 notebooks of Dr Francis Crossle containing histories of families in the Newry area.

LINEN HALL LIBRARY
    17 Donegal Square North
    Belfast
    BT1 5GD
    Telephone (028) 90 321707
    Fax (028) 90 438586
    Email info@linenhall.com
    Website www.linenhall.com

The Linen Hall Library serves as a 'national' library for Northern Ireland and Ulster. It has the most complete file of the Belfast Newsletter dating back to 1737. A former governor, Pinkerton, extracted all death and marriage entries up to 1800 and the Linen Hall staff also indexed births, deaths and marriages in the *Newsletter* right up until civil registration began in 1864. They have a complete set of the printed version of the tenement valuation of 1864 for County Armagh and indeed for all of Northern Ireland and also major genealogical collections in the working papers of former governors such as Ronald Greeves and Reginald Blackwood. Their holdings include some 500 volumes of printed histories of families. This can justly claim to be the leading centre for Irish and local studies in the North of Ireland.

NATIONAL ARCHIVES
  Bishop Street
  Dublin 8
  Telephone (01) 4783711
  Fax (01) 407 2333
  Email mail@nationalarchives.ie
  Website www.nationalarchives.ie

The National Archives holds records for all counties in Ireland including Armagh. The main collection of official papers is the archive of the Chief Secretary's office dating from c.1790. A lot of these are police intelligence papers entitled the Rebellion Papers and State of the Country Papers. There are also transportation files and registers, and Relief Commission papers for the Great Famine. Recent discoveries include an archive with thousands of names of tithe defaulters c.1830 (mainly in counties like Kilkenny and Tipperary) and some 200,000 signatories petitioning for the release of William Smith O'Brien who was transported for involvement in the '1848 Rebellion'. With the help of the Crowley bequest it is hoped that this massive collection will be adequately catalogued and made generally available through the Internet.

Official papers include the 1901 and 1911 census returns for all Ireland and a set of manuscript field books of the first valuation of the 1830s for Armagh and all counties in Northern Ireland except Tyrone. There are also early records of the National Board of Education including registers of correspondence and records of schools and payment of teachers c.1832–c.1855 (records from c.1855 relating to Northern Ireland were transferred and these are now deposited in PRONI). Private deposits include the working papers of genealogical researchers such as Tenison Groves, Gertrude Thrift and Francis and Philip Crossle and these probably contain hundreds, perhaps thousands, of copies and abstracts of Armagh wills.

NATIONAL LIBRARY OF IRELAND
  Kildare Street
  Dublin 2
  Telephone (01) 6030200
  Email info@nli.ie
  Website www.nli.ie

The National Library houses a number of collections of estate papers relating to County Armagh: microfilm copies of pre-1880 Roman Catholic parish registers; printed version of Griffith's valuation; landed estate court printed rentals; professional and trade directories.

THE CARDINAL TOMAS O FIAICH MEMORIAL LIBRARY & ARCHIVE
  Ara Coeli
  Armagh
  BT61 7QY
  Telephone (028) 37 522905

This library is temporarily housed in the Archdiocesan Records Centre. The library contains approximately 10,000 volumes and 600 periodicals arranged by subject and includes genealogical material.

PUBLIC RECORD OFFICE OF NORTHERN IRELAND
  66 Balmoral Avenue
  Belfast
  BT9 6NY
  Telephone (028) 90 251318
  Email proni@nics.gov.uk
  Website http://proni.nics.gov.uk/index.htm

The Public Record Office of Northern Ireland is the major repository for records relating to County Armagh. Important collections include the papers of many landed estates; church records of most denominations; government records; local authority records; 1901 census. It is worth checking your local library for the various guides produced by PRONI.

REGISTRY OF DEEDS
King's Inns
Henrietta Street
Dublin 1
Telephone (01) 6707500

The memorials in the Registry of Deeds are a massive source with volumes of transcripts containing a million folios for the period 1708–1832. There is a limited personal name index and a place – name index. All are available on microfiche in PRONI and in the National Archives, Dublin.

ULSTER AMERICAN FOLK PARK
Mellon Road
Castletown
Omagh
County Tyrone
Northern Ireland
BT78 5QY
Telephone (028) 82 256315
Fax (028) 82 242241
Email uafp@iol.ie
Websites www.qub.ac.uk/cms/ & www.folkpark.com

The research library at the Centre for Migration Studies comprises a specialist collection of printed material and an emigration database. Material includes books, periodicals, micro-forms and audiovisual materials. The emigration database is a computerised collection of primary source documents on Irish emigration to the United States and Canada in the 18th and 19th centuries. This database can also be accessed in the Local Studies Departments of the Education and Library Boards in Armagh, Ballymena, Ballynahinch, Belfast, Enniskillen, Londonderry and Omagh.

ULSTER HISTORICAL FOUNDATION
  Balmoral Buildings
  12 College Square East
  Belfast
  BT1 6DD
  Telehone (028) 90 332288
  Fax (028) 90 239885
  E-mail enquiry@uhf.org.uk
  Website www.ancestryireland.com

Located in Belfast city centre, the Ulster Historical Foundation is a not-for-profit organisation that was founded in 1956 to promote interest in Irish history and genealogy, with particular reference to the province of Ulster. UHF offers a comprehensive Irish ancestral research service, publishes books on Irish history and genealogy, organises conferences and lecture tours and runs a membership club (Guild) that acts as a research co-operative. The Foundation's growing computerised archive includes a range of sources for County Armagh, including transcripts of gravestone inscriptions for all cemeteries in the county, 1631 Muster Roll, 1740 Protestant Householders, 1770 Census for Armagh city, 1796 Flax Growers List, 1821 census fragments and an index to wills 1858–1900. Some of these sources are available through the UHF website and this site also includes an online bookstore with titles relating to County Armagh. Since 1956 the Foundation has undertaken over one thousand in depth searches on Armagh families.

APPENDIX 3

COUNTY ARMAGH
ADMINISTRATIVE DIVISIONS

(alphabetical by townland)

TOWNLAND	CIVIL PARISH	BARONY	POOR LAW UNION	DISTRICT ELECTORAL DIVISION
Abbey Park	Armagh	Armagh	Armagh	Armagh Rural 1 *
Acton	Ballymore	Orior Lower	Newry	Poyntzpass 68
Acton town	Ballymore	Orior Lower	Newry	Poyntzpass 68
Aghacommon	Seagoe	Oneilland East	Lurgan	Brownlowsderry 48
Aghadavoyle	Killevy	Orior Upper	Newry	Jonesborough 60
Aghamoat	Armagh	Armagh	Armagh	Armagh Rural 1
Aghanergill or Corglass	Drumcree	Oneilland West	Lurgan	Breagh 54
Aghanore	Grange	Armagh	Armagh	Grange 9
Aghantaraghan	Ballymore	Orior Lower	Newry	Poyntzpass 68
Aghavellan or West Richmount	Drumcree	Oneilland	Lurgan	Breagh 54
Aghavilly	Lisnadill	Armagh	Armagh	Ballyards 5
Aghayalloge	Killevy	Orior Upper	Newry	Killevy 61
Aghincurk	Ballymyre	Fews Upper	Newry	Ballymyre 62
Aghinlig	Loughgall	Armagh	Armagh	Charlemont 7
Aghmakane	Killevy	Orior Upper	Newry	Camlough 65
Aghnacloy	Shankill	Oneilland East	Lurgan	Lurgan Rural 46
Aghory	Kilmore	Oneilland West	Armagh	Rich Hill 26
Allistragh	Grange	Armagh	Armagh	Grange 9
Altaturk	Loughgall	Oneilland West	Armagh	Hockley 24
Altnamackan	Newtownhamilton	Fews Upper	Castleblayney	Lisleitrim 42
Altnaveigh	Newry	Orior Upper	Newry	Ballybot 57
Annacloghmullin	Killevy	Orior Upper	Newry	Latbirget 59
Annaboe	Kilmore	Oneilland West	Armagh	Kilmore 25
Annaclare	Grange	Oneilland West	Armagh	Hockley 24
Annaclarey	Eglish	Tiranny	Armagh	Ballymartrim 6
Annacramph	Grange	Oneilland West	Armagh	Loughgall 18
Annagh West	Drumcree	Oneilland	Lurgan	Portadown Rural 52
Annagh	Tynan	Tiranny	Armagh	Glenaul 8
Annaghananny	Tynan	Tiranny	Armagh	Glenaul 8
Annagharap	Tynan	Tiranny	Armagh	Glenaul 8
Annaghboy or Rosebrook	Armagh	Armagh	Armagh	Armagh Rural 1
Annaghgad	Creggan	Fews Upper	Castleblayney	Moybane 39
Annaghmacmanus	Loughgall	Armagh	Armagh	Charlemont 7
Annaghmare	Creggan	Fews Upper	Castleblayney	Cullyhanna 38
Annaghmore	Loughgall	Oneilland West	Armagh	Annaghmore 16
Annagora	Drumcree	Oneilland West	Lurgan	Breagh 54
Annahagh	Grange	Armagh	Armagh	Grange 9
Annahaia	Killevy	Orior Upper	Newry	Jonesborough 60
Annahugh	Kilmore	Oneilland West	Armagh	Kilmore 25

*This sub-number and sub-division is used in the arrangement and cataloguing of 1901 Census Returns for all Ireland (NAI) and it is also used in the cataloguing of valuation revision books c.1859-c.1930 in PRONI (VAL 12B/1).

TOWNLAND	CIVIL PARISH	BARONY	POOR LAW UNION	DISTRICT ELECTORAL DIVISION
Annakeera	Drumcree	Oneilland West	Lurgan	Breagh 54
Annaloist	Seagoe	Oneilland East	Lurgan	Brownlowsderry 44
Annamoy	Eglish	Tiranny	Armagh	Ballymartrim 6
Annareagh	Kilmore	Oneilland West	Armagh	Rich Hill 26
Annasamry	Loughgall	Oneilland West	Armagh	Tullyroan 19
Ardgonnell	Tynan	Tiranny	Armagh	Middletown 28
Ardmore	Montiaghs	Oneilland East	Lurgan	Montiaghs 49
Ardrea	Grange	Oneilland West	Armagh	Kilmore 25
Ardress	Loughgall	Oneilland East	Armagh	Annaghmore 16
Ardress	Loughgall	Oneilland West	Armagh	Tullyroan 19
Armagh town	Armagh	Armagh	Armagh	Armagh Urban E2, N3, S4
Armaghbrague	Lisnadill	Fews Upper	Armagh	Armaghbrague 10
Artabrackagh	Drumcree	Oneilland West	Lurgan	Portadown Rural 52
Artassooly	Eglish	Tiranny	Armagh	Glenaul 8
Aughadanove	Forkill	Orior Upper	Newry	Latbirget 59
Aughanduff	Forkill	Orior Upper	Castleblayney	Dorsy 41
Aughantarragh and Corr	Eglish	Tiranny	Armagh	Glenaul 8
Aughlish	Ballymore	Orior Lower	Banbridge	Ballysheil 30
Aughnacloy	Grange	Armagh	Armagh	Aughnacloy Urban 16
Aughnagurgan	Keady	Armagh	Armagh	Armaghbrague 10
Aughrafin	Eglish	Armagh	Armagh	Ballymartrim 6
Ballaghy	Eglish	Armagh	Armagh	Ballymartrim 6
Ballard	Killevy	Orior Upper	Newry	Camlough 65
Balleer	Lisnadill	Fews Lower	Armagh	Ballyards 5
Ballenan	Loughgilly	Orior Lower	Newry	Poyntzpass 68
Ballindarragh	Kilclooney	Fews Lower	Armagh	Markethill 23
Ballinlare	Newry	Orior Upper	Newry	Ballybot 57
Ballinliss	Killevy	Orior Upper	Newry	Killevy 61
Ballintaggart	Kilmore	Oneilland West	Armagh	Rich Hill 26
Ballintate	Ballymyre	Fews Upper	Newry	Ballymyre 62
Ballintemple	Ballymyre	Fews Upper	Newry	Ballymyre 62
Ballintemple	Killevy	Orior Upper	Newry	Killevy 61
Ballyanny	Mullaghbrack	Fews Lower	Armagh	Markethill 23
Ballyards	Lisnadill	Armagh	Armagh	Ballyards 5
Ballyargan	Ballymore	Orior Lower	Banbridge	Ballysheil 30
Ballyblagh	Shankill	Oneilland East	Lurgan	Lurgan Rural 46
Ballybrannan	Grange	Oneilland West	Armagh	Hockley 24
Ballybreagh	Kilmore	Oneilland West	Armagh	Rich Hill 26
Ballybrocky	Eglish	Tiranny	Armagh	Ballymartrim 6
Ballybrolly	Lisnadill	Fews Lower	Armagh	Lisnadill 15
Ballybrolly	Eglish	Armagh	Armagh	Ballymartrim 6
Ballycoffey or Ballyhoy	Lisnadill	Armagh	Armagh	Brootally 27
Ballycullen or Drumask	Clonfeacle	Armagh	Armagh	Armagh Rural 1
Ballycullen or Shanmullagh	Clonfeacle	Armagh	Armagh	Charlemont 7
Ballydogherty	Loughgilly	Orior Lower	Newry	Tullyhappy 67
Ballydonaghy	Seagoe	Oneilland East	Lurgan	Carrowbrack 50
Ballydoo	Eglish	Armagh	Armagh	Ballymartrim 6
Ballyfodrin	Drumcree	Oneilland West	Lurgan	Breagh 54
Ballygargan	Seagoe	Oneilland East	Lurgan	Carrowbrack 50
Ballygasey	Loughgall	Oneilland West	Armagh	Loughgall 18
Ballygassoon	Grange	Armagh	Armagh	Grange 9

TOWNLAND	CIVIL PARISH	BARONY	POOR LAW UNION	DISTRICT ELECTORAL DIVISION
Ballygorman	Loughgilly	Orior Lower	Newry	Mountnorris 64
Ballygroobany	Mullaghbrack	Fews Lower	Armagh	Hamilton's Bawn 21
Ballyhagan	Kilmore	Oneilland West	Armagh	Kilmore 25
Ballyhannon	Seagoe	Oneilland East	Lurgan	Carrowbrack 50
Ballyheridan	Lisnadill	Armagh	Armagh	Ballyards 5
Ballyhoy or Ballycoffey	Lisnadill	Armagh	Armagh	Brootally 27
Ballykeel	Forkill	Orior Upper	Newry	Latbirget 59
Ballyknick	Grange	Oneilland West	Armagh	Loughgall 18
Ballyknock	Kilmore	Orior Lower	Banbridge	Mullahead 32
Ballylane	Kilclooney	Fews Lower	Armagh	Clady 20
Ballyleny	Kilmore	Oneilland West	Armagh	Rich Hill 26
Ballylisk	Kilmore	Orior Lower	Banbridge	Mullahead 32
Ballyloughan	Kilmore	Oneilland West	Armagh	Rich Hill 26
Ballymacanab	Lisnadill	Fews Lower	Armagh	Lisnadill 15
Ballymacawley	Kilclooney	Fews Lower	Armagh	Killeen 22
Ballymacdermot	Killevy	Orior Upper	Newry	Killevy 61
Ballymackilmurry	Grange	Armagh	Armagh	Grange 9
Ballymacrandral	Seagoe	Oneilland East	Lurgan	Carrowbrack 50
Ballymacully Lower	Eglish	Tiranny	Armagh	Glenaul 8
Ballymacully Upper	Eglish	Tiranny	Armagh	Glenaul 8
Ballymagerny	Loughgall	Oneilland West	Armagh	Loughgall 18
Ballymakeown	Drumcree	Oneilland West	Lurgan	Breagh 54
Ballymartrim Etra	Eglish	Armagh	Armagh	Ballymartrim 6
Ballymartrim Otra	Eglish	Armagh	Armagh	Ballymartrim 6
Ballymoran	Lisnadill	Fews Lower	Armagh	Lisnadill 15
Ballymore	Ballymore	Orior Lower	Banbridge	Tanderagee Rural 33
Ballynacarry	Creggan	Fews Upper	Castleblayney	Crossmaglen 37
Ballynaclosha	Creggan	Fews Upper	Dundalk	Creggan Lower 36
Ballynacor	Seagoe	Oneilland East	Lurgan	Kernan 51
Ballynagalliagh	Lisnadill	Fews Lower	Armagh	Ballyards 5
Ballynaghy	Seagoe	Oneilland East	Lurgan	Carrowbrack 50
Ballynagolan	Derrynoose	Armagh	Armagh	Brootally 27
Ballynagowan	Drumcree	Oneilland West	Lurgan	Drumcree 55
Ballynagreagh	Ballymore	Orior Lower	Newry	Poyntzpass 68
Ballynahinch	Kilmore	Oneilland West	Armagh	Rich Hill 26
Ballynahone Beg	Lisnadill	Armagh	Armagh	Ballyards 5
Ballynahone More	Armagh	Armagh	Armagh	Armagh Rural 1
Ballynalack	Killevy	Orior Upper	Newry	Camlough 65
Ballynaleck	Ballymore	Orior Lower	Newry	Poyntzpass 68
Ballynameta or Wood Park	Tynan	Tiranny	Armagh	Tynan 29
Ballynamony	Seagoe	Oneilland East	Lurgan	Brownlowsderry 48
Ballynarea	Newtownhamilton	Fews Upper	Castleblayney	Lisleitrim 42
Ballynarry	Tartaraghan	Oneilland West	Lurgan	Tartaraghan 56
Ballynery	Montiaghs	Oneilland East	Lurgan	Montiaghs 49
Ballynewry	Mullaghbrack	Fews Lower	Armagh	Hamilton's Bawn 21
Ballyoran	Drumcree	Oneilland West	Lurgan	Portadown Rural 52
Ballyrath	Armagh	Armagh	Armagh	Armagh Rural 1
Ballyrea	Armagh	Armagh	Armagh	Armagh Rural 1
Ballyreagh	Ballymore	Orior Lower	Newry	Poyntzpass 68
Ballyscandal	Eglish	Armagh	Armagh	Ballymartrim 6
Ballysheil Beg	Ballymore	Orior Lower	Banbridge	Ballysheil 30
Ballysheil More	Ballymore	Orior Lower	Banbridge	Ballysheil 30
Ballytroddan	Clonfeacle	Armagh	Armagh	Charlemont 7
Ballytrue	Kilmore	Oneilland West	Armagh	Kilmore 25

TOWNLAND	CIVIL PARISH	BARONY	POOR LAW UNION	DISTRICT ELECTORAL DIVISION
Ballytyrone	Loughgall	Oneilland West	Armagh	Kilmore 25
Ballyvally	Loughgilly	Orior Lower	Newry	Mountnorris 64
Ballywilly	Kilmore	Oneilland West	Armagh	Kilmore 25
Ballyworkan	Drumcree	Oneilland West	Lurgan	Portadown Rural 52
Baltarran	Lisnadill	Armagh	Armagh	Ballyards 5
Balteagh	Tynan	Armagh	Armagh	Brootally 27
Balteagh	Seagoe	Oneilland East	Lurgan	Kernan 51
Baltylum	Drumcree	Oneilland West	Lurgan	Portadown Rural 52
Belleek	Loughgilly	Orior	Upper Newry	Belleek 63
Belleektown	Loughgilly	Orior Upper	Newry	Belleek 63
Blackwatertown or Lisbofin	Clonfeacle	Armagh	Armagh	Charlemont 7
Blackwatertown	Clonfeacle	Armagh	Armagh	Charlemont 7
Bocombra	Seagoe	Oneilland East	Lurgan	Kernan 51
Boconnell	Seagoe	Oneilland East	Lurgan	Brownlowsderry 48
Bolton	Loughgilly	Orior Lower	Newry	Mountnorris 64
Bondville Etra or Tullybrick	Tynan	Tiranny	Armagh	Tynan 29
Borough of Loughgall	Armagh	Armagh	Charlemont	Charlemont 7
Bottlehill	Kilmore	Oneilland West	Armagh	Kilmore 25
Brackagh	Loughgilly	Orior Lower	Newry	Poyntzpass 68
Brackagh	Kilmore	Orior Lower	Banbridge	Mullahead 32
Brackly	Kilclooney	Fews Lower	Armagh	Markethill 23
Brackly	Keady	Tiranny	Armagh	Derrynoose 12
Bracknagh	Eglish	Armagh	Armagh	Ballymartrim 6
Breagh	Seagoe	Oneilland East	Lurgan	Carrowbrack 50
Breagh	Drumcree	Oneilland West	Lurgan	Breagh 54
Breagh	Tartaraghan	Oneilland West	Lurgan	Tartaraghan 56
Breaghey	Tynan	Tiranny	Armagh	Tynan 29
Brootally	Derrynoose	Armagh	Armagh	Brootally 27
Broughan	Lisnadill	Fews Lower	Armagh	Ballyards 5
Brughas	Tartaraghan	Oneilland West	Armagh	Annaghmore 16
Bryandrum	Mullaghbrack	Fews Lower	Armagh	Markethill 23
Cabragh	Grange	Armagh	Armagh	Grange 9
Cabragh	Mullaghbrack	Fews Lower	Armagh	Markethill 23
Cabragh	Mullaghbrack	Oneilland West	Banbridge	Mullaghbrack 31
Cabragh	Eglish	Tiranny	Armagh	Glenaul 8
Calone	Lisnadill	Fews Lower	Armagh	Killeen 22
Camagh	Derrynoose	Armagh	Armagh	Keady Rural 13
Camlough town	Killevy	Orior Upper	Newry	Camlough 65
Camly (Ball)	Newtownhamilton	Fews Upper	Castleblayney	Camly 40
Camly Macullagh	Newtownhamilton	Fews Upper	Castleblayney	Camly 40
Canary	Clonfeacle	Oneilland West	Armagh	Tullyroan 19
Cannagola Beg	Drumcree	Oneilland West	Lurgan	Breagh 54
Cannagola More	Drumcree	Oneilland West	Lurgan	Breagh 54
Canoneill	Drumcree	Oneilland West	Lurgan	Breagh 54
Cappagh	Creggan	Fews Upper	Castleblayney	Moybane 39
Cargaclogher	Keady	Armagh	Armagh	Keady Rural 13
Cargagh	Armagh	Armagh	Armagh	Ballyards 5
Cargalisgorran	Derrynoose	Tiranny	Armagh	Derrynoose 12
Carganamuck	Grange	Armagh	Armagh	Grange 9
Cargans	Ballymore	Orior Lower	Banbridge	Tanderagee Rural 33
Carn	Seagoe	Oneilland East	Lurgan	Kernan 51
Carnacally	Forkill	Orior Upper	Newry	Latbirget 59
Carnagat	Killevy	Orior Upper	Newry	Ballybot 57
Carnally	Creggan	Fews Upper	Dundalk	Creggan Lower 36

TOWNLAND	CIVIL PARISH	BARONY	POOR LAW UNION	DISTRICT ELECTORAL DIVISION
Carnavanaghan	Kilclooney	Fews Lower	Armagh	Killeen 22
Carnbane	Newry	Orior Upper	Newry	Ballybot 57
Carran	Creggan	Fews Upper	Castleblayney	Cloghoge 35
Carran	Loughgilly	Orior Lower	Newry	Poyntzpass 68
Carrick	Seagoe	Oneilland East	Lurgan	Carrowbrack 50
Carrickabolie	Derrynoose	Tiranny	Armagh	Derrynoose 12
Carrickacullion	Newtownhamilton	Fews Upper	Castleblayney	Camly 40
Carrickaldreen	Forkill	Orior Upper	Newry	Latbirget 59
Carrickaloughran	Grange	Armagh	Armagh	Grange 9
Carrickamone	Creggan	Fews Upper	Castleblayney	Crossmaglen 37
Carrickananny	Loughgilly	Orior Upper	Newry	Belleek 63
Carrickaness	Eglish	Tiranny	Armagh	Glenaul 8
Carrickastickan	Forkill	Orior Upper	Newry	Forkill 58
Carrickbrack	Ballymore	Orior Lower	Newry	Poynzpass 68
Carrickbrackan	Killevy	Orior Upper	Newry	Camlough 65
Carrickbroad	Killevy	Orior Upper	Newry	Jonesborough 60
Carrickcloghan	Killevy	Orior Upper	Newry	Camlough 65
Carrickcroppan	Killevy	Orior Upper	Newry	Camlough 65
Carrickduff	Keady	Tiranny	Armagh	Derrynoose 12
Carrickgallogly	Loughgilly	Orior Upper	Newry	Belleek 63
Carricklane	Kilclooney	Fews Lower	Armagh	Markethill 23
Carricklane	Tynan	Tiranny	Armagh	Middletown 28
Carricknagalliagh	Killevy	Orior Upper	Newry	Latbirget 59
Carricknagavna	Forkill	Orior Upper	Newry	Latbirget 59
Carrickrovadddy (Macdonald) or Dorsy	Newtownhamilton	Fews Upper	Castleblayney	Camly 40
Carricktroddan	Grange	Armagh	Armagh	Armagh Rural 1
Carrigans	Forkill	Orior Upper	Newry	Forkill 58
Carrive	Forkill	Orior Upper	Newry	Forkill 58
Carrivekeeny	Killevy	Orior Upper	Newry	Ballybot 57
Carrivemaclone	Killevy	Orior Upper	Newry	Killevy 61
Carrowmenagh	Loughgilly	Orior Upper	Newry	Belleek 63
Carrowmoney	Mullaghbrack	Fews Lower	Armagh	Hamilton's Bawn 21
Carryhugh	Derrynoose	Armagh	Armagh	Keady Rural 13
Cashel	Lisnadill	Fews Lower	Armagh	Lisnadill 15
Cashel	Forkill	Orior Upper	Castleblayney	Dorsy 41
Castleraw	Kilmore	Oneilland West	Armagh	Loughgall 18
Causanagh	Loughgall	Oneilland West	Armagh	Loughgall 18
Cavan	Kilmore	Oneilland West	Armagh	Kilmore 25
Cavanacaw	Lisnadill	Armagh	Armagh	Ballyards 5
Cavanagarvan	Tynan	Armagh	Armagh	Crossmore 11
Cavanagrow	Kilclooney	Fews Lower	Armagh	Killeen 22
Cavanakill	Ballymyre	Fews Upper	Newry	Ballymyre 62
Cavanapole	Tynan	Tiranny	Armagh	Tynan 29
Cavanballaghy	Eglish	Tiranny	Armagh	Glenaul 8
Cavandoogan	Tynan	Tiranny	Armagh	Middletown 28
Charlemont town	Loughgall	Armagh	Armagh	Charlemont 7
Charlemont, Borough of	Loughgall	Armagh	Armagh	Charlemont 7
Charlestown town	Montiaghs	Oneilland East	Lurgan	Montiaghs 49
Church View	Kilmore	Orior Lower	Banbridge	Mullahead 32
Clady Beg	Kilclooney	Fews Lower	Armagh	Clady 20
Clady More	Kilclooney	Fews Lower	Armagh	Clady 20
Clankilvoragh	Magheralin	Oneilland East	Lurgan	Cornakinnegar 45
Clanrolla	Seagoe	Oneilland East	Lurgan	Kernan 51
Clanrolla	Shankill	Oneilland East	Lurgan	Cornkinnegar 45

TOWNLAND	CIVIL PARISH	BARONY	POOR LAW UNION	DISTRICT ELECTORAL DIVISION
Claranagh	Creggan	Fews Upper	Castleblayney	Moybane 39
Clarbane	Creggan	Fews Upper	Castleblayney	Crossmaglen 37
Clare	Ballymore	Orior Lower	Banbridge	Tanderagee Rural 33
Clarkill	Forkill	Orior Upper	Newry	Latbirget 59
Clay	Keady	Armagh	Armagh	Keady Rural 13
Cloghan	Kilmore	Oneilland West	Armagh	Hockley 24
Clogharevan	Killevy	Orior Upper	Newry	Camlough 65
Cloghfin	Eglish	Armagh	Armagh	Ballymartrim 6
Cloghinny	Forkill	Orior Upper	Newry	Forkill 58
Cloghinny	Killevy	Orior Upper	Newry	Mullaghglass 66
Cloghoge	Ballymore	Orior Lower	Banbridge	Ballysheil 30
Cloghoge	Killevy	Orior Upper	Newry	Ballybot 57
Cloghoge	Creggan	Fews Upper	Castleblayney	Cloghoge 35
Cloghreagh	Killevy	Orior Upper	Newry	Mullaghglass 66
Clonakle	Tartaraghan	Oneilland West	Armagh	Annaghmore 16
Clonalig	Creggan	Fews Upper	Castleblayney	Moybane 39
Clonamola	Drumcree	Oneilland West	Lurgan	Drumcree 55
Cloncarrish	Tartaraghan	Oneilland West	Lurgan	Tartaraghan 56
Cloncore	Tartaraghan	Oneilland West	Lurgan	Tartaraghan 56
Clonlum	Killevy	Orior Upper	Newry	Killevy 61
Clonmacash	Tartaraghan	Oneilland West	Armagh	Annaghmore 16
Clonmain	Loughgall	Oneilland West	Armagh	Tullyroan 19
Clonmakate	Tartaraghan	Oneilland West	Lurgan	Tartaraghan 56
Clonmartin	Drumcree	Oneilland West	Lurgan	Breagh 54
Clonmore	Killyman	Oneilland West	Armagh	Killyman 17
Clonroot	Kilmore	Oneilland West	Armagh	Kilmore 25
Clontycarty	Tynan	Tiranny	Armagh	Glenaul 8
Clontyclay	Killyman	Oneilland West	Armagh	Killyman 17
Clontygora	Killevy	Orior Upper	Newry	Killevy 61
Clontylew	Tartaraghan	Oneilland West	Lurgan	Tartaraghan 56
Cloven Eden	Loughgall	Oneilland West	Armagh	Tullyroan 19
Clownagh	Drumcree	Oneilland West	Lurgan	Portadown Rural 52
Coharra	Drumcree	Oneilland West	Lurgan	Breagh 54
College Hall or Marrassit	Tynan	Armagh	Armagh	Tynan 29
Coney Island	Tartaraghan	Oneilland West	Lurgan	Tartaraghan 56
Cooey	Tynan	Tiranny	Armagh	Tynan 29
Coolderry	Creggan	Fews Upper	Dundalk	Creggan Lower 36
Coolkill	Tynan	Tiranny	Armagh	Tynan 29
Coolmillish	Mullaghbrack	Fews Lower	Armagh	Markethill 23
Coolyhill	Ballymore	Orior Lower	Banbridge	Tanderagee Rural 33
Copney	Clonfeacle	Oneilland West	Armagh	Killyman 17
Cor Tynan	Tynan	Tiranny	Armagh	Tynan 29
Coragh	Loughgall	Oneilland West	Armagh	Loughgall 18
Corbracky	Drumcree	Oneilland West	Lurgan	Drumcree 55
Corcrain	Drumcree	Oneilland West	Lurgan	Portadown Urban 53
Corcreevy	Kilmore	Oneilland West	Armagh	Rich Hill 26
Corcrum	Ballymore	Orior Lower	Newry	Poyntzpass 68
Corcullentragh Beg	Drumcree	Oneilland West	Lurgan	Portadown Rural 52
Corcullentragh More	Drumcree	Oneilland West	Lurgan	Portadown Rural 52
Cordrain	Kilmore	Orior Lower	Banbridge	Mullahead 32
Cordrummond	Kilclooney	Fews Lower	Armagh	Markethill 23
Corernagh	Ballymore	Orior Lower	Banbridge	Ballysheil 30
Corfehan	Tynan	Tiranny	Armagh	Tynan 29
Corglass or West Aghanergill	Drumcree	Oneilland	Lurgan	Breagh 54

TOWNLAND	CIVIL PARISH	BARONY	POOR LAW UNION	DISTRICT ELECTORAL DIVISION
Corhammock	Kilclooney	Fews Lower	Armagh	Markethill 23
Corkley	Keady	Armagh	Armagh	Armaghbrague 10
Corlat	Ballymyre	Fews Upper	Newry	Ballymyre 62
Corliss	Creggan	Fews Upper	Castleblayney	Cullyhanna 38
Corlust	Ballymore	Orior Lower	Banbridge	Ballysheil 30
Cormeen	Derrynoose	Armagh	Armagh	Brootally 27
Cornacrew	Mullaghbrack	Fews Lower	Armagh	Hamilton's Bawn 21
Cornagrally	Loughgilly	Orior Lower	Newry	Mountnorris 64
Cornahove	Creggan	Fews Upper	Castleblayney	Crossmaglen 37
Cornakinnegar	Shankill	Oneilland East	Lurgan	Cornakinnegar 45
Cornalack	Drumcree	Oneilland West	Lurgan	Drumcree 55
Cornamucklagh	Drumcree	Oneilland West	Lurgan	Breagh 54
Cornascreeb	Kilmore	Orior Lower	Banbridge	Mullahead 32
Cornoonagh	Creggan	Fews Upper	Dundalk	Creggan Lower 36
Corporation	Armagh	Armagh	Armagh	Armagh Rural 1
Corr and Aughantarragh	Eglish	Tiranny	Armagh	Glenaul 8
Corr and Dunavally	Loughgall	Armagh	Armagh	Charlemont 7
Corran	Lisnadill	Fews Upper	Armagh	Armaghbrague 10
Corrinare	Loughgilly	Orior Lower	Newry	Poyntpass 68
Corrinshigo	Killevy	Orior Upper	Newry	Ballybot 57
Corrinure	Loughgilly	Orior Lower	Newry	Mountnorris 64
Corry	Mullaghbrack	Fews Lower	Armagh	Hamilton's Bawn 21
Cortamlat	Newtownhamilton	Fews Upper	Castleblayney	Lisleitrim 42
Craigmore	Killevy/Newry	Orior Lower		Mullaghglass 66
Craigmore	Newry	Orior Lower		Ballybot 57
Cranagill	Tartaraghan	Oneilland West	Armagh	Annaghmore 16
Crankey	Killevy	Orior Lower	Newry	Tullyhappy 67
Crankey	Loughgilly	Orior Lower	Newry	Tullyhappy 67
Crann	Tynan	Tiranny	Armagh	Middletown 28
Creaghan	Clonfeacle	Armagh	Armagh	Grange 9
Crearum or Fellows Hall	Tynan	Armagh	Armagh	Tynan 29
Creenagh	Kilmore	Oneilland West	Armagh	Kilmore 25
Creenkill	Creggan	Fews Upper	Castleblayney	Crossmaglen 37
Creeve	Loughgilly	Orior Lower	Newry	Poyntzpass 68
Creevekeeran	Creggan	Fews Upper	Castleblayney	Crossmaglen 37
Creevekeeran	Tynan	Tiranny	Armagh	Middletown 28
Creeveroe	Eglish	Armagh	Armagh	Ballymartrim 6
Creggan Bane Glebe	Creggan	Fews Upper	Castleblayney	Crossmaglen 37
Creggan Duff	Creggan	Fews Upper	Castleblayney	Cloghoge 35
Creggan Lower	Loughgilly	Orior Upper	Newry	Mountnorris 64
Creggan Upper	Loughgilly	Orior Upper	Newry	Mountnorris 64
Crew Beg	Ballymore	Orior Lower	Banbridge	Ballysheil 30
Crew More	Ballymore	Orior Lower	Newry	Poyntzpass 68
Crewcat	Kilmore	Oneilland West	Armagh	Rich Hill 26
Cromeen	Derrynoose	Armagh	Armagh	Brootally 27
Cronkill	Tartaraghan	Oneilland West	Armagh	Killyman 17
Cross	Killevy	Orior Upper	Newry	Camlough 65
Crossbane	Derrynoose	Tiranny	Armagh	Derrynoose 12
Crossdall	Tynan	Tiranny	Armagh	Middletown 28
Crossdened	Keady	Armagh	Armagh	Keady Rural 13
Crossmacahilly	Seagoe	Oneilland East	Lurgan	Kernan 51
Crossmaglen	Creggan	Fews Upper	Castleblayney	Crossmaglen 37
Crossmaglen town	Creggan	Fews Upper	Castleblayney	Crossmaglen 37
Crossmore	Keady	Armagh	Armagh	Crossmore 11

TOWNLAND	CIVIL PARISH	BARONY	POOR LAW UNION	DISTRICT ELECTORAL DIVISION
Crossnamoyle	Keady	Tiranny	Armagh	Derrynoose 12
Crossnenagh	Keady	Tiranny	Armagh	Derrynoose 12
Crossreagh or Doonat	Derrynoose	Tiranny	Armagh	Derrynoose 12
Crunagh	Loughgilly	Fews Lower	Armagh	Markethill 23
Crunaght	Mullaghbrack	Fews Lower	Armagh	Markethill 23
Culkeeran	Eglish	Tiranny	Armagh	Glenaul 8
Cullaville	Creggan	Fews Upper	Castleblayney	Crossmaglen 37
Cullentragh	Eglish	Armagh	Armagh	Ballymartrim 6
Cullentragh	Ballymore	Orior Lower	Newry	Tullyhappy 67
Cullyanna Big	Creggan	Fews Upper	Castleblayney	Cullyhanna 38
Cullyanna Little	Creggan	Fews Upper	Castleblayney	Cullyhanna 38
Cullyhanna town	Creggan	Fews Upper	Castleblayney	Cullyhanna 38
Cusheny	Drumcree	Oneilland West	Lurgan	Breagh 54
Damoily	Kilclooney	Fews Lower	Armagh	Clady 20
Darkley	Keady	Armagh	Armagh	Keady Rural 13
Darton	Tynan	Armagh	Armagh	Tynan 29
Demesne	Shankill	Oneilland East	Lurgan	Lurgan Rural 46
Demesne or Parkmore	Armagh	Armagh	Armagh	Armagh Rural 1
Demoan	Ballymore	Orior Lower	Newry	Poyntzpass 68
Derlett	Loughgilly	Fews Lower	Armagh	Markethill 23
Dernalea	Derrynoose	Armagh	Armagh	Brootally 27
Dernasigh	Eglish	Tiranny	Armagh	Glenaul 8
Derrinraw	Tartaraghan	Oneilland West	Lurgan	Tartaraghan 56
Derry	Shankill	Oneilland East	Lurgan	Lurgan Rural 46
Derryadd	Montiaghs	Oneilland East	Lurgan	Montiaghs 49
Derryadd	Tartaraghan	Oneilland West	Armagh	Killyman 17
Derryall	Drumcree	Oneilland West	Lurgan	Drumcree 55
Derryallen	Ballymore	Orior Lower	Banbridge	Tanderagee Rural 33
Derryane	Tartaraghan	Oneilland West	Armagh	Killyman 17
Derryanvil	Drumcree	Oneilland West	Lurgan	Drumcree 55
Derryaugh	Tartaraghan	Oneilland West	Lurgan	Tartaraghan 56
Derrybrughas	Drumcree	Oneilland West	Lurgan	Drumcree 55
Derry Beg	Newry	Orior Upper	Newry	Ballybot 57
Derrycaw	Drumcree	Oneilland West	Lurgan	Drumcree 55
Derrycaw	Tartaraghan	Oneilland West	Lurgan	Tartaraghan 56
Derrycaw	Clonfeacle	Oneilland West	Armagh	Tullyroan 19
Derrycoose	Loughgall	Oneilland West	Armagh	Annaghmore
Derrycor	Montiaghs	Oneilland East	Lurgan	Montiaghs 49
Derrycor	Tartaraghan	Oneilland West	Armagh	Annaghmore 16
Derrycorry North	Killyman	Oneilland West	Armagh	Killyman 17
Derrycorry South	Killyman	Oneilland West	Armagh	Killyman 17
Derrycory	Drumcree	Oneilland West	Lurgan	Drumcree 55
Derrycrew	Loughgall	Oneilland West	Armagh	Loughgall 18
Derrycughan	Kilclooney	Orior Lower	Armagh	Markethill 23
Derrydorragh	Eglish	Tiranny	Armagh	Glenaul 8
Derryhale	Kilmore	Oneilland West	Armagh	Rich Hill 26
Derryhaw	Tynan	Armagh	Armagh	Brootally 27
Derryhennet	Derrynoose	Armagh	Armagh	Crossmore 11
Derryhirk	Killyman	Oneilland West	Armagh	Killyman 17
Derryhubbert	East Killyman	Oneilland West	Armagh	Killyman 17
Derryhubbert South	Killyman	Oneilland West	Armagh	Killyman 17
Derryhubbert West	Killyman	Oneilland West	Armagh	Killyman 17
Derryinver	Montiaghs	Oneilland East	Lurgan	Montiaghs 49
Derrykeeran	Tartaraghan	Oneilland West	Lurgan	Tartaraghan 56
Derrykeevan	Tartaraghan	Oneilland West	Lurgan	Tartaraghan 56
Derrykeran	Drumcree	Oneilland West	Lurgan	Drumcree 55

TOWNLAND	CIVIL PARISH	BARONY	POOR LAW UNION	DISTRICT ELECTORAL DIVISION
Derrylard	Tartaraghan	Oneilland West	Lurgan	Tartaraghan 56
Derrylee	Tartaraghan	Oneilland West	Armagh	Killyman 17
Derrylettiff	Drumcree	Oneilland West	Lurgan	Breagh 54
Derrylileagh	Tartaraghan	Oneilland West	Lurgan	Tartaraghan 56
Derrylisnahavil	Magheralin	Oneilland	Lurgan	Cornakinnegar 45
Derryloste	Montiaghs	Oneilland	Lurgan	Montiaghs 49
Derryloughan	Kilmore	Oneilland West	Armagh	Loughgall 18
Derrymacash	Montiaghs	Oneilland East	Lurgan	Montiaghs 49
Derrymacfall	Drumcree	Oneilland West	Lurgan	Drumcree 55
Derrymagowan	Clonfeacle	Oneilland West	Armagh	Tullyroan 19
Derrymattry	Drumcree	Oneilland West	Lurgan	Drumcree 55
Derry More	Newry	Orior Upper	Newry	Ballybot 57
Derrynaught	Mullaghbrack	Fews Lower	Armagh	Hamilton's Bawn 21
Derryneskan	Drumcree	Oneilland West	Lurgan	Drumcree 55
Derryraine	Mullaghbrack	Fews Lower	Armagh	Hamilton's Bawn 21
Derryscollop	Clonfeacle	Oneilland West	Armagh	Tullyroan 19
Derryscollop town	Clonfeacle	Oneilland West	Armagh	Tullyroan 19
Derrytagh North	Montiaghs	Oneilland East	Lurgan	Montiaghs 49
Derrytagh South	Montiaghs	Oneilland East	Lurgan	Montiaghs 49
Derrytrasna	Montiaghs	Oneilland East	Lurgan	Montiaghs 49
Derryvane	Drumcree	Oneilland West	Lurgan	Drumcree 55
Derryvore	Seagoe	Oneilland East	Lurgan	Kernan 51
Derrywilligan	Killevy	Orior Upper	Newry	Mullaghglass 66
Dillay	Tynan	Tiranny	Armagh	Tynan 29
Dinnahorra	Mullaghbrack	Oneilland West	Banbridge	Mullaghbrack 31
Diviny	Drumcree	Oneilland West	Lurgan	Breagh 54
Doctor's Quarter	Forkill	Orior Upper	Newry	Latbirget 59
Donagreagh	Magheralin	Oneilland East	Lurgan	Cornakinnegar 45
Doogary	Tynan	Tiranny	Armagh	Middletown 28
Doohat or Crossreagh	Derrynoose	Tiranny	Armagh	Derrynoose 12
Dorsy	Creggan	Fews Upper	Castleblayney	Dorsy 41
Dorsy (Cavan O'Hanlon) or Roxborough	Newtownhamilton	Fews Upper	Castleblayney	Camly 40
Dorsy (Hearty)	Newtownhamilton	Fews Upper	Castleblayney	Camly 40
Dorsy (Macdonald) or Carrickrovaddy	Newtownhamilton	Fews Upper	Castleblayney	Camly 40
Dorsy (Mullaghglass)	Newtownhamilton	Fews Upper	Castleblayney	Camly 40
Dougher	Shankill	Oneilland East	Lurgan	Lurgan Rural 46
Downs or Drumarg	Armagh	Armagh	Armagh	Armagh Rural 1
Dressogagh	Tartaraghan	Oneilland West	Armagh	Annaghmore 16
Dressogagh	Eglish	Tiranny	Armagh	Glenaul 8
Drum	Tynan	Armagh	Armagh	Tynan 29
Drumacanver	Derrynoose	Armagh	Armagh	Crossmore 11
Drumachee	Mullaghbrack	Fews Lower	Armagh	Hamilton's Bawn 21
Drumadd T	Armagh	Armagh	Armagh	Armagh Rural 1
Drumadd	Armagh	Armagh	Armagh	Armagh Rural 1
Drumahean	Tynan	Tiranny	Armagh	Middletown 28
Drumalane	Newry	Orior Upper	Newry	Ballybot 57
Drumalaragh	Kilclooney	Orior Lower	Armagh	Markethill 23
Drumalis	Drumcree	Oneilland West	Lurgan	Breagh 54
Drumaltnamuck	Newtownhamilton	Fews Upper	Castleblayney	Camly 40
Drumanphy	Tartaraghan	Oneilland West	Armagh	Annaghmore 16
Drumard (Jones)	Kilmore	Oneilland West	Armagh	Rich Hill 26
Drumard (Primate)	Kilmore	Oneilland West	Armagh	Kilmore 25
Drumarg or Downs	Armagh	Armagh	Armagh	Armagh Rural 1

TOWNLAND	CIVIL PARISH	BARONY	POOR LAW UNION	DISTRICT ELECTORAL DIVISION
Drumarn	Clonfeacle	Armagh	Armagh	Charlemont 7
Drumart	Mullaghbrack	Oneilland West	Banbridge	Loughgall 18
Drumart	Grange	Oneilland West	Armagh	Mullaghbrack 31
Drumart	Loughgall	Oneilland West	Armagh	Loughgall 18
Drumask or Ballycullen	Clonfeacle	Armagh	Armagh	Charlemont 7
Drumatee	Mullaghbrack	Fews Lower	Armagh	Hamilton's Bawn 21
Drumbally	Creggan	Fews Upper	Castleblayney	Crossmaglen 37
Drumbanagher	Killevy	Orior Lower	Newry	Poyntzpass 68
Drumbee	Eglish	Armagh	Armagh	Ballymartrim 6
Drumbee Beg	Lisnadill	Fews Lower	Armagh	Killeen 22
Drumbee Cross	Mullaghbrack	Fews Lower	Armagh	Hamilton's Bawn 21
Drumbee More	Lisnadill	Fews Lower	Armagh	Killeen 22
Drumboy	Creggan	Fews Upper	Castleblayney	Moybane 39
Drumcarn	Grange	Armagh	Armagh	Grange 9
Drumconwell	Lisnadill	Fews Lower	Armagh	Ballyards 5
Drumcoote	Armagh	Armagh	Armagh	Armagh Rural 1
Drumcree	Drumcree	Oneilland West	Lurgan	Drumcree 55
Drumcrow	Loughgilly	Orior Lower	Newry	Drumcree 55
Drumcullen	Clonfeacle	Armagh	Armagh	Charlemont 7
Drumderg	Keady	Armagh	Armagh	Crossmore 11
Drumduff	Eglish	Tiranny	Armagh	Genaul 8
Drumennis	Mullaghbrack	Fews Lower	Armagh	Hamilton's Bawn 21
Drumfergus	Mullaghbrack	Fews Lower	Armagh	Hamilton's Bawn 21
Drumgane	Loughgilly	Fews Lower	Armagh	Markethill 23
Drumgar	Derrynoose	Armagh	Armagh	Tynan 29
Drumgarran	Tynan	Tiranny	Armagh	Middletown 28
Drumgask	Seagoe	Oneilland East	Lurgan	Kernan 51
Drumgaw	Lisnadill	Fews Lower	Armagh	Killeen 22
Drumgolliff	Tynan	Tiranny	Armagh	Glenaul 8
Drumgoose	Drumcree	Oneilland West	Lurgan	Drumcree 55
Drumgor	Seagoe	Oneilland East	Lurgan	Kernan 51
Drumgose	Creggan	Fews Upper	Castleblayney	Crossmaglen 37
Drumgose	Tynan	Tiranny	Armagh	Crossmore 11
Drumgreenagh	Derrynoose	Armagh	Armagh	Middletown 28
Drumharriff	Loughgall	Oneilland West	Armagh	Loughgall 18
Drumharriff	Loughgilly	Orior Upper	Newry	Belleek 63
Drumharriff	Drumcree	Oneilland West	Lurgan	Breagh 54
Drumherney	Derrynoose	Tiranny	Armagh	Derrynoose 12
Drumhillery	Tynan	Tiranny	Armagh	Middletown 28
Drumhirk	Derrynoose	Armagh	Armagh	Crossmore 11
Drumilly	Loughgall	Oneilland West	Armagh	Kilmore 25
Drumilly	Killevy	Orior Upper	Newry	Belleek 63
Druminallyduff	Drumcree	Oneilland West	Lurgan	Breagh 54
Druminargal	Ballymore	Orior Lower	Banbridge	Ballysheil 30
Drumintee	Killevy	Orior Upper	Newry	Jonesborough 60
Druminure	Ballymore	Orior Lower	Banbridge	Tanderagee Rural 33
Drumlack	Mullaghbrack	Fews Lower	Armagh	Markethill 23
Drumlellum	Drumcree	Oneilland West	Lurgan	Breagh 54
Drumlisnagrilly	Seagoe	Oneilland East	Lurgan	Carrowbrack 50
Drumlougher	Creggan	Fews Upper	Castleblayney	Lisleitrim 42
Drumman	Mullaghbrack	Fews Lower	Armagh	Hamilton's Bawn 21
Drumman Beg	Grange	Oneilland West	Armagh	Hockley 24
Drumman More	Grange	Oneilland West	Armagh	Hockley 24
Drummannon	Tartaraghan	Oneilland West	Armagh	Annaghmore 16
Drummeland	Derrynoose	Tiranny	Armagh	Derrynoose 12

TOWNLAND	CIVIL PARISH	BARONY	POOR LAW UNION	DISTRICT ELECTORAL DIVISION
Drummenagh	Drumcree	Oneilland West	Lurgan	Drumcree 55
Drummilt	Loughgilly	Orior Lower	Newry	Tullyhappy 67
Drummond	Tynan	Armagh	Armagh	Crossmore 11
Drummond	Loughgilly	Orior Lower	Newry	Tullyhappy 67
Drummuck	Creggan	Fews Upper	Castleblayney	Moybane 39
Drummuckavall	Creggan	Fews Upper	Castleblayney	Moybane 39
Drumnacanvy	Seagoe	Oneilland East	Lurgan	Carrowbrack 50
Drumnaglontagh	Ballymore	Orior Lower	Banbridge	Tanderagee Rural 33
Drumnagloy	Mullaghbrack	Fews Lower	Armagh	Hamilton's Bawn 21
Drumnagoon	Seagoe	Oneilland East	Lurgan	Kernan 51
Drumnahavil	Derrynoose	Tiranny	Armagh	Derrynoose 12
Drumnahoney	Loughgilly	Orior Upper	Newry	Belleek 63
Drumnahunshin	Kilmore	Oneilland West	Armagh	Rich Hill 26
Drumnahunshin	Loughgilly	Orior Upper	Newry	Belleek 63
Drumnakelly	Drumcree	Oneilland West	Lurgan	Portadown Rural 52
Drumnakelly	Seagoe	Oneilland East	Lurgan	Brownlowsderry 44
Drumnaleg	Ballymore	Orior Lower	Banbridge	Tanderagee Rural 33
Drumnamether	Mullaghbrack	Oneilland West	Banbridge	Mullaghbrack 31
Drumnamoe	Shankill	Oneilland East	Lurgan	Lurgan Rural 46
Drumnasoo	Loughgall	Oneilland West	Armagh	Hockley 24
Drumnasoo	Drumcree	Oneilland West	Lurgan	Portadown Rural 52
Drumnevan	Drumcree	Oneilland West	Lurgan	Breagh 54
Drumnykerne	Shankill	Oneilland East	Lurgan	Cornakinnegar 45
Drumogher	Grange	Oneilland West	Armagh	Hockley 24
Drumorgan	Mullaghbrack	Fews Lower	Armagh	Hamilton's Bawn 21
Drumrusk	Eglish	Tiranny	Armagh	Glenaul 8
Drumsallan Lower	Eglish	Tiranny	Armagh	Glenaul 8
Drumsallan Upper	Eglish	Tiranny	Armagh	Glenaul 8
Drumsavage	Mullaghbrack	Fews Lower	Armagh	Hamilton's Bawn 21
Drumshallan	Mullaghbrack	Fews Lower	Armagh	Hamilton's Bawn 21
Drumsill	Grange	Armagh	Armagh	Grange 9
Duburren	Killevy	Orior Upper	Newry	Camlough 65
Dunavally and Corr	Loughgall	Armagh	Armagh	Charlemont 7
Dundrum	Keady	Armagh	Armagh	Keady Rural 13
Dunesmullan	Mullaghbrack	Fews Lower	Armagh	Markethill 23
Dunlarg	Keady	Armagh	Armagh	Crossmore 11
Duvernagh	Killevy	Orior Upper	Newry	Camlough 65
Eagralougher	Loughgall	Oneilland West	Armagh	Tullyroan 19
Edenappa	Jonesborough	Orior Upper	Newry	Jonesborough 60
Edenaveys	Lisnadill	Fews Lower	Armagh	Killeen 22
Edenderry	Seagoe	Oneilland East	Lurgan	Portadown Urban 53
Edenderry	Eglish	Tiranny	Armagh	Glenaul 8
Edenknappagh	Lisnadill	Fews Lower	Armagh	Killeen 22
Edenykennedy	Kilclooney	Fews Lower	Armagh	Markethill 23
Eglish	Tartaraghan	Oneilland West	Armagh	Annaghmore 16
Eglish	Eglish	Tiranny	Armagh	Glenraul 8
Ellisholding	Killevy	Orior Upper	Newry	Killevy 61
Elm Park or Mullaghatinny	Eglish	Tiranny	Armagh	Ballymartrim 6
Enagh	Lisnadill	Armagh	Armagh	Tynan 29
Enagh	Kilclooney	Fews Lower	Armagh	Clady 20
Enagh	Killevy	Orior Lower	Newry	Tullyhappy 67
Enagh	Tynan	Tiranny	Armagh	Tynan 29
Ennislare	Lisnadill	Fews Lower	Armagh	Ballyards 5
Eshwary	Killevy	Orior Upper	Newry	Camlough 65
Fairview or Mucklagh	Tynan	Tiranny	Armagh	Tynan 29

TOWNLAND	CIVIL PARISH	BARONY	POOR LAW UNION	DISTRICT ELECTORAL DIVISION
Farmacaffly	Lisnadill	Armagh	Armagh	Ballyards 5
Farnaloy	Derrynoose	Armagh	Armagh	Crossmore 11
Farra	Drumcree	Oneilland West	Lurgan	Breagh 54
Farranamucklagh	Lisnadill	Fews Upper	Armagh	Lisnadill 15
Fathom Lower	Newry	Orior Upper	Newry	Ballybot 57
Fathom Upper	Newry	Orior Upper	Newry	Ballybot 57
Federnagh	Ballymore	Orior Lower	Newry	Poyntzpass 68
Fellows Hall or Crearum	Tynan	Armagh	Armagh	Tynan 29
Fergort	Derrynoose	Tiranny	Armagh	Derrynoose 12
Fernagreevagh	Loughgall	Oneilland West	Armagh	Loughgall 18
Finiskin	Creggan	Fews Upper	Castleblayney	Dorsy 41
Foley	Lisnadill	Fews Lower	Armagh	Lisnadill 15
Forkill town	Forkill	Orior Upper	Newry	Forkill 58
Foughill Etra	Jonesborough	Orior Upper	Newry	Jonesborough 60
Foughill Otra	Jonesborough	Orior Upper	Newry	Jonesborough 60
Foyarr	Tynan	Tiranny	Armagh	Glenaul 8
Foy Beg	Drumcree	Oneilland West	Lurgan	Drumcree 55
Foy More	Drumcree	Oneilland West	Lurgan	Drumcree 55
Foyduff	Tynan	Tiranny	Armagh	Middletown 28
Freeduff	Creggan	Fews Upper	Castleblayney	Cloghoge 35
Gallrock	Tartaraghan	Oneilland West	Armagh	Annaghmore 16
Garvagh	Mullaghbrack	Fews Upper	Armagh	Hamilton's Bawn 21
Garvaghy	Drumcree	Oneilland West	Lurgan	Ballymartrim 6
Garvaghy	Eglish	Tiranny	Armagh	Portadown Urban 53
Gillis	Armagh	Armagh	Armagh	Armagh Rural 1
Glasdrumman	Creggan	Fews Upper	Dundalk	Creggan Lower 36
Glasdrumman	Ballymore	Orior Lower	Newry	Poyntzpass 68
Glasdrummanaghy	Creggan	Fews Upper	Castleblayney	Crossmaglen 37
Glasdrummond	Kilclooney	Fews Lower	Armagh	Markethill 23
Glasdrummond	Killevy	Orior Upper	Newry	Mullaghglass 66
Glasdrummond	Tynan	Tiranny	Armagh	Middletown 28
Glebe	Forkill	Orior Upper	Newry	Forkill 58
Glenanne T.	Loughgill	Fews Lower	Armagh	Markethill 23
Goragh	Killevy	Orior Upper	Newry	Mullaghglass 66
Gortalegg	Tynan	Tiranny	Armagh	Tynan 29
Gosford Demesne	Mullaghbrack	Fews Lower	Armagh	Markethill 23
Granemore	Keady	Armagh	Armagh	Armaghbrague 10
Grange Blundel	Grange	Armagh	Armagh	Grange 9
Grange Lower	Newry	Oneilland West	Armagh	Loughgall 18
Grange More	Grange	Armagh	Armagh	Grange 9
Grange Upper	Newry	Oneilland West	Armagh	Loughgall 18
Greenan	Grange	Oneilland West	Armagh	Loughgall 18
Greyhillan	Loughgilly	Orior Upper	Newry	Belleek 63
Hacknahay	Seagoe	Oneilland East	Lurgan	Carrowbrack 50
Hamiltons Bawn town	Mullaghbrack	Fews Lower	Armagh	Hamilton's Bawn 21
Hamiltonsbawn	Mullaghbrack	Fews Lower	Armagh	Hamilton's Bawn 21
Hanslough	Tynan	Tiranny	Armagh	Middletown 28
Iskymeadow	Keady	Armagh	Armagh	Crossmore 11
Island Spa	Tynan	Tiranny	Armagh	Tynan 29
Johnstown	Mullaghbrack	Fews Lower	Armagh	Hamilton's Bawn 12
Jonesborough town	Jonesborough	Orior Upper	Newry	Jonesborough 60
Keady Beg	Loughgilly	Orior Lower	Newry	Tullyhappy 67
Keady More	Loughgilly	Orior Lower	Newry	Tullyhappy 67
Keady town	Keady	Armagh	Armagh	Keady Urban 14
Keenaghan	Loughgall	Armagh	Armagh	Charlemont 7

TOWNLAND	CIVIL PARISH	BARONY	POOR LAW UNION	DISTRICT ELECTORAL DIVISION
Keggall	Killevy	Orior Upper	Newry	Camlough 65
Kennedies	Tynan	Armagh	Armagh	Tynan 29
Kennedies	Lisnadill	Armagh	Armagh	Ballyards 5
Kernan	Seagoe	Oneilland East	Lurgan	Kernan 51
Kilbracks	Kilclooney	Fews Lower	Armagh	Markethill 23
Kilcam	Keady	Tiranny	Armagh	Derrynoose 12
Kilcarn	Eglish	Tiranny	Armagh	Glenaul 8
Kilcon	Loughgilly	Orior Lower	Newry	Mountnorris 64
Kilcreevy Etra	Derrynoose	Armagh	Armagh	Brootally 27
Kilcreevy Otra	Derrynoose	Armagh	Armagh	Brootally 27
Killaghy	Shankill	Oneilland East	Lurgan	Cornakinnegar 45
Killeen	Lisnadill	Fews Lower	Armagh	Killeen 22
Killeen	Killevy	Orior Upper	Newry	Killevy 61
Killuney	Armagh	Oneilland West	Armagh	Hockley 24
Killybodagh	Killevy	Orior Lower	Newry	Poyntzpass 68
Killycapple	Lisnadill	Fews Lower	Armagh	Killeen 22
Killycarn Lower	Loughgilly	Orior Lower	Newry	Mountnorris 64
Killycarn Upper	Loughgilly	Orior Lower	Newry	Mountnorris 64
Killycomain	Seagoe	Oneilland East	Lurgan	Carrowbrack 50
Killyfaddy	Lisnadill	Fews Lower	Armagh	Lisnadill 15
Killylea	Tynan	Armagh	Armagh	Tynan 29
Killylea town	Tynan	Armagh	Armagh	Tynan 29
Killylyn	Grange	Armagh	Armagh	Grange 9
Killymaddy	Eglish	Tiranny	Armagh	Glenaul 8
Killynure	Lisnadill	Armagh	Armagh	Ballyards 5
Killyquin	Eglish	Tiranny	Armagh	Glenaul 8
Killeavy	Derrynoose	Armagh	Armagh	Crossmore 11
Killyrudden	Mullabrack	Fews Lower	Armagh	Hamilton's Bawn 21
Kilmacanty	Kilmore	Oneilland West	Armagh	Kilmore 25
Kilmachugh	Grange	Oneilland	Armagh	Hockley 24
Kilmachugh	Kilclooney	Fews Lower	Armagh	Clady 20
Kilmagamish	Drumcree	Oneilland West	Lurgan	Drumcree 55
Kilmatroy	Eglish	Tiranny	Armagh	Glenaul 8
Kilmonaghan	Killevy	Orior Lower	Newry	Mullaghglass 66
Kilmore	Kilmore	Oneilland West	Armagh	Kilmore 25
Kilmore	Clonfeacle	Armagh	Armagh	Charlemont 7
Kilmoriarty	Drumcree	Oneilland West	Lurgan	Portadown Rural 52
Kilrea	Killevy	Orior Lower	Newry	Poyntzpass 68
Kiltubbrid	Tynan	Tiranny	Armagh	Middletown 28
Kiltybane or Lisleitrim	Newtownhamilton	Fews Upper	Castleblayney	Lisleitrim 42
Kilvergan	Seagoe	Oneilland East	Lurgan	Brownlowsderry 48
Kincon	Kilmore	Oneilland West	Armagh	Loughgall 18
Kingarve	Drumcree	Oneilland	Lurgan	Breagh 54
Kinnegoe	Loughgall	Armagh	Armagh	Charlemont 7
Kinnegoe	Seagoe	Oneilland East	Lurgan	Brownlowsderry 44
Kishaboy	Loughgall	Armagh	Armagh	Charlemont 7
Knappagh	Eglish	Tiranny	Armagh	Glenaul 8
Knock	Seagoe	Oneilland East	Lurgan	Carrowbrack 50
Knockaconny	Grange	Armagh	Armagh	Grange 9
Knockagraffy	Eglish	Armagh	Armagh	Ballymartrim 6
Knockaneagh	Tynan	Tiranny	Armagh	Glenaul 8
Knockavannon	Ballymyre	Fews Upper	Newry	Ballymyre 62
Knockbane	Tynan	Tiranny	Armagh	Middletown 28
Knockduff	Killevy	Orior Lower	Newry	Mullaghglass 66
Knockmenagh	Seagoe	Oneilland East	Lurgan	Kernan 51
Knocknamuckley	Seagoe	Oneilland East	Lurgan	Carrowbrack 50

TOWNLAND	CIVIL PARISH	BARONY	POOR LAW UNION	DISTRICT ELECTORAL DIVISION
Knocknashane	Shankill	Oneilland East	Lurgan	Lurgan Rural 46
Knockramer	Seagoe	Oneilland East	Lurgan	Brownlowsderry 48
Knockrevan	Derrynoose	Armagh	Armagh	Crossmore 11
Lagan	Keady	Armagh	Armagh	Keady Rural 13
Laurelvale T.	Kilmore	Orior Lower	Banbridge	Mullahead 32
Laraghshankill	Eglish	Tiranny	Armagh	Glenaul 8
Latbirget	Forkill	Orior Upper	Newry	Latbirget 59
Latmacollum	Lisnadill	Fews Lower	Armagh	Killeen 22
Latt	Killevy	Orior Upper	Newry	Mullaghglass 66
Lattery	Mullaghbrack	Fews Lower	Armagh	Markethill 23
Legacorry or Rich Hill	Kilmore	Oneilland West	Armagh	Rich Hill 26
Legaghory	Shankill	Oneilland East	Lurgan	Lurgan Rural 46
Legagilly or Tyross	Armagh	Armagh	Armagh	Armagh Rural 1
Leganny	Drumcree	Oneilland West	Lurgan	Breagh 54
Legarhill	Armagh	Armagh	Armagh	Armagh Rural 1
Legavilly	Loughgall	Oneilland West	Armagh	Hockley 24
Legmoylin	Creggan	Fews Upper	Dundalk	Creggan Lower 36
Lemnagore	Tynan	Tiranny	Armagh	Tynan 29
Lenalea	Mullaghbrack	Fews Lower	Armagh	Hamilton's Bawn 21
Lesh	Killevy	Orior Lower	Newry	Tullyhappy 67
Lesh	Loughgilly	Orior Lower	Newry	Tullyhappy 67
Levaghery	Seagoe	Oneilland East	Lurgan	Carrowbrack 50
Levalleglish	Loughgall	Oneilland West	Armagh	Loughgall 18
Levallymore	Forkill	Orior Upper	Newry	Latbirget 59
Lisadian	Eglish	Armagh	Armagh	Ballymartim
Lisadian	Loughgilly	Orior Lower	Newry	Tullyhappy 67
Lisamry	Creggan	Fews Upper	Castleblayney	Crossmaglen 37
Lisbane	Ballymore	Orior Lower	Banbridge	Tanderagee Rural 33
Lisavague	Kilmore	Orior Lower	Banbridge	Mullahead 32
Lisbane	Eglish	Tiranny	Armagh	Ballymartrim 6
Lisbanoe	Lisnadill	Armagh	Armagh	Ballyards 5
Lisbofin or Blackwatertown	Clonfeacle	Armagh	Armagh	Charlemont 7
Liscalgat	Creggan	Fews Upper	Castleblayney	Moybane 39
Liscorran	Shankill	Oneilland East	Lurgan	Cornakinnegar 45
Lisdonwilly	Grange	Armagh	Armagh	Grange 9
Lisdown	Eglish	Tiranny	Armagh	Ballymartrim 6
Lisdromafarna	Eglish	Tiranny	Armagh	Ballymartrim 6
Lisdrumard	Lisnadill	Armagh	Armagh	Brootally 27
Lisdrumbrughas	Derrynoose	Armagh	Armagh	Brootally 27
Lisdrumchor Lower	Loughgilly	Fews Lower	Armagh	Markethill 23
Lisdrumchor Upper	Loughgilly	Fews Lower	Armagh	Markethill 23
Lisdrumgullion	Newry	Orior Upper	Newry	Ballybot 57
Lisdrumliska	Newry	Orior Upper	Newry	Ballybot 57
Lisglynn	Derrynoose	Armagh	Armagh	Crossmore 11
Liskyborough	Kilmore	Oneilland West	Armagh	Rich Hill 26
Lislasly	Loughgall	Armagh	Armagh	Charlemont 7
Lislea	Killevy	Orior Upper	Newry	Camlough 65
Lislea	Derrynoose	Tiranny	Armagh	Derrynoose 12
Lislea	Lisnadill	Fews Upper	Armagh	Lisnadill 15
Lislea	Lisnadill	Armagh	Armagh	Ballyards 5
Lisleitrim or Kiltybane	Newtownhamilton	Fews Upper	Castleblayney	Lisleitrim 42
Lislooney	Tynan	Tiranny	Armagh	Tynan 29
Lisnadill	Lisnadill	Fews Upper	Armagh	Lisnadill 15
Lisnafeedy	Eglish	Tiranny	Armagh	Glenaul 8
Lisnagat	Kilclooney	Fews Lower	Armagh	Markethill 23

TOWNLAND	CIVIL PARISH	BARONY	POOR LAW UNION	DISTRICT ELECTORAL DIVISION
Lisnagree	Ballymore	Orior Lower	Newry	Tullyhappy 67
Lisnakea	Ballymore	Orior Lower	Banbridge	Tanderagee Rural 33
Lisnalee	Forkill	Orior Lower	Newry	Tullyhappy 67
Lisnalee	Loughgilly	Orior Lower	Newry	Tullyhappy 67
Lisnamintry	Seagoe	Oneilland East	Lurgan	Kernan 51
Lisneany	Loughgall	Oneilland West	Armagh	Loughgall 18
Lisnisk	Loughgilly	Orior Lower	Newry	Poyntzpass 68
Lisnisky	Seagoe	Oneilland East	Lurgan	Kernan 51
Lisraw	Ballymore	Orior Lower	Newry	Poyntzpass 68
Lissagally	Derrynoose	Armagh	Armagh	Brootally 27
Lissaraw	Creggan	Fews Upper	Castleblayney	Moybane 39
Lissaraw	Killevy	Orior Upper	Newry	Camlough 65
Lissheagh or Mount Irwin	Tynan	Tiranny	Armagh	Tynan 29
Lissheffield	Kilmore	Oneilland West	Armagh	Kilmore 25
Lissheffield	Loughgall	Oneilland West	Armagh	Kilmore 25
Lisslanly	Tynan	Tiranny	Armagh	Middletown 28
Lissummon	Killevy	Orior Lower	Newry	Poyntzpass 68
Listarkelt	Derrynoose	Tiranny	Armagh	Derrynoose 12
Longfield	Forkill	Orior Upper	Newry	Latbirget 59
Longstone	Armagh	Armagh	Armagh	Armagh Rural 1
Loughgall	Loughgall	Oneilland West	Armagh	Loughgall 18
Loughgall town	Loughgall	Oneilland West	Armagh	Loughgall 18
Loughross	Creggan	Fews Upper	Castleblayney	Crossmaglen 37
Lurgaboy	Mullaghbrack	Fews Lower	Armagh	Hamilton's Bawn 21
Lurgan	Shankill	Oneilland East	Lurgan	Lurgan Urban 47
Lurgana	Ballymyre	Fews Upper	Newry	Ballymyre 62
Lurgancot	Kilmore	Oneilland West	Armagh	Kilmore 25
Lurgancullenboy	Creggan	Fews Upper	Dundalk	Creggan Lower 36
Lurgantarry	Shankill	Oneilland East	Lurgan	Cornakinnegar 45
Lurgan Urban District	Shankill	Oneilland East	Lurgan	Lurgan Urban 47
Lurgyross	Loughgilly	Fews Lower	Armagh	Markethill 23
Lurgyvallen	Armagh	Armagh	Armagh	Armagh Rural 1
Lylo	Seagoe	Oneilland East	Lurgan	Kernan 51
Macantrim	Mullaghbrack	Fews Lower	Armagh	Hamilton's Bawn 21
Maddan	Derrynoose	Armagh	Armagh	Crossmore 11
Magaraty	Tartaraghan	Oneilland West	Armagh	Annaghmore 16
Magherarville	Lisnadill	Armagh	Armagh	Ballyards 5
Maghernahely	Killevy	Orior Upper	Newry	Camlough 65
Maghery	Tartaraghan	Oneilland West	Lurgan	Tartaraghan 56
Maghery Kilcrany	Derrynoose	Armagh	Armagh	Brootally 27
Maghery town	Tartaraghan	Oneilland West	Lurgan	
Magherydogherty	Mullaghbrack	Fews Lower	Armagh	Hamilton's Bawn 21
Maghnavery	Kilclooney	Orior Lower	Armagh	Markethill 23
Maghon	Drumcree	Oneilland West	Lurgan	Portadown Rural 52
Manooney	Tynan	Armagh	Armagh	Tynan 29
Maphoner	Forkill	Orior Upper	Newry	Labirget 59
Markethill town	Kilclooney	Fews Lower	Armagh	Markethill 23
Markethill town	Mullaghbrack	Fews Lower	Armagh	Markethill 23
Marlacoo Beg	Mullaghbrack	Oneilland West	Banbridge	Mullaghbrack 31
Marlacoo More	Mullaghbrack	Oneilland West	Banbridge	Mullaghbrack 31
Marrassit or College Hall	Tynan	Armagh	Armagh	Tynan 29
Mavemacullen	Loughgilly	Orior Lower	Banbridge	Mullaghbrack 31
Mavemacullen	Ballymore	Orior Lower	Banbridge	Ballysheil 30
Maydown	Eglish	Tiranny	Armagh	Glenaul 8

TOWNLAND	CIVIL PARISH	BARONY	POOR LAW UNION	DISTRICT ELECTORAL DIVISION
Maynooth	Kilmore	Oneilland West	Armagh	Rich Hill 26
Maytone	Loughgilly	Orior Lower	Newry	Mountnorris 64
Maytown	Killevy	Orior Upper	Newry	Mullaghglass 66
Meigh	Killevy	Orior Upper	Newry	Killevy 61
Middletown	Tynan	Tiranny	Armagh	Middletown 28
Middletown town	Tynan	Tiranny	Armagh	Middletown 28
Millford T.	Lisnadill	Armagh	Armagh	Ballyards 5
Milltown	Tartaraghan	Oneilland West	Lurgan	Tartaraghan 56
Monaguillagh	Creggan	Fews Upper	Castleblayney	Crossmaglen 37
Monbrief	Shankill	Oneilland East	Lurgan	Lurgan Rural 46
Monclone	Ballymore	Orior Lower	Banbridge	Ballysheil 30
Money	Kilmore	Oneilland West	Armagh	Kilmore 25
Moneycree	Grange	Armagh	Armagh	Grange 9
Moneypatrick	Lisnadill	Armagh	Armagh	Ballyards 5
Moneyquin	Lisnadill	Armagh	Armagh	Ballyards 5
Monog	Creggan	Fews Upper	Castleblayney	Crossmaglen 37
Moodoge	Ballymore	Orior Lower	Banbridge	Tanderagee Rural 33
Mount Irwin or Lissheagh	Tynan	Tiranny	Armagh	Tynan 29
Mount Norris town	Loughgilly	Orior Lower	Newry	Mountnorris 64
Mounthill	Creggan	Fews Upper	Dundalk	Creggan Lower 36
Mountnorris	Loughgilly	Orior Lower	Newry	Mountnorris 64
Mowillin	Derrynoose	Armagh	Armagh	Crossmore 11
Moybane	Creggan	Fews Upper	Castleblayney	Moybane 39
Moyraverty	Seagoe	Oneilland East	Lurgan	Kernan 51
Moyrourkan	Mullaghbrack	Oneilland West	Banbridge	Mullaghbrack 31
Muckery	Drumcree	Oneilland West	Lurgan	Drumcree 55
Mucklagh or Fairview	Tynan	Tiranny	Armagh	Tynan 29
Mulladry	Kilmore	Oneilland West	Armagh	Rich Hill 26
Mullaghatinny or Elm Park	Eglish	Tiranny	Armagh	Ballymartrim 6
Mullaghbane	Kildarton	Oneilland West	Armagh	Hockley 24
Mullaghbane	Mullaghbrack	Fews Lower	Armagh	Hamilton's Bawn 21
Mullaghbane	Forkill	Orior Upper	Newry	Forkill 58
Mullaghbrack	Mullaghbrack	Fews Lower	Armagh	Hamilton's Bawn 21
Mullaghduff	Newtownhamilton	Fews Upper	Castleblayney	Lisleitrim 42
Mullaghglass	Ballymore	Orior Lower	Banbridge	Tanderagee Rural 33
Mullaghglass	Killevy	Orior Upper	Newry	Mullaghglass 66
Mullaghmore	Loughgall	Armagh	Armagh	Charlemont 7
Mullaghmore	Loughgilly	Orior Lower	Newry	Mountnorris 64
Mullahead	Kilmore	Orior Lower	Banbridge	Mullahead 32
Mullalelish	Kilmore	Oneilland West	Armagh	Rich Hill 26
Mullaletragh	Kilmore	Oneilland West	Armagh	Rich Hill 26
Mullan	Tynan	Tiranny	Armagh	Tynan 29
Mullanary	Ballymore	Orior Lower	Banbridge	Ballysheil 30
Mullanary	Clonfeacle	Armagh	Armagh	Charlemont 7
Mullanary	Tynan	Tiranny	Armagh	Middletown 28
Mullanasilla	Loughgall	Oneilland West	Armagh	Hockley 24
Mullantine	Drumcree	Oneilland West	Lurgan	Portadown Rural 52
Mullantur	Eglish	Tiranny	Armagh	Glenaul 8
Mullantur	Ballymore	Orior Lower	Banbridge	Tanderagee Rural 33
Mullavilly	Kilmore	Orior Lower	Banbridge	Mullahead 32
Mullenakill North	Killyman	Oneilland West	Armagh	Killyman 17
Mullenakill South	Killyman	Oneilland West	Armagh	Killyman 17
Mullenakill West	Killyman	Oneilland West	Armagh	Killyman 17
Mullurg	Mullaghbrack	Fews Lower	Armagh	Hamilton's Bawn 21

TOWNLAND	CIVIL PARISH	BARONY	POOR LAW UNION	DISTRICT ELECTORAL DIVISION
Mullyard	Derrynoose	Tiranny	Armagh	Derrynoose 12
Mullyleggan	Clonfeacle	Armagh	Armagh	Charlemont 7
Mullyloughan	Eglish	Tiranny	Armagh	Glenaul 8
Mullyloughran	Kildarton	Oneilland West	Armagh	Hockley 24
Mullynure	Grange	Armagh	Armagh	Grange 9
Naul	Tynan	Armagh	Armagh	Tynan 29
Navan	Eglish	Armagh	Armagh	Ballymartrim 6
Newry Urban District	Newry	Orior Upper	Newry	Newry West 99
Newtown	Killevy	Orior Upper	Newry	Killevy 61
Newtown Hamilton ton	Newtownhamilton	Fews Upper	Castleblayney	Newtown Hamilton 43
Outlack	Lisnadill	Fews Lower	Armagh	Killeen 22
Outleckan	Ballymyre	Fews Upper	Newry	Ballymyre 62
Parkmore or Demesne	Armagh	Armagh	Armagh	Armagh Rural 1
Pollnagh	Tynan	Tiranny	Armagh	Glenaul 8
Portadown town	Drumcree	Oneilland West	Lurgan	Portadown Urban 53
Portadown town	Seagoe	Oneilland East	Lurgan	Portadown Urban 53
Portnelligan	Tynan	Tiranny	Armagh	Middletown 28
Poyntz Pass town	Ballymore	Orior Lower	Newry	Scarva 23
Racarbry	Keady	Armagh	Armagh	Keady Rural 13
Ratarnet	Mullaghbrack	Fews Lower	Armagh	Hamilton's Bawn 21
Rathcarbry	Loughgilly	Orior Lower	Newry	Tullyhappy 67
Rathconvil	Loughgilly	Orior Lower	Newry	Poyntzpass 68
Rathcumber	Tynan	Tiranny	Armagh	Middletown 28
Rathdrumgran	Loughgall	Oneilland West	Armagh	Hockley 24
Rathkeelan	Creggan	Fews Upper	Castleblayney	Crossmaglen 37
Rathtrillick	Tynan	Tiranny	Armagh	Middletown 28
Rawes	Tynan	Tiranny	Armagh	Middletown 28
Reedyflat	Montiaghs	Oneilland East	Lurgan	Montiaghs 49
Reen	Tynan	Tiranny	Armagh	Middletown 28
Rich Hill or Legacorry	Kilmore	Oneilland West	Armagh	Rich Hill 26
Rich Hill town	Kilmore	Oneilland West	Armagh	Rich Hill 26
Richmount or Aghavellan	Drumcree	Oneilland West	Lurgan	Breagh 45
Rockmacreeny	Kilmore	Oneilland West	Armagh	Rich Hill 26
Rocks	Mullaghbrack	Fews Lower	Armagh	Hamilton's Bawn 21
Rosebrook or Annaghboy	Armagh	Armagh	Armagh	Armagh Rural 1
Roughan	Drumcree	Oneilland West	Lurgan	Breagh 54
Roughan	Derrynoose	Armagh	Armagh	Crossmore 11
Rowan	Derrynoose	Tiranny	Armagh	Derrynoose 12
Roxborough or Dorsy (Cavan O'Hanlon)	Newtownhamilton	Fews Upper	Castleblayney	Camly 40
Salters Grange	Grange	Oneilland West	Armagh	Hockley 24
Seaboughan	Kilclooney	Fews Lower	Armagh	Market Hill 23
Seafin	Killevy	Orior Upper	Newry	Killevy 61
Seagahan	Lisnadill	Fews Lower	Armagh	Lisnadill 15
Seagoe Lower	Seagoe	Oneilland East	Lurgan	Kernan 51
Seagoe Upper	Seagoe	Oneilland East	Lurgan	Kernan 51
Selshion	Drumcree	Oneilland West	Lurgan	Portadown Rural 52
Serse	Killevy	Orior Lower	Newry	Mullaghglass 66
Shanecrackan Beg	Mullaghbrack	Oneilland West	Banbridge	Mullaghbrack 31
Shanecrackan More	Mullaghbrack	Oneilland West	Banbridge	Mullaghbrack 31
Shaneglish	Ballymore	Orior Lower	Banbridge	Ballysheil 30
Shankill	Shankill	Oneilland East	Lurgan	Lurgan Rural 46
Shanmullagh or Ballycullen	Clonfeacle	Armagh	Armagh	Charlemont 7

TOWNLAND	CIVIL PARISH	BARONY	POOR LAW UNION	DISTRICT ELECTORAL DIVISION
Shanroe	Forkill	Orior Upper	Newry	Forkill 58
Shantally	Tynan	Tiranny	Armagh	Middletown 28
Shean	Forkill	Orior Upper	Newry	Forkill 58
Sheeroe	Creggan	Fews Upper	Castleblayney	
Sheetrim	Creggan	Fews Upper	Castleblayney	Cullyhanna 38
Sheetrim	Tynan	Tiranny	Armagh	Middletown 28
Sheiland	Creggan	Fews Upper	Castleblayney	Moybane 39
Shewis	Kilmore	Oneilland West	Armagh	Rich Hill 26
Silverwood	Seagoe	Oneilland East	Lurgan	Brownlowsderry 44
Skegatillida	Ballymore	Orior Lower	Newry	Poyntzpass 68
Skerries	Tynan	Tiranny	Armagh	Middleton 28
Skerriff (Tickburn)	Newtownhamilton	Fews Upper	Castleblayney	Lisleitrim 42
Skerriff (Trueman)	Newtownhamilton	Fews Upper	Castleblayney	Lisleitrim 42
Slieve Gullion	Forkill	Orior Upper	Newry	Latbirget 59
Sturgan	Killevy	Orior Upper	Newry	Camlough 65
Taghnevan East	Shankill	Oneilland	Lurgan	Lurgan Rural 46
Tamlaght	Derrynoose	Armagh	Armagh	Brootally 27
Tamlaght	Eglish	Armagh	Armagh	Ballymartrim 6
Tamnaficarbet	Seagoe	Oneilland East	Lurgan	Kernan 51
Tamnafiglassan	Seagoe	Oneilland East	Lurgan	Kernan 51
Tamnaghbane	Killevy	Orior Upper	Newry	Killevy 61
Tamnaghmore	Kilmore	Orior Lower	Banbridge	Mullahead 32
Tamnaghvelton	Kilmore	Orior Lower	Banbridge	Mullahead 32
Tanderagee	Lisnadill	Fews Lower	Armagh	Tanderagee Urban 34
Tanderagee Urban District	Ballymore	Orior Lower	Banbridge	Tanderagee Urban 34
Tannaghmore	Mullaghbrack	Oneilland West	Banbridge	Mullaghbrack 31
Tannaghmore North	Shankill	Oneilland East	Lurgan	Cornakinnegar 45
Tannaghmore South	Shankill	Oneilland East	Lurgan	Cornakinnegar 45
Tannaghmore West	Seagoe	Oneilland East	Lurgan	Brownlowsderry 48
Tannyoky	Ballymore	Orior Lower	Newry	Poyntzpass 68
Tarsan East	Seagoe	Oneilland	Lurgan	Kernan 51
Tarthlogue West	Tartaraghan	Oneilland	Lurgan	Tartaraghan 56
Tassagh	Keady	Armagh	Armagh	Crossmore 11
Tavanagh	Drumcree	Oneilland West	Lurgan	Portadown Urban 53
Teagy West	Tartaraghan	Oneilland	Armagh	Annaghmore 16
Teemore	Mullaghbrack	Oneilland West	Banbridge	Mullaghbrack 31
Teer	Creggan	Fews Upper	Castleblayney	Cullyhanna 38
Teer Island	Creggan	Fews Upper	Castleblayney	Cullyhanna 38
Teeraw	Grange	Armagh	Armagh	Grange 9
Terraskane	Eglish	Armagh	Armagh	Ballymartrim 6
Terryhoogan	Ballymore	Orior Lower	Banbridge	Tanderagee Rural 39
Tievecoghoge	Forkill	Orior Upper	Newry	
Tievecrom	Forkill	Orior Upper	Newry	Forkill 58
Tievenamara	Keady	Tiranny	Armagh	Derrynoose 12
Timakeel	Drumcree	Oneilland West	Lurgan	Breagh 54
Timukenny	Drumcree	Oneilland West	Lurgan	Breagh 54
Tireagerty	Clonfeacle	Armagh	Armagh	Charlemont 7
Tirearly	Lisnadill	Armagh	Armagh	Brootally 27
Tirgarriff	Eglish	Armagh	Armagh	Ballymartrim 6
Tirgarve	Grange	Armagh	Armagh	Grange 9
Tirmacrannon	Loughgall	Armagh	Armagh	Charlemont 7
Tirnascobe	Armagh	Oneilland West	Armagh	Hockley 24
Tirsogue	Shankill	Oneilland East	Lurgan	Lurgan Rural 46
Tivnacree	Derrynoose	Tiranny	Armagh	Derrynoose 12
Toberhewny	Shankill	Oneilland East	Lurgan	Lurgan Rural 46

TOWNLAND	CIVIL PARISH	BARONY	POOR LAW UNION	DISTRICT ELECTORAL DIVISION
Tonnagh	Eglish	Armagh	Armagh	Ballymartrim 6
Tray	Eglish	Armagh	Armagh	Ballymartrim 6
Tullyah	Loughgilly	Orior Upper	Newry	Belleek 63
Tullyallen	Loughgilly	Orior Lower	Newry	Mountnorris 64
Tullyard	Creggan	Fews Upper	Castleblayney	Crossmaglen 37
Tullyard	Grange	Armagh	Armagh	Grange 9
Tullyargle	Armagh	Armagh	Armagh	Armagh Rural 1
Tullybrick (Hamilton)	Tynan	Tiranny	Armagh	Middletown 28
Tullybrick Etra or Bondville	Tynan	Tiranny	Armagh	Tynan 29
Tullybrone	Lisnadill	Fews Upper	Armagh	Armaghbrague 10
Tullycallidy	Derrynoose	Armagh	Armagh	Brootally 27
Tullydagan East	Shankill	Oneilland	Lurgan	Cornakinnegar 45
Tullydonnell (Gage)	Creggan	Fews Upper	Dundalk	Creggan Lower 36
Tullydonnell (O'Callaghan)	Creggan	Fews Upper	Dundalk	Creggan Lower 36
Tullyelmer	Armagh	Armagh	Armagh	Armagh Rural 1
Tullygally	Shankill	Oneilland East	Lurgan	Lurgan Rural 46
Tullygarden	Kilmore	Oneilland West	Armagh	Kilmore 25
Tullygarran	Grange	Armagh	Armagh	Grange 9
Tullyglush	Keady	Armagh	Armagh	Keady Rural 13
Tullyglush (Kane)	Tynan	Tiranny	Armagh	Middletown 28
Tullyglush (Nevin)	Tynan	Tiranny	Armagh	Middletown 28
Tullygoonigan	Grange	Armagh	Armagh	Grange 9
Tullyhappy	Killevy	Orior Lower	Newry	Tullyhappy 67
Tullyherron	Loughgilly	Orior Lower	Newry	Mountnorris 64
Tullyhirm	Derrynoose	Tiranny	Armagh	Derrynoose 12
Tullyhugh	Ballymore	Orior Lower	Banbridge	Tanderagee Rural 33
Tullykevan	Clonfeacle	Armagh	Armagh	Charlemont 7
Tullylinn	Ballymore	Orior Lower	Newry	Poyntzpass 68
Tullylost	Armagh	Armagh	Armagh	Armagh Rural 1
Tullymacann	Ballymore	Orior Lower	Banbridge	Ballysheil 30
Tullymacreeve	Forkill	Orior Upper	Newry	Latbirget 59
Tullymore	Kilmore	Oneilland West	Armagh	Loughgall 18
Tullymore	Armagh	Armagh	Armagh	Armagh Rural 1
Tullymore Agawan	Eglish	Tiranny	Armagh	Ballymartrim 6
Tullymore Etra	Eglish	Tiranny	Armagh	Glenaul 8
Tullymore Otra	Eglish	Tiranny	Armagh	Glenaul 8
Tullynacross	Ballymore	Orior	Lower Newry	Poyntzpass 68
Tullynagin	Lisnadill	Fews Upper	Armagh	Lisnadill 15
Tullynamalloge	Keady	Armagh	Armagh	Crossmore 11
Tullynavall	Creggan	Fews Upper	Castleblayney	Cloghoge 35
Tullyneagh	Eglish	Tiranny	Armagh	Ballymartrim 6
Tullynichol	Eglish	Armagh	Armagh	Ballymartrim 6
Tullyogallaghan	Newtownhamilton	Fews Upper	Castleblayney	Dorsy 41
Tullyroan	Clonfeacle	Oneilland West	Armagh	Tullyroan 19
Tullyronnelly	Shankill	Oneilland East	Lurgan	Cornakinnegar 45
Tullysaran	Eglish	Tiranny	Armagh	Ballymartrim 6
Tullyvallan	Newtownhamilton	Fews Upper	Castleblayney	Newtownhamilton 43
Tullyvallan (Hamilton) East	Newtownhamilton	Fews Upper	Castleblayney	Dorsy 41
Tullyvallan (Hamilton) West	Newtownhamilton	Fews Upper	Castleblayney	Dorsy 41
Tullyvallan (Macullagh)	Newtownhamilton	Fews Upper	Castleblayney	Dorsy 41
Tullyvallan (Tipping) East	Newtownhamilton	Fews Upper	Castleblayney	Dorsy 41

TOWNLAND	CIVIL PARISH	BARONY	POOR LAW UNION	DISTRICT ELECTORAL DIVISION
Tullyvallan (Tipping) West	Newtownhamilton	Fews Upper	Castleblayney	Dorsy 41
Tullywinny	Loughgilly	Orior Upper	Newry	Belleek 63
Tullyworgle	Armagh	Armagh	Armagh	Armagh Rural 1
Turcarra	Loughgall	Oneilland West	Armagh	Hockley 24
Turmoyra	Seagoe	Oneilland East	Lurgan	Brownlowsderry 44
Turry	Tynan	Tiranny	Armagh	Glenaul 8
Tynan	Tynan	Tiranny	Armagh	Tynan 29
Tynan town	Tynan	Tiranny	Armagh	Tynan 29
Tyross or Legagilly	Armagh	Armagh	Armagh	Armagh Rural 1
Umgola	Armagh	Armagh	Armagh	Armagh Rural 1
Ummeracam (Ball) North	Creggan	Fews Upper	Castleblayney	Dorsy 41
Ummeracam (Ball) South	Creggan	Fews Upper	Castleblayney	Dorsy 41
Ummeracam (Johnston)	Creggan	Fews Upper	Castleblayney	Dorsy 41
Ummerinvore	Newtownhamilton	Fews Upper	Castleblayney	Dorsy 41
Unshinagh	Kilmore	Orior Lower	Banbridge	Mullahead 32
Unshinagh	Drumcree	Oneilland West	Lurgan	Breagh 54
Unshog	Tynan	Tiranny	Armagh	Middletown 28
Urcher	Creggan	Fews Upper	Castleblayney	Crossmaglen 37
Wood Park or Ballynameta	Tynan	Tiranny	Armagh	Tynan 29

APPENDIX 4

COUNTY ARMAGH
LIST OF UNOFFICIAL PLACENAMES
(alphabetical by placename)

UNOFFICIAL PLACENAME	TOWNLAND	CIVIL PARISH	OS MAP REF
Abrahams Bog	Derrymacash	Montiaghs	6
Anna Hill	Ballyleny	Kilmore	13
Annahone	Blackwaterstown or Lisbofin	Clonfeacle	8
Assan	Drumlougher	Creggan	27
Anglesey Mountain	Clontygora	Killevy	29
Babylon Hill	Mullaghglass	Ballymore & Killevy	18
Badger Island	Cargans	Ballymore	14
Ballsmill	Glassdrumman & Ballynaclosha	Creggan	31
Ballyclanowen	Carrickbroad	Killevy	32
Ballynamadda	Carrickbroad	Killevy	32
Ballynamona	Carrickbroad	Killevy	32
Bannfoot or Charlestown	Derryinver	Montiaghs	2
Bawn Hill	Derrycrew & Fernagreevagh	Loughgall	8
Bellville	Derrytagh North	Montiaghs	2
Blackbank or Deadman's Hill	Clady Beg	Kilclooney	21
Black Hill	Cavanakill	Ballymyre	25
Black Hill	Tievenamara	Keady	24
Black Island	Annaghmore	Loughgall	4
Black Mullyard	Mullyard	Derrynoose	19
Blackrock	Belleek	Loughgilly	25
The Black Rocks	Corliss	Creggan	30
Black Quarter	Clady More	Kilclooney	21
Blasoor	Cortamlat	Newtownhamilton	24
Blackey	Derryall	Drumcree	5
Bloody Bog	Tullyvallan	Newtownhamilton	24
Blue Hill	Drumnahavil	Derrynoose	19
Borough Hill	Derryscallop	Clonfeacle	4
Botany	Mullenakill	North Killyman	4
Bradagh Bog	Kilcam & Tivenamara	Keady	24
Brocker Hill	Tullydagan	Shankill	6
Bullays Hill	Drumnakelly	Seagoe & Drumcree	6
Bunanvillla	Fathom Upper	Newry	29
Burnt Island	Annaghmore	Loughgall	4
Cairnan Hill	Shean	Forkill	31
Cannon Hill	Turcarra	Loughgall	8
Carewamean	Carrickbroad	Killevy	32
Cargy	Listarkelt	Derrynoose	19
Carnagh	Crossnenagh & Tievenamara	Keady	23

UNOFFICIAL PLACENAME	TOWNLAND	CIVIL PARISH	OS MAP REF
Carn Glen	Carnavanaghan	Kilclooney	16
Carn Hill	Cavanakill	Ballymyre	25
Carn Hill	Clady Bag	Kilcloney	21
Carn Hill	Seafin	Killevy	29
Carrick	Derryall	Drumcree	5
Carrickawilkin	Clay	Keady	24
Carrick's Hill	Leganny	Drumcree	9
Carrigatuke	Armaghbrague	Lisnadill	20
Carrowbane	Drumilly	Killevy	25
Carrowbane	Tullyglush	Keady	20
Carryoghill	Clay	Keady	20
Charlestown or Bannfoot	Derryinver	Montiaghs	2
Cherry's Hill	Ballynahinch	Kilmore	13
Church Hill Demesne	Mullenakill South/ Derryhubbert/ East & North & Derryane	Killyman /Tartaraghan	4
Clady Milltown	Clady More	Kilclooney	21
Cloghbane	Aghincurk	Ballymyre	21
Cloghoge Mountain	Ellisholding	Killevy	29
The Cluster	Cashel	Forkill	16
Coal Hill	Ballyloughan	Kilmore	13
Cock Hill	Kilcam	Keady	24
Cockle Hill	Cloven Eden	Loughgall	8
Cold Brae Bog	Cavanakill	Ballymyre	25
Cold Brae	Cavanakill	Ballymyre	25
Columbkille	Derrylard	Tartaraghan	2
Conlan's Rocks	Cornoonagh	Creggan	31
Conlon Hill	Tallyvallon (Tipping) East	Newtownhamilton	28
Con's Hill	Artabrackagh	Drumcree	9
Cooey's Hill	Tullyvallan	Newtownhamilton	27
Connory's Hill	Crossnenagh	Keady	23
Cor Hill	Cor Tynan	Tynan	11
Cortreasla	Glasdrumman	Creggan	31
Courtneys Island	North Louth	Derryadd & Tartaraghan	4
Courtney Mountain	Duburren	Killevy	25
Crabtreelane	Derryall	Drumcree	5
Craigaquillin	Clonalig	Creggan	30
Craigmore Hill	Derry Beg	Newry	26
Crammon Hill	Carricklane	Kilclooney	17
Cran Island	Tullyroan	Clonfeacle	8
Craveernagh	Lisdrumbrughas	Derrynoose	15
Craveernagh	Lisdrumbrughas	Derrynoose	16
Craveernagh	Lisdrumbrughas	Derrynoose	17
Crockafeeka	Clady More	Kilclooney	21
Crockanroe	Blackwatertown or Lisbofin	Clonfeacle	8
Crocket's Hill	Leganny	Drumcree	9
Croslieve	Shean	Forkill	31
Crow Hill	Maydown	Eglish	7
Crumlin Hill	Keenaghan	Loughgall	8
Curragh	Mullyard	Derrynoose	19
Daaikilmore	Carrickbroad	Killevy	32

UNOFFICIAL PLACENAME	TOWNLAND	CIVIL PARISH	OS MAP REF
Dairy	Aghincurk	Ballymyre	21
Dangary	Tullyvallan	Newtownhamilton	24
Deadman's Hill or Blackbank	Clady Beg	Kilclooey	21
Deer Park	Belleek	Loughgilly	25
Dernaroy	Aghadavoyle	Killevy	32
Derryadd	Derryhubbert North	Killyman	4
Derryardry	Derryhubbert East	Killyman	4
Derrycarib	Derrinraw	Tartaraghan	5
Derrycarran	Derrinraw	Tartaraghan	5
Derrycrew	Clonmore	Killyman	4
Derrycrow	Derrinver	Montiaghs	2
Derrycush	Ballynarry	Tartaraghan	5
Derryesker	Derryhubbert South	Killyman	4
Derryesog	Clontyclay	Killyman	4
Derrygavad	Annaghmore	Loughgall	4
Derrygavel	Derryhubbert East	Killyman	4
Derryhohan	Clontyclay	Killyman	4
Derrykiniff	Ballynarry	Tartaraghan	5
Derrykinlough	Derryhubbert East	Killyman	4
Derryloughanbane	Derryhubbert East	Killyman	4
Derryloughanclave	Derryhubbert East	Killyman	4
Derrynasool	Derrymagowan	Clonfeacle	4
Derrywarragh Is.	Maghery	Tartaraghan	2
Derryore	Derrcorry North	Killyman	4
Derryruddery	Derrymagowan	Clonfeacle	4
Derryvar	Derrylard	Tartaraghan	2
Derryveen	Derryhubbert South	Killyman	4
Dobbin's Valley	Parkmore or Demesne	Armagh	12
Dog Street	Clady Beg	Kilclooney	21
Dougan's Mountain	Ballymacawley	Kilclooney	16
Drapers Hill	Gosford Demesne	Mullaghbrack	17
Drumbunion	Racarbry	Keady	20
Drumcarn	Drumnahavil	Derrynoose	23
Drumcultar	Kilcreevy Etna	Derrynoose	16
Drumcultar	Kilcreevy Etna	Derrynoose	15
Drumduff	Cor Tynan	Tynan	15
Drummill	Tullynavall	Creggan	28
Drumnot	Derrycorry North	Killyman	4
Dungormley	Tullyvallan	Newtownhamilton	24
Dunreavy Wood	Glasdrumman	Ballymore & Creggan	31
Edenard	Clady Beg	Kilclooney	21
Edenfore	Clady Beg	Kilclooney	21
Edenfore	Clontygora	Killevy	29
Englishtown	Annamoy	Eglish	8
Faughert Hill	Tullymore	Armagh & Kilmore	9
Feigh	Drumgose	Creggan & Tynan	15
Fisher's Hill	Tullycallidy	Derrynoose	11
Fonfield	Tievecrom	Forkill	31
Garvagh Hill	Hamilton's Bawn	Mullaghbrack	13
Glebe Hill	Drumnaleg	Ballymore	14

UNOFFICIAL PLACENAME	TOWNLAND	CIVIL PARISH	OS MAP REF
Glen Hill	Lisdrumliska	Newry	26
Glenny's Hill	Ballintemple	Ballymyre	25
Grabbagh	Clady Beg	Kilclooney	21
Gravel Hill	Corr And Dunavally	Loughgall	8
Groobany Hill	Ballygroobany	Mullaghbrack	13
Grove Hill	Creenagh	Kilmore	9
Hamilton's Bawn	Drumorgan	Mullaghbrack & Mullaghbane	13
Harrisons Hill	Ballynahinch	Kilmore	13
Harnessey's Rooks	Mounthill	Creggan	31
Heath Hall Demesne	Ballymacdermot	Killevy	29
Hemp Hill	Annagharap	Tynan	11
Highway Gap	Clonroot	Kilmore	9
Hill Farm	Derryhale	Kilmore	13
Hockley	Mullanasilla	Loughgall	12
The Island	Ballintemple	Ballymyre	25
The Island	Bolton	Loughgilly	21
The Island	Derrymacfall	Drumcree	5
The Island	Kilmore	Clonfeacle & Kilmore	8
Island Hill	Druminargal	Ballymore	18
Irish Corran	Corran	Lisnadill	20
Johnston's Hill	Ballintemple	Ballymyre	25
Kane's Hill	Tullyglush	Keady	15
Kieran's Rocks	Mounthill	Creggan	31
Kildarragh	Drummannon	Tartaraghan	9
Killyleh Bog	Annaghananny	Tynan	11
Kilmore	Cordrain	Kilmore	14
Kingsmills	Lisadian & Drumharriff	Drumcree & Loughgall & Loughgilly	21
Kirk Hill	Ballymoran	Lisnadill	16
Knockmaney	Greenan	Grange	8
Knocknagor	Breagh	Seagoe & Drumcree & Tartaraghan	10
Knockowen	Corkley	Keady	24
Laurel Vale	Tamnaghvelton	Kilmore	13
Legar Hill	Corr/Dunavally	Loughgall	8
Levin	Outleckan	Ballymyre	25
Lisdoo	Marlacco Beg	Mullaghbrack	13
Lochnanaram	Clonalig	Creegan	30
Lough Hill	Farnamucklagh	Lisnadill	20
Love's Hill	Richmount or Aghavallan	Kilmore	9
Mcginn's Rocks	Tullyvallan	Newtownhamilton	24
Mcgoggin's Hill	Kilcarn	Eglish	7
Mckinley's Hill	Carricklane	Kilclooney	17
Magee's Bog	Ballintemple	Ballymyre	25
Mallawee	Clady More	Kilclooney	21
The Man Of War	Clay	Keady	19
Meadow Hill	Cavanakill	Ballymyre	25
Millford	Kennedies	Lisnadill & Tynan	12
Milltown	Aghory	Kilmore	13

UNOFFICIAL PLACENAME	TOWNLAND	CIVIL PARISH	OS MAP REF
Milltown	Balteagh	Tynan & Seagoe	15
Milltown	Derryaugh	Tartaraghan	2
Milltown	Tullymore Etra	Eglish	7
Millvale	Mullaghglass	Ballymore & Killevy	26
Moore's Island	Grange Blundel	Grange	8
Mount St. Catherine	Corporation	Armagh	12
Mount Caulfield	Derrymore	Newry	26
Mountnab	Ballymacawley	Kilclooney	17
Mouse Hill	Clady More	Kilclooney	21
Mowhan	Drumgane	Loughgilly	17
Muckery Lower	Derryloste	Montiaghs	2
Mullaboy	Drummannon	Tartaraghan	5
Mullaghbane	Glebe	Forkill	28
Mullaghdoy	Crossdened	Keady	20
Mullaghcrick	Carricklane	Kilclooney	19
Mullanayarvy	Cladymore	Kilclooney	21
Mullin's Hill	Ballymore	Ballymore	14
Mullen's Hill	Derrymagowan	Clonfeacle	4
Mino Mile Hill	Ballintemple	Ballymyre	25
Oak Hill	Foy Beg	Drumcree	5
Oak Hill	Magherydogherty	Mullaghbrack	13
Oxford Island	Annaloist	Seagoe	6
Pattersons Hill	Kilmore	Clonfeacle	8
Piper Hill	Cornakinnegar	Shankill	6
Pisgah Hill	Crossmore	Keady	20
Pollramer Meadows	Mulladry	Kilmore	9
Proctor's Hill	Corcreey	Kilmore	13
Queen's Island	Tullyroan	Clonfeacle	4
Quilly	Mullaghbane	Mullaghbrack & Loughgall & Forkhill	31
Rathlin Island	Derrymacash	Montiaghs	6
The Reagh Bog	Brackagh	Kilmore & Loughgilly	10
Ring Hill	Mullanasilla	Loughgall	12
Roughan Hill	Lurgancot	Kilmore	9
Round Hill	Clankilvoragh	Magheralin	6
Rover	Glasdrumman	Creggan & Ballymore	31
Sailors Street	Cooldery	Creggan	31
Sargony	Fergort	Derrynose	19
Scotch Corran	Corran	Lisnadill	20
Silverbridge	Legmoylin	Creggan	28
Sinclairs Hill	Tullyroan	Clonfeacle	4
Slievebrack	Shanroe	Forkill	31
Slievenbolea	Carrickbroad	Killery	32
Slievenappel	Carricknagavna	Forkill	28
Star Hill	Maytone	Loughgilly	21
Stockingsman's Hill	Ballynahone More	Lisnadill	V
Sugarloaf Hill	Duburren	Killevy	25
Tassagh	Dundrum	Keady	20
Tole's Island	Grange Lower	Newry	9
Tullygeasy	Tullyvallan	Newtownhamilton	24
Tullynawood	Tullyglush	Keady	24
Tullyneill	Tullyvallan	Newtownhamilton	24
Tullyvoney Bog	Cashel	Forkill	16
Tullywill	Clady Beg	Kilclooey	21

UNOFFICIAL PLACENAME	TOWNLAND	CIVIL PARISH	OS MAP REF
Tyrone's Ditches	Ballenan	Loughgilly	18
The Waste Lands	Tirnascobe & Altaturk	Armagh	12
Water Hill	Ballymacully Lower	Eglish	11
Whitecross	Corlat	Ballymyre	21
White Hill	Tullyvallan	Newtownhamilton	24
White Rock	Armaghbrague	Lisnadill	24
Whitlas Hill	Drumachunshin	Kilmore & Loughgilly	9
Wilson's Hill	Mulladry	Kilmore	13
Windmill Hill	Ballyleny	Kilmore	9
Wolf Island Bog	Aughnagurgan & Corkley	Keady	20
Wolf's Island	Derrymacash	Montiaghs	6
Wood Hill	Cor Tynan	Tynan	11

APPENDIX 5

PRONI REFERENCES FOR TITHE APPLOTMENT BOOKS 1823–1838 [FIN]; VALUATION RECORDS 1830s, TENEMENT VALUATION 1864 AND ANNUAL REVISIONS 1864–c.1930 [VAL]. NATIONAL ARCHIVES, DUBLIN REFERENCES TO VALUATIONS 1830s [OL4.]

PARISH	TITHES 1823–38 FIN 5A/	VALUATION 1830s VAL 1B/ FIELD BOOKS [OL4.]	TENEMENT VALUATION c.1864 VAL 2B/2/	VALUATION REVISIONS c.1860–c.1930 VAL 12B/
Acton (Ballymore)			32D	
Armagh	20	21A & B, 224 234, [.0090] [.0110]	1A-G, 22	10/4A-H, 5A-C, 6A-C, 7A-C, 8A-C, 9A-E, 25A-E
Ballymore	41	214, 248 [.0120]	32A-C, 32E	11/1A-C, 11/5A-G, 15/23A-D, 15/24A-D
Ballymyre	42	239, [.0102]	13	15/2A-D
Blackwatertown (Clonfeacle)		249	2B	
Camlough (Killevy)		178		
Charlemont (Loughgall)		249	2B	
Clonfeacle	79	22, 225A & B 234, [.0111]	2A, 23	10/12A-F, 23A-E, 30A-E, 38A-D,
Creggan	86	240A & B [.0103]	14A-G	12/2A-E, 3A-4E, 5A-E, 6A-E, 7A-D, 13/1A-F
Crossmaglen (Creggan)			14G	
Derrynoose	95	23, 235, 248 [.0091, .0131]	3A-C, 40	10/11A-E, 17A-E, 19A-D, 26A-C, 28A, 39A-E
Drumcree	119	226A & B, 234, [.0112]	24A-H	14/2A-C, 6A-C, 12A-13B, 14A
Eglish	136	24, 236, 248 [.0092, .0132]	4, 41	10/10A-D, 22A-E
Forkill	143	215, 247, 248 [.0121, .0126]	32E, 35A-C	12/5A-C, 15/13A-B, 18A-D, 24A-C
Grange	150	25, 227, 234 [.0093, .0113]	5, 25	10/23A-E, 25A-E, 31A-E, 33A-E
Jonesborough	160	243, 248 [.0127]	36	15/15A-C
Keady	161	26A-D, 237 248-9, [.0094] [.0133]	6A-D, 3B-C, 42	10/3A-B, 17A-E, 19A-D, 26A-C, 27A-C, 28A-B
Kilclooney	225	210A & B 216, 248, 249 [.0098, .0122]	9A-C	10/13A-D, 29A-D, 34A-E
Kildarton	20 etc			10/24A-D, 25A-E, 29A-C

PARISH	TITHES 1823–38 FIN 5A/	VALUATION 1830s VAL 1B/ FIELD BOOKS [OL4.]	TENEMENT VALUATION c.1864 VAL 2B/2/	VALUATION REVISIONS c.1860–c.1930 VAL 12B/
Killevy	178	217, 244A & B 248, [.0123] [.0128]	32E, 34C, 37A-J	12B, 15/1A-D, 1F, 1H, 3A-E, 6A-J, 15A-C, 17A-C, 18A-D, 22A-24C
Killylea (Tynan)		249		
Killyman	183	228, 234, [.0114]	27	10/30A-C
Kilmore	186	218, 248 229A & B [.0115, .0124]	26A-D, 33	10/25A-E, 11/4A-F, 31A-E, 33A-E, 37A-F
Lisnadill	202	27, 211, 241 [.0095, .0099] [.0104]	8A, 10A-B 12B, 15	10/3A-D, 9A-E, 11A-E, 29A-D, 32A-E
Loughgall	206	28, 230, 234 249, [.0096]	7, 28A-C	10/2A-E, 10/25A-E, 31A-E, 33A-E, 38A-D
Loughgilly	207	212, 219 245A & B, 248 [.0100, .0125]	11, 29, 34A-C, 38A -B	10/34A-C, 11/3A-D, 15/3A-E, 19A-D, 23A-D, 24A-D
Lurgan (Shankill)			20C-G	14/9A-H
Magheralin	219	220, 234, [.0106]	17	14/5A-C
Markethill (Mullaghbrack)			12C	
Middletown (Tynan)				43D
Montiaghs	223	221, 234 [.0107]	18	14/11A-C
Mountnorris (Loughgilly)				32D
Mullaghbrack	225	213, 231, 234 [.0101, .0117]	12A-B, 29	10/24A-D, 34A-E, 11/3A-E
Newry	226	232, 234, 246A-E, 248 [.0118, .0130]	39A-C	10/33A-D, 15/1A-H 22/16A-C, 17A-C, 18A-D
Newtownhamilton	229	242A & B [.0105]	16A-D	12/1A-D, 5A-E, 6A-E, 8A-E
Poyntzpass (Ballymore)				32D
Portadown (Drumcree etc)			24E-H	14/13A-N
Richhill (Kilmore)			26E	
Seagoe	245	222, 234, [.0108]	19A-D	14/3A-C, 4A-C, 7A-C
Shankill	248	223A & B 234, [.0109]	20A-G	14/5A-C, 9H
Tandragee (Ballymore)			11	11/5A-G
Tartaraghan	255	233A & B 234, [.0119]	21A-C	10/2A-C, 30A-C, 14/15A-D
Tynan	270	29A & B 238, 248 [.0097, .0134]	8A, B 43A-D	10/11A-E, 17A-E, 22A-E, 35A-E, 39A-E

APPENDIX 6
COUNTY ARMAGH
MAP OF CIVIL PARISHES

1 ARMAGH
2 BALLYMORE
3 BALLYMYRE
4 CLONFEACLE
5 CREGGAN
6 DERRYNOOSE
7 DRUMCREE
8 EGLISH
9 FORKILL/FORKHILL
10 GRANGE
11 JONESBOROUGH
12 KEADY

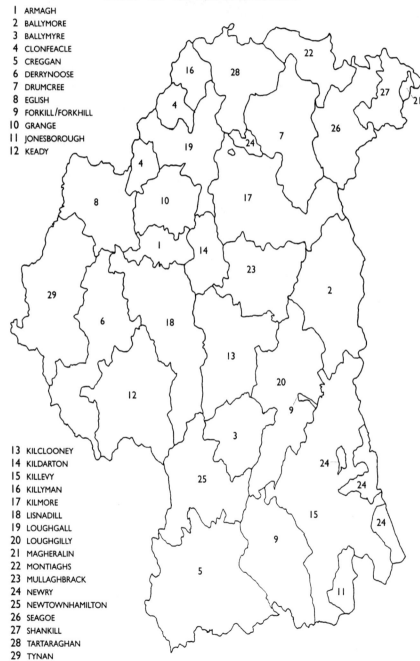

13 KILCLOONEY
14 KILDARTON
15 KILLEVY
16 KILLYMAN
17 KILMORE
18 LISNADILL
19 LOUGHGALL
20 LOUGHGILLY
21 MAGHERALIN
22 MONTIAGHS
23 MULLAGHBRACK
24 NEWRY
25 NEWTOWNHAMILTON
26 SEAGOE
27 SHANKILL
28 TARTARAGHAN
29 TYNAN

APPENDIX 7
MAP OF ROMAN CATHOLIC PARISHES

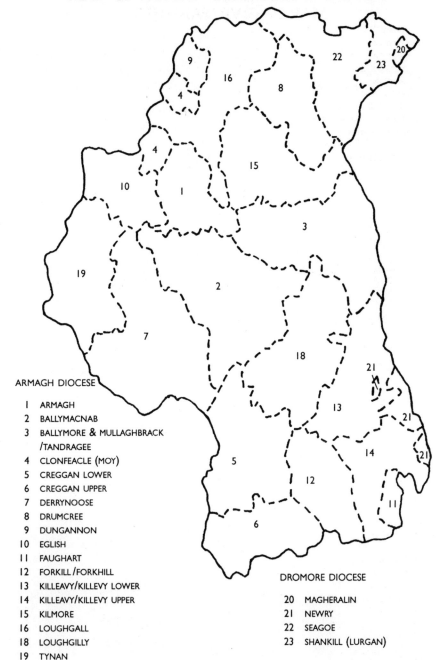

ARMAGH DIOCESE

1   ARMAGH
2   BALLYMACNAB
3   BALLYMORE & MULLAGHBRACK
     /TANDRAGEE
4   CLONFEACLE (MOY)
5   CREGGAN LOWER
6   CREGGAN UPPER
7   DERRYNOOSE
8   DRUMCREE
9   DUNGANNON
10   EGLISH
11   FAUGHART
12   FORKILL /FORKHILL
13   KILLEAVY/KILLEVY LOWER
14   KILLEAVY/KILLEVY UPPER
15   KILMORE
16   LOUGHGALL
18   LOUGHGILLY
19   TYNAN

DROMORE DIOCESE

20   MAGHERALIN
21   NEWRY
22   SEAGOE
23   SHANKILL (LURGAN)

Courtesy of John Grenham, *Tracing your Irish Ancestors*, Dublin 1992

INDEX

Ball Estate Papers
Cullyhanna